PRAISE FOR
THE RIGHT SIDE OF WRONG

"Leon Trotsky once famously observed that you may not be interested in war, but war may be interested in you. Nowhere is this more true than in Ruth Hillelson's touching story of her family, the Dindingers, who started the twentieth century living in the German Empire, then spent the inter-war period living in Poland, only to be annexed to the Third Reich. It is a beautiful story of how a family remained together, even when pulled apart by the vicissitudes of war."

—**Richard DiNardo, PhD,** author of *Germany's Panzer Arm* and Professor of National Security Affairs at the United States Marine Corps University

"This is the multigenerational saga of one extended family's struggles—spanning several countries and two world wars—and their indomitable determination to persevere and prosper. A gripping and often lyrical narrative."

—**Robert Goldsborough,** Nero Book Award–winning author and retired editor of the *Chicago Tribune Sunday Magazine*

"This fascinating and exceptionally well-told history follows a German-Russian family through two world wars. Their story is uncovered by an American surgeon who unexpectedly inherited two dusty suitcases filled with photos, documents, and tender letters. With detective-like research and determination, Dr. Hillelson reveals perspectives seldom told, capturing a family's joys, perils, secrets, and losses in a vivid and deeply human portrait of its time."

—**Julie Glowacki, PhD,** Professor Emerita of Orthopedic Surgery and of Oral and Maxillofacial Surgery at Brigham and Women's Hospital, Harvard Medical School, and Harvard School of Dental Medicine

THE RIGHT SIDE OF WRONG

Renegades Against the Reich

RUTH L. HILLELSON, MD

This book is a memoir and historical account based on documented events, records, and recollections. The story reflects both the author's personal perspective and historical research. All details are presented as accurately as possible. No names or identifying characteristics have been changed intentionally.

Published by River Grove Books
Austin, TX
www.gbgpresss.com

Distributed by River Grove Books

Design and composition by Greenleaf Book Group
Cover design by Sergio Porto

Publisher's Cataloging-in-Publication data is available.

Print ISBN: 979-8-90052-052-0

eBook ISBN: 979-8-90052-053-7

First Edition

To my beloved husband Terry L. Whipple,
the wind beneath my wings.

CONTENTS

PREFACE xi

PROLOGUE: Two Suitcases (2017) 1

PART I. A TRUE HOME

ONE: Forbidden Love (1914) 15

TWO: Revolution and Escape (1917) 28

THREE: Building a Life in Bydgoszcz (1918) 34

FOUR: New Arrivals (1920) 41

FIVE: Uncertain Peace (1921) 47

SIX: Holding Close (1925–1932) 53

PART II. HEADING TOWARD WAR

SEVEN: The Rise of Hitler (1933) 63

EIGHT: Order Inside Chaos (1936) 71

NINE: The Strangling Angel (1937) 78

TEN: A World Gone Mad (1938) 86

ELEVEN: Invasion (1939) 91

PART III. THE WAR BEGINS

TWELVE: Reclaiming the Light (1939) 101

THIRTEEN: Death March (1939) 107

FOURTEEN: Learning the Truth (1939) 112

FIFTEEN: A Bond Is Forged (1939) 117

SIXTEEN: Unbroken (1939) 124

SEVENTEEN: Changes at Home (1940) 131

EIGHTEEN: Conscription (1941) 139

PART IV. PURPOSE

NINETEEN: Part of the Machine (1941) 145

TWENTY: Come What May (1942) 153

TWENTY-ONE: A Kind of Survival (1942) 163

TWENTY-TWO: The White Rose (1942–1943) 173

TWENTY-THREE: Hohenlychen (1943) 181

TWENTY-FOUR: Loss (1943) 187

TWENTY-FIVE: Revelations from Ravensbrück (1943) 194

TWENTY-SIX: Pekari (1943) 205

PART V. HEARTBREAK

TWENTY-SEVEN: Hardened Resolve (1944) 215

TWENTY-EIGHT: Arrest (1944) 221

TWENTY-NINE: Capture (1945) 227

THIRTY: Keeping Hope Alive (1945) 232

THIRTY-ONE: Remembering How to Heal (1945) 238

PART VI. NEW BEGINNINGS

THIRTY-TWO: The Will to Go On (1945) 249

THIRTY-THREE: Rescue (1945–1946) 257

THIRTY-FOUR: Seeking Refuge (1946) 264

THIRTY-FIVE: Stuttgart (1946) 270

THIRTY-SIX: Newfound Purpose (1946) 276

THIRTY-SEVEN: Rejoining the World (1946) 283

THIRTY-EIGHT: Onward to Freedom (1948) 293

EPILOGUE: Reflections (2022) 299

ACKNOWLEDGMENTS 307

ABOUT THE AUTHOR 309

PREFACE

IS A STORY EVER TRULY at its beginning, or does it merely loop in a timeless dance? For me, this story began unexpectedly one evening in Strasbourg, France, not in the throes of grand events but in the quiet convergence of past and present during a dinner party. It was there, amid the clinking of glasses and the soft drone of conversation, that I found an unexpected connection to Stuttgart, Germany—the city where I thought my mother had been born and raised.

The tendrils of friendship formed that night would reach back through time, pulling a shrouded past into the light, leading me to two small suitcases filled to the brim and heavy with history: photographs whispering in sepia tones, documents bearing silent testimony to incredible resilience, letters scrawled in ink and pencil. Together, these files wove the narrative of my German family's valiant struggle against the suffocating grip of Nazi occupation in Poland.

Each item was a snapshot, part of a puzzle waiting to be pieced together, revealing a tapestry of courage and survival. It was in these fragments of a fractured past that I would begin to truly understand the essence of where, and from whom, I had come from.

Within those fragile pages lay an account of one of humanity's darkest periods—not only a chronicle of war and the search for peace but also an intimate record of how love, duty, and fear shaped the choices my family made. Starting with these documents, I would unearth complex, heartbreaking truths that revealed far more about my beloved late mother than I'd ever imagined.

Though I did not know it on that marvelous evening in a serene corner of Strasbourg, I stood on the cusp of a journey into the shadowed corridors of history, poised to uncover the story of a family steadfast in their German identity yet rooted in Polish soil, shepherded by a matriarch of secret Russian Jewish lineage. Against the dark backdrop of a world at war, that family had clung steadfastly to hope and to each other.

World War II is often recalled as a monochrome tableau of tragedies, its history etched in the stark black of the Holocaust's darkest moments— Babi Yar, Auschwitz, Bergen-Belsen. Yet among these tales of unspeakable sorrow, there exists a constellation of stories aglow with valor, love, and an ironclad allegiance to ideals and homeland. My family's saga is one such story, an odyssey of courage and hope seen through the eyes of German nationals who opposed totalitarian ideology.

A family history stretches back endlessly through time, but a story has to start somewhere. This one starts with the cousins of two crowns: Kaiser Wilhelm II and Tsar Nicholas II, bridged by blood and politics, who unwittingly became the architects of my grandparents' fate and my family's future. Adolf "Adi" Dindinger, my grandfather, was head of the Kaisergarde during the First World War—the Great War, as it was known in the early decades of the twentieth century. His world, defined by duty and honor under Kaiser Wilhelm, was starkly different from that of young Tatjana Wiczewski, my grandmother, whose cradle was the lush wilderness of the Białowieża Forest in Russia. Imperial meetings between the royal cousins, cloaked in the diplomacy of hunts and hushed dialogues, aimed to dam the swelling currents of war between their nations. Amid these noble endeavors, Adolf's heart found its compass in Tatjana—a love kindled in the embers of a world on the brink of igniting.

Their love was not a mere footnote in the annals of time, but a declaration that even amid the cacophony of war and the tumultuous tides of history, love can flourish.

TWO SUITCASES (2017)

THE CHRISTMAS MARKET HAS just come alive in Strasbourg, scattering warmth and color across cobblestone streets. Twinkling lights drape the buildings, and festive music drifts through the frosty air. But I'm not here for the holiday celebration. Attending an international surgery conference with my husband, I am focused more on lectures and networking than on carols and cinnamon.

The winter chill quickens our pace to the brasserie at the Les Haras Hôtel, and something stirs inside me—a subtle thrill laced with unease. Maybe it's the beauty of the eighteenth-century architecture glowing with golden light, or the city's unique fusion of French and German cultures. Or maybe it's something deeper: the quiet anticipation I've carried for years, waiting for something to break the silence that has gripped my mother's past. Maybe it's our proximity to Stuttgart.

The bar, nestled gracefully between two spiral staircases, is awash in an elegant amber hue, its leather armchairs offering islands of comfort. Laughter and the rhythm of martini shakers float like music all around us.

"Good evening," the bartender greets us warmly, his voice rising above the chatter and clinking ice. "What can I get for you?"

"A French seventy-five, s'il vous plaît," my husband says, indulging in his new favorite cocktail. He glances my way. "And for my lovely wife . . . ?"

I smile, taking in the polished wood, the subtle elegance, the luxury and ease of the moment. "A white wine, please. Alsatian Riesling would be perfect."

"Oui, madame," the bartender replies with a knowing smile.

Our drinks arrive with a flourish, echoing the city's balance of efficiency and charm. Tucked into two armchairs by the window, we watch Strasbourg's evening life unfold: couples strolling hand in hand, vendors calling out over bright stalls, the charming city sparkling under Christmas lights. I'm warm behind the glass, enjoying our front-row seats, yet that uneasy thrill continues to stir, just beneath a distant memory.

Upstairs, dinner awaits. Conference attendees—surgeons, scientists, spouses—gather around large banquet tables, voices chiming in a mosaic of languages and laughter. We find ourselves seated with a handsome German-speaking gentleman whose curious accent immediately catches my ear.

He introduces himself as Max, and I learn that he is a prominent surgeon. In that moment he is simply a friendly stranger—though he will soon become far more significant in my life than I could have imagined.

"Excuse me," I say, threading my voice into the ambient hum. "Your accent—it's familiar. May I ask where you're from?"

"Stuttgart, my dear." Max smiles, warm and open. "Are you familiar with it?"

Emotion wells up unexpectedly, softening the edges of the room. "My mother," I reply quietly. "She grew up there, as far as I know."

The pain of my mother's death at age eighty-three has stretched across a decade, yet my memory of her remains vivid, a constant presence in my daily thoughts. In the years since her passing, I have become something of a digital archaeologist, combing through online archives and genealogy sites in search of her European childhood. The trail she left behind is faint, scattered like crumbs leading nowhere. Each clue hints at a larger story but dissolves into silence before I can follow it to the end.

Across the table, Max leans forward, his expression alert. "Really?" His voice is a gentle nudge in the space between us, and all other noise in the room fades into the background. "Stuttgart was her home?" He pauses, as if weighing the moment. "Then perhaps our meeting isn't mere coincidence."

Our conversation, initially polite and casual, has transformed subtly, taking on the gravity of something more personal—an old connection newly discovered, suspended between past and present.

"Christa," I hear myself saying. "Her name was Christa Dindinger." Uttering the syllables of her identity feels like a sacred act.

"Dindinger," Max repeats, turning the name over carefully, testing its weight. Recognition, however, does not seem to land. He touches a finger to his temple and offers a rueful smile. "If our paths ever crossed, I'm afraid the memory has slipped away. That's what age does," he adds with a quiet shrug. "It grants wisdom and steals memories in equal measure."

His gentleness disarms me. His voice carries no forced sentiment—just the honest tug of years lived and memories misplaced. Still, a small ache opens inside me. I had hoped, if not for revelation, then at least for a sign of familiarity.

Even after many years, my heart holds tight to fondness for the days when my mother's family was more than a distant reminder of the past—precious days that my mother and I spent in Stuttgart with my grandfather Adi and my mother's siblings. Each of these kin was a surviving thread of the fabric of my mother's history. Now those threads have frayed, and I've been fumbling for something solid to hold on to. Max's accent and cadence have taken me somewhere close to memory, to the border of something I've been chasing for years.

As the evening draws to a close, I don't want to let the import of the moment dim with disappointment. "It has been an absolute pleasure, Max," I say, trying to match his warmth with my own.

Max meets my hesitation with a kindhearted, determined smile. "Ah, but I'm not ready to give up," he says, shaking his head resolutely. "I may not remember your family right now, but give me a little time. I can find anyone." He regards me expectantly, the offer hanging in the space between us.

His confidence catches me off guard. The notion—that a chance dinner conversation could somehow peel back years of silence and mystery—is both ridiculous and totally irresistible. Laughter, light and unbidden, bubbles up from within me. The idea may be absurd, yet suddenly it feels possible.

"It's a generous proposal," I say at last, cautious yet intrigued. "But our time here in Europe is tight. It doesn't seem likely that we'll be able to meet long-lost relatives before we leave."

Max nods, his smile softening. "Of course. Still, my offer stands," he says, slipping a business card into my hand. "Just in case." Then he unclasps his hand, returning us both to the hum of the room.

Our conversation was simple, yet something has shifted—like a door long shut, now slowly creaking open. That exchange, over a shared meal in a distant land, is the first whisper of a story that has been waiting for me—a legacy that will soon lead me back through time.

In the days that follow, Max's casual comment lingers in my thoughts, echoing with unexpected significance. It isn't just the thrill of solving a mystery that entices me but also the hope of recovering a piece of my mother's life that I've never fully understood.

The thought tugs at me with the persistence of an unfulfilled wish. Saying no to Max's offer would mean closing a door that I hadn't even known was open. It would mean letting apathy win. The years continue to pass relentlessly, and the generation that knew my mother is fading. Am I prepared to let the shadows claim their stories forever?

As my husband and I drive in thoughtful quiet toward the airport in Frankfurt, the prospect of reconnecting with that lost history begins to feel so urgent, I can't ignore it anymore. This isn't just curiosity. It's responsibility. The chance to bridge the gap between my mother's past and my present is a gift. And I am finally ready to accept it.

The silence in the car grows heavy. My husband reaches over and gives my hand a gentle squeeze. "Penny for your thoughts?" he asks quietly, his smile patient.

I hesitate. The idea forming in my mind feels impulsive yet oddly necessary. "Do you think it would be crazy to ask Max to help with my mother's family history?"

He glances at me, half amused and half serious, as though he knows this has been bothering me for a while. "Max is genuine, so there's no harm in asking," he says, eyes on the road. His tone is steady and pensive. "Maybe it's not so far-fetched. It could be the start of something."

The idea, with all its uncertainties and possibilities, amplifies that thrill I felt in Strasbourg. My husband's belief in the venture gives it the affirmation I've been seeking.

"I'll contact Max when we're back," I announce, settling into the decision.

The question of my mother's past accompanies me, restless and insistent, throughout the rest of our trip back to America. I send Max a message the moment I've returned home, before I even unpack.

The phone rings soon after that. "You're not going to believe this," Max says, laughter crackling through the line. "Your mother's cousin is right here in Stuttgart. She's quite the respected ophthalmologist." The sheer delight in his tone is infectious.

It seems destiny had a hand in our meeting after all.

That's how fate works, though, isn't it? Serendipity is all about finding the right moment, the right people, the right path. In the intricate dance of life, fate often conspires to guide us exactly where we need to be. That dinner in Strasbourg wasn't just a meal. It was a turning point.

I haven't seen my mother's cousin Helga for decades. Conversations with her soon punctuate the calendar as, with a mix of hope and curiosity, we make plans to reunite in Germany. Stuttgart is no longer just a place on a map but also a thread in the story I'm only beginning to piece together. What awaits is more than a destination; it's a chance to step into a past I've only glimpsed until now.

Preparing to board a plane back to Europe, I feel as though this trip is a homecoming—but to a place where I have never lived and a family I'm only beginning to understand.

———

"Komm, setz Dich hin. Sit and have some tea," Helga says, gesturing to the dining room table with the familiar ease that defines the women in our family. Her movements seem instinctive, graceful—an unspoken choreography of welcome passed down through generations. This is the kind of hospitality I remember from my teenage years: warm, quiet, enveloping. It's part of what made me feel visible again, after years of treatment for my spinal disorder dulled the way others looked at me.

As we settle into the rhythm of reminiscence, Helga's living room becomes a threshold—an entryway to memory. Her stories, infused with the scent of black tea and nostalgia, are vibrant but incomplete, flecked with both the familiar and the unknown. They paint a portrait of her own youth and my mother's, backlit by the long aftermath of the Great War and the looming threat of another brewing storm.

I listen not as a distant, indifferent cousin but as someone trying to find her own place in the family's unfinished map. I ponder the early lives of these children who grew up in a world still licking its wounds, only to find themselves on the cusp of new turmoil. The rumblings of conflict were the lullabies of their youth. For them, the abnormal had been normalized.

"What was it like for them, growing up in Stuttgart?" I muse aloud, my hands wrapped around the warm teacup. "Did they ever really know peace?"

Despite Helga's vivid recollections and the comforting timbre of her voice, the complete image of their lives eludes me. I knew my mother's siblings as adults and witnessed the full richness of their being: their mannerisms, the cadence of their laughter, the subtle shifts of expressions when words failed, hinting at something underneath. But the weight of what had shaped them—the shadows they walked through before I ever knew them—remained just out of reach.

In my mind's eye, I can almost see them in their youth, a band of siblings whose days were woven with the simple pleasures of childhood—games played in sun-dappled courtyards, laughter echoing through hallways, the innocent mischief that is the hallmark of unfettered spirits. The simplicity of those imagined scenes clashes with what later surrounded them: war, displacement, silence. By the time my mother and her siblings reached adulthood, a hush had fallen over the past, a heaviness that dimmed the brightness of childhood.

Helga lifts her shoulders in a slight, uncertain shrug, a gesture that carries the weariness of a time when clarity was a luxury. "How much can children grasp of war—the strife, the loss?" she says quietly. "Adi and Tatjana tried to build a shelter around them, a sense of normal life. But no, not here in Stuttgart."

"Not here?" I echo, trying to understand.

Helga's gaze is kind but steady. "Your mother spoke little of it, true?" she asks gently.

"Yes," I admit, the enormity of her silence hitting me once again. "She remained silent on so much." My voice drops. "I've been trying to piece things together ever since she died. But every answer seems to bring more questions."

"Such is the nature of life, isn't it?" Helga's smile is tender and resolute, soothing the sting of the unknown. "But your grandparents didn't raise your mother here. Adi and Tatjana made their home in Bydgoszcz, in Poland. That's where they weathered the real storms—the ones that came with invasion, with change, with history turning on itself."

"Bydgoszcz . . ." I repeat. The name feels foreign on my tongue, an unexpected glimpse of a world I never knew existed. The image I had so carefully constructed, of my mother's childhood framed by the city of Stuttgart, begins to dim.

Helga's next words pull me back from the drift of memory. "I have something—something you must see," she says, rising with unexpected agility. "A legacy from your grandfather, my beloved Adi. He was never Adolf to me. I loved him even more than my own father. You are his blood."

From the corner of the room, Helga retrieves a small wooden suitcase, an unassuming item that nonetheless charges the air between us. Her eyes shine as she says softly, "This has been waiting for you."

The suitcase is heavier than it looks. Crafted from wood, its surface bears the patina of age, unlike the slick, modern luggage we all use today. My fingers trace the contours of its history, feeling the weight of generations in its grain.

"This is beautiful," I murmur, my voice low, reverent.

On the lid of the suitcase, in the upper corner—stained by water, wear, and time—is an inscription:

Ich bleib Dir treu, 1916

"I remain true to you." Helga leans closer, her voice soft as she smiles, the memory lighting her face. "Surprisingly romantic, isn't it? Especially knowing World War I had already begun. That was no small promise."

I can only nod, overwhelmed by the intimacy of the inscription. The pledge between my grandparents, inscribed in that humble suitcase, seems to defy the passing years. It is still alive, reaching out to me.

When I undo the brass clasps of the suitcase, the lid opens with a faint sigh.

The case is full of yellowing papers, piles of letters and photographs and other documents. But these aren't just papers and photos—they are traces of Adi, of Aunt Erika and Uncle Hellmuth, etched in ink and pencil, and of Uncle Joachim, his early battlefield letters written in the ornate Old German Sütterlin script. As I sift through the dated pages, the war continues, and his handwriting shifts into something plainer, more utilitarian, as if even his pencil was worn down and reshaped by the relentless crucible of conflict.

In the sea of letters, the handwriting of my mother, Christa, attracts my eye like a magnet. Her script is a dance of ink: precise, elegant, every character arranged with the care of an artist's brushstroke. Her disciplined, graceful spirit infuses every curve and flourish. In the symmetry of her script, I find the mirror image of a soul that has been both my guide and my greatest mystery.

Filtered throughout are the letters of Tatjana, my grandmother, flowing from Russian to Polish to German, as fluid and adaptable as she was in life. Her words reflect a mind that conversed in six tongues, a spirit unconfined by borders.

Tucked among this correspondence are photographs revealing moments from the lives they once lived. Here is Tatjana, small and striking, her blue eyes luminous even in black and white. Here is Adi, calm and still, carrying a presence that needs no words. Joachim and Hellmuth look impossibly young, their energy captured just before time and war began to reshape their faces. And Erika and Christa, so close in age, radiating promise in every frame, their expressions full of a future not yet complicated by the burden of history.

Upon lifting the next letter, written by Joachim from the Eastern Front, I flinch. A chill runs through me as I lean closer to the page, staring at the unmistakable symbols stamped across the top: the Reich eagle, the swastikas.

The swastikas are small—I had not noticed them in my first pangs of excitement—but their impact is immediate. Stark and black against the brittle parchment, they stare back with quiet violence. Their presence is a jarring contrast to the tenderness of the writing, a grim reminder of the era that swallowed so many lives whole.

"Most letters from '33 to '45 bear this mark." Helga's voice is gentle. She must have noticed my involuntary flinch. "It was a sign of the times."

"Of course," I reply softly, reaching for another paper, my voice nearly lost in the stillness that has settled over us.

"Remember," Helga says, her voice cutting through the silence, steady and clear. "Joachim and Hellmuth were conscripted. They were never Nazis. Joachim joined the Wehrmacht because the pay was better, and the family needed it. Hellmuth . . . well, he was born to fly."

Her words ground me. These aren't caricatures from history books.

These were sons, brothers, young men swept into something larger than themselves. As my fingertips wander across the faded German script, a quiet warmth rises through me. These letters carry more than ink. They hold love, loyalty, and the quiet defiance of those who stayed connected even as the world fractured around them.

The communications from Joachim, each one signed with an affectionate farewell to his parents and siblings, feel like whispers from another time, fragments of a family bond that refused to break, even under siege. "Liebe Eltern und Tita und Eka . . . Viele Grüße und Küsse," Helga reads aloud, her voice soft with memory. "Dear Parents and Tita and Eka . . . many greetings and kisses . . ."

A surge of emotion swells within me. Joachim, the brother that my mother spoke of with wet eyes and a distant smile, suddenly feels near. Overwhelmed, I pause. The letters and photographs blur as I fight back tears.

"I came searching for traces of the past, but I've found so much more, Helga. You've bridged gaps in my history that I never knew existed," I admit with profound gratitude.

Helga's smile is a quiet reminder of what we share, a kinship that runs deeper than names on a family tree. "No need for thanks," she says, her eyes kind. "And there is another suitcase, a twin to this one. Take these treasures. And when you're ready, let them lead you. You'll find more than you expect."

I nod, feeling the weight of it—not just the suitcase but the journey it promises. "I will," I reply, the anticipation building within me. "My German is rusty, and my Polish by ear only, but I will manage." My fingers pause on a laminated document, its age evident in the yellowing edges and the gentle curl of the paper.

"This forged document—it was Tatjana's lifeline," Helga says carefully. "Your grandfather had it made for her."

As I study the signatures, faded and delicate with age, something tightens in my chest. This ink, this paper, carried them across borders and into a new life of hope. Their defiance, preserved in secrecy and script, feels alive in my hands.

I return the document to its place with care. "So I guess it all began in . . . Bydgoszcz?"

Helga dismisses my inquiry with a shake of her head, and her eyes sparkle with the mischief of a shared secret. "The essence of the tale lies deep within the ancient woods of Białowieża. *That's* where it all began," she hints, her voice lowering to a conspiratorial whisper. "The answers you seek exist within the folds of these modest suitcases."

Her words are both mystery and invitation. I will have to find the rest on my own.

Later, with the contents of the two small suitcases spread before me, the significance of Helga's words begins to crystallize. The primeval Białowieża Forest, shrouded in the mists of time and family lore, beckons as the birthplace of my forebears' saga.

Białowieża . . . where it all began.

One of Adolf's two small suitcases from World War I,
brimming with documents and letters.

Ich bleib Dir treu.
1916
"I remain true to you."
The inscription to Tatjana inside one of the suitcases.
These small suitcases escaped Russia with Adi and Tatjana
during the Bolshevik Revolution.

PART I

A True Home

CHAPTER ONE

FORBIDDEN LOVE (1914)

THE YEAR WAS 1914, AND a storm was coming.

Adolf Dindinger sat motionless in his saddle, scanning the tree line of the ancient Białowieża Forest. The woods stretched across the borderlands between Poland and the Russian Empire—a vast, primeval wilderness unlike any he had ever known. As head of the Kaisergarde, Adolf had seen his share of majesty and beauty, but this forest humbled him. Each time he returned, it caught him off guard. Its silence wasn't empty; it pulsed.

Through the trees, he could just make out the hulking shapes of a herd of bison lazily grazing in a sunny glade without a care in the world. From a distance, the beasts seemed like gentle giants, furry and warm—almost cuddly. But Adolf knew better. Looks could be deceiving, and Adi had seen bison in action more than once, especially when startled. Few natural predators in the forest could best them. They were the kings here.

The bison, with their formidable presence, struck Adi as a living metaphor for the Russian Empire: immense, regal, a vestige of a bygone era. They moved through the forest with a slow, deliberate grace that belied their power, much like the empire itself—grandiose and seemingly imperturbable on the precipice of the modern age, with the currents of change lapping at its foundations.

In the hush of the forest, Adi couldn't help but draw the quiet parallel between nature and nation—both majestic, both seemingly unshakable, yet each vulnerable to the tremors of an approaching storm. And there was wisdom in the caution of a soldier, in his unwillingness to tempt the might lurking beneath that calm exterior, whether of the creature or the crown.

Adi understood the delicate dance of power and the importance of alliance, especially when it came to the Kaiser and his Imperial cousin. The political tapestry of Europe was a precarious one, and the fabric of the Russian Empire was fraying more visibly with each passing day. The world had shifted underfoot over the past four years. The Russian Empire, once sprawling and unquestioned, was crumbling.

Revolution simmered in salons and spread in the fields. The Imperial court was restless. Rumors traveled faster than decrees. Something was coming, though no one yet knew how far it would go—or how much it would take with it.

When the sound of hoofbeats came, it was sharp and sudden—there, from the underbrush to Adi's left—and shattered the tranquility of the morning. His horse reared slightly, nostrils flaring, but Adi was poised to confront any threat that dared disturb the calm. The imperative of his role was clear: protect the Kaiser at all costs.

His hand went instinctively to the hilt of his sword. "Who goes there?" he called out, voice crisp and commanding.

The trees parted as a horse and rider emerged, but it wasn't a brigand. It was a woman—alone, upright in her saddle, framed by shafts of morning light. She moved with a quiet self-assurance, her posture too composed for a peasant or a courier. Her blonde hair caught the sun, and her clear blue eyes met Adi's without hesitation.

"I am called Tatjana," she announced, her German words tinged with the melody of a Russian accent. Her tone was steady but not serious—in fact, she sounded almost amused.

She didn't look lost or uncertain, just out of place in a way that made Adi sit a little straighter. The grace with which she handled her reins, the quiet control in her movements—it all hinted at a life far from the border villages and their harsh rhythms.

"Adolf Dindinger," he replied, offering a formal nod. He tried not to smile but failed. A moment ago, he had been prepared to draw steel. Now he couldn't stop staring. "Is it customary for a woman of your standing to ride unaccompanied in these parts?"

Tatjana's smile was as light as the breeze that tussled the leaves above them. "Customary?" she echoed playfully, her eyes shining. "I might ask the same of a German officer riding alone this deep into the forest."

Her words danced between teasing and testing. They made something spark in the air—unexpected but not unwelcome. Her wit, sharp as the edge of a blade, drew a genuine smile from Adi.

"Do you live in one of the neighboring villages?" he asked, watching her with renewed interest.

"My family owns land nearby, yes." She looked him up and down carefully, as her horse slowly approached his. "And you? I know without asking that you are not from one of the villages."

"You are correct," he conceded, his nod a silent acknowledgment of her perceptiveness. Their conversation felt like a game of chess, and she had skillfully met his opening moves. "My home is Berlin."

"Ah," she mused, her expression unreadable for a beat. "You have traveled here with the Kaiser then?" she probed further, a playful lilt in her voice.

Adi could not conceal his surprise. "You know he is here?"

Tatjana only shook her head and laughed. "You think two royal trains, dozens of ministers and bodyguards, hundreds of servants, and thousands of pounds of food rumbling through town go unnoticed? Everyone knows the Tsar and the Kaiser are meeting here."

She had a point—and one difficult to ignore.

Adi cleared his throat. "So. You're educated, beautiful, and clearly at ease on a horse. You are either a spy or the most fascinating woman I've ever met."

She arched a brow, her mouth curling at the edges. "I could be both," she said, her voice light but firm. "But I'll take that as a compliment."

Something about her confidence was disarming. That unexpected spark, he realized, came from her. Intelligent, composed, and versed in humor, she spoke with ease, but her eyes watched everything. Was she flirting or gathering intelligence?

Somehow, the uncertainty only intrigued him more.

She was rare—that much was clear. Even in Berlin, Adi doubted he would have met her equal. Her presence was inescapable, like sunlight breaking through the trees: subtle at first but with a brilliance impossible to ignore.

In her company, Adi felt something change. The instincts that usually kept him guarded gave way to a curiosity he couldn't quite contain. She was poised, yes—but also unpredictable, unafraid. There was no easy name for what drew him in.

He only knew one thing for certain: He wanted to see her again.

Białowieża Hunting Lodge for Tsar Nicholas II, circa 1914. Interesting inclusion of Kaiser Wilhelm at bottom left.

Amid the ancient whispers of the Białowieża Forest, a connection was forged. For the length of the Tsar's stay at the Białowieża Hunting Lodge, Adolf and Tatjana managed to meet for enchanting horseback rides through the forest and stolen moments in the quiet corners of her small village. When the day inevitably arrived for his departure with the Kaisergarde, Adi promised to write often—and to return one day to Białowieża.

Tatjana, with her quick wit and piercing gaze, had kindled something within Adi that he could not explain, only feel. Whether it would last or fade, he couldn't know. But in that moment, it felt like the beginning of everything.

As a member of the 8ten Kompanie Garde-Füsilier-Regiments and head of the Kaisergarde, Adi continued to move in the highest circles of power, shuttling between the Kaiser and the Tsar, whose armies were now adversaries on the battlefield. Meanwhile, Adi's letters to Tatjana were full of words that could never be spoken aloud, describing a love that lived in shadows and in small acts of defiance, even as their countries were entering a brutal war.

As the months passed, Adi's elegant script described his longing for a time when the two lovers could reunite. Tatjana's replies, more cautious but no less passionate, hinted at the dangers of their bond—of a German soldier and a Russian Jew daring to imagine a life together in a world that would never permit it.

JUNE 1914

My dearest Adi,
How I cherish each letter that arrives from you, though they come
with less frequency than before. The post has become frustratingly

unreliable of late, yet I cling to the hope that this missive will somehow reach your hands.

Each word you pen is a beacon, illuminating my solitude with the light of your presence. How I cherish these paper messengers, fraught with the warmth of your touch and the depth of your sentiments.

Here, in the seclusion of my village, life moves to the quiet rhythm of the untouched, and yet the faintest ripples of unrest from the cities manage to reach even my ears. The lines you write are etched with concern, the ink a testament to your love, now shadowed by the weight of separation. I am cocooned in our sylvan retreat, a world away from the storm that brews on the distant horizon.

Nonetheless, the air is charged with the rumblings of change. Dire tales of riots and revolt against the Tsar spill from the lips of weary travelers, painting St. Petersburg as a canvas of chaos. Workers and peasants, their spirits ground down by want and woe, have banded together in a chorus of despair, crying out for justice and sustenance. Though my abode remains a sanctuary from these nightmarish realities, I cannot turn a deaf ear to the cries that rise in the dark.

Your Tatjana

JULY 1914

My dear Adi,

Through the long night I stand at my window, gazing out over moon-drenched meadows toward the woods that witnessed the building of our love. I imagine you riding out from that tree line as you once did, handsome upon your noble steed. In my dreams I run to meet you, throwing myself into your welcoming embrace with tears of joy. Alas, the forest remains still and empty, devoid of my gallant German officer.

But though world forces keep us cruelly separated, nothing can conquer the love burning in my heart. It spans the hundreds of miles between us. Eventually there will come renewed optimism for Russia's future. I know you have come to speak with Tsar Nicholas on behalf of the Kaiser. What a dangerous time this is. Russia has weathered countless hard seasons, and though her people suffer greatly now, I trust she will bloom again.

My time here feels increasingly transient, a way station before our fates guide us together. Have faith, dearest love. Keep your chin high and your heart courageous. We have endured the blistering prejudice of small minds and emerged unbroken. Compared to that, surely, we can weather whatever caprices Mother Russia throws at her children. A quiet strength resides within these lands themselves, the spirt of endurance that has borne generation after generation through many winters. It stirs now in her downtrodden people and in my soul.

With abiding affection,
Your Tatjana

OCTOBER 1914

My dearest Tatjana,
Forgive the prolonged silence that has stretched between my words and your heart—such an absence is a grievous burden that weighs heavily upon my soul. The relentless demands of duty have bound me to Berlin, each moment consumed by the service of the Kaiser. Time, once a steadfast companion, now trickles through my fingers, leaving me bereft of the solace of our correspondence.

The somber cloak of war has enshrouded our nations since August, casting a long shadow over the tender memories we have cultivated. The Kaiser, despite his most ardent endeavors, could not turn the tides of conflict that now surge between our homelands. Oh, how fervently I yearn to stand beside you, to be your bastion against the creeping dread that this war brings to your doorstep. Instead, I am ensnared by distance, my spirit tormented by the specters of calamity that may befall you.

My dearest, to envision your smile is to recall the splendor of a time when the sun shone upon our union, unclouded by the specter of war. Your voice now resonates only in the echoes of my memory. This chasm that divides us is a chalice of sorrow from which I drink deeply, each day more bitter than the last. We danced once in the light of a golden summer, our souls entwined in a halcyon embrace. The thought of our lost refuge gnaws at my conscience, for I am haunted by the choices of a man who saw not the storm's approach.

The Jewish plight under the Tsar fills me with dread, and my heart trembles for your safety. It is a merciless irony that our love now flickers in the gale of history's unforgiving tempest. In these moments of solitude, I cling to the promise of our love—a love that remains defiant in the face of the chaos that encircles us.

These halls of power, once the symbol of order and authority, now seem but hollowed shells to me, echoing with the signs of desolation. As I tread these marbled corridors, the grandeur of bygone days jeers at me, a stark reminder of the life that you, my dearest Tatjana, might be enduring. Your village, once a sanctuary of simple joys, may now shiver in the cold grip of want, the shadow of violence looming ominously at its edges. The opulence that surrounds me here in Berlin is but a cruel mirage when I think of you, possibly besieged by hunger and the encroaching darkness of uncertain times.

Our mighty Germany, a colossus with feet of clay, stands teetering on the verge of tumultuous upheaval. The whispers of discontent murmur through the Kaiser's courts, a cacophony of disquiet that heralds the crumbling of foundations once deemed unshakable. Our celebrated military shows the strain of internal strife, mirroring the faltering pulse of an economy that once surged with vitality. And the people, weary from the gaudy display of aristocratic indulgence and the crush of relentless inflation, now find themselves on the cusp of insurrection. I sense a reckoning on the horizon, a storm that threatens to sweep away all that we have known.

Day upon day, I beseech my superiors for leave, seeking even a momentary respite from this gilded cage, but to no avail. They speak of chaos beyond our borders, of a world unhinged, insisting that the Kaiser's need for steadfast guardians supersedes all personal entreaties. They fail to grasp that my truest duty, the very essence of my being, resides not within the imposing walls of this palace, but in the wintry embrace of the Russian wilderness where you await.

With each denied request, I am reminded that my place is here, shackled to the fate of an empire that may soon know the bitter winds of change. Yet in my heart, I yearn for nothing more than the comfort of your presence, to return to the haven of our forest, where the silence speaks more profoundly than the clamor of a thousand courts.

I find solace only at the window, my gaze cast eastward across the breadth of Prussia's ancient forests, reaching for the whisper of your village. In the quietude of my mind, I see you—the pulse of life in our secluded world, your laughter a melody that defies the encroaching gloom. Oh, how I long for the simple grace of your presence, for the lustrous dance of candlelight in your hair. My heart aches to reclaim the softness of your hand, to vow with the certainty of the stars that I shall never part from your side again.

Hold fast to the belief, my dearest, that this chasm that lies between us will soon be bridged. For every moment of solitude, every trial that tests our resolve, is but a fleeting shadow against the enduring flame of our union.

The day will come when I shall cast off these chains and rush to your embrace. Let the resilience that has long defined us be your cloak against the chill of uncertainty. Our love, unfettered by the bounds of tyrants or the cruel hands of fate, will find its way. You are the keeper of my heart, Tatjana, and in the sanctuary of your arms, I will discover my true home, now and forevermore.

With unwavering love,
Your Adi

Adolf Dindinger, 8ten Kompanie Garde-Füsilier-Regiments (an infantry unit of the Guards Corps of the Prussian Army, garrisoned in Berlin), 1913.

№ *12* der Truppenstammrolle für 191*1*

Führungszeugnis.

Der *Gefreite Füsilier, Adolf Dindinger*

geboren am *4*ten *November* 18*89* zu *Forst Wallitsch*
Kreis: Briesen, Provinz: Westpreußen
hat vom *14*ten *Oktober* 19*11* bis *22*ten *September* 191*3*
bei der *8*ten **Kompagnie Garde-Füsilier-Regiments**
gedient und sich während dieser Dienstzeit *sehr gut* geführt.

Strafen:
a) Gerichtliche Strafen:

Keine

b) Disziplinar-Bestrafungen mit strengem Arrest:

Keine

Berlin, den *21*ten September 191*1*

v. Koler.

Hauptmann und Kompagnie-Chef.

Certificate of good conduct for Adolf Dindinger in the 8ten Kompanie Garde-Füsilier-Regiments, 1911–1913.

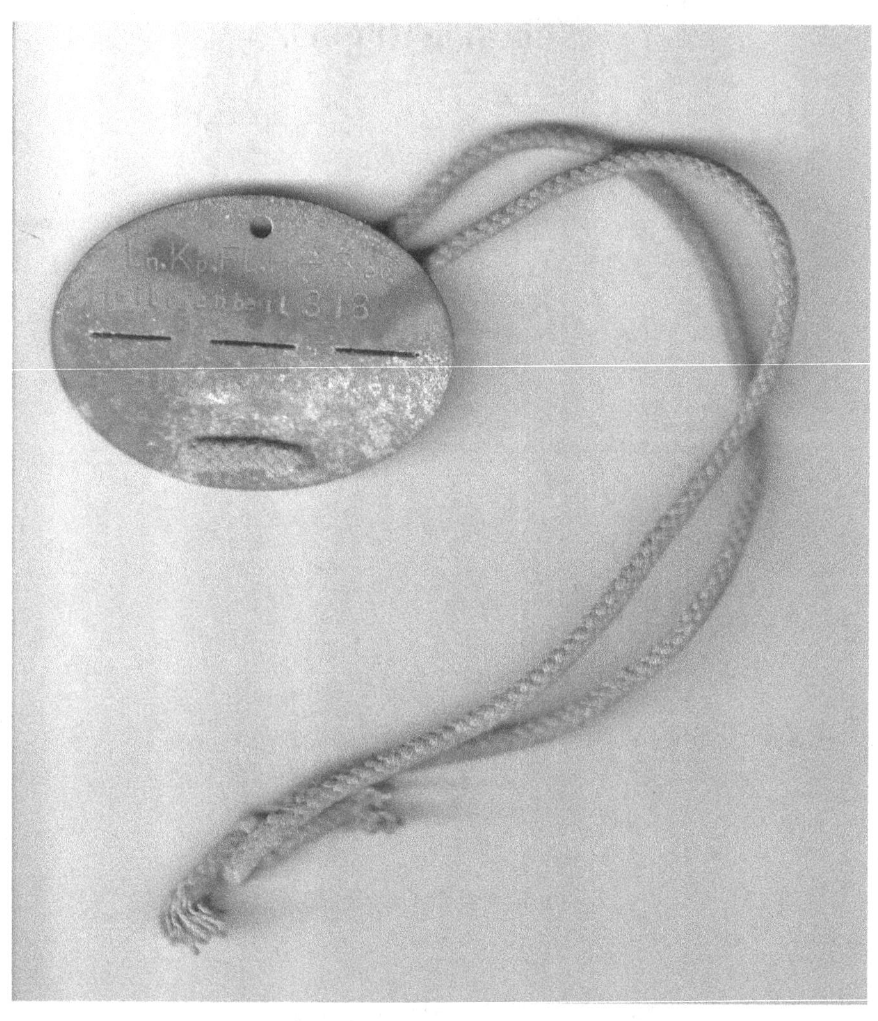

Adi's World War I dog tag, manufactured so it could be split in half.
The use of two separate dog tags was not introduced until World War II.

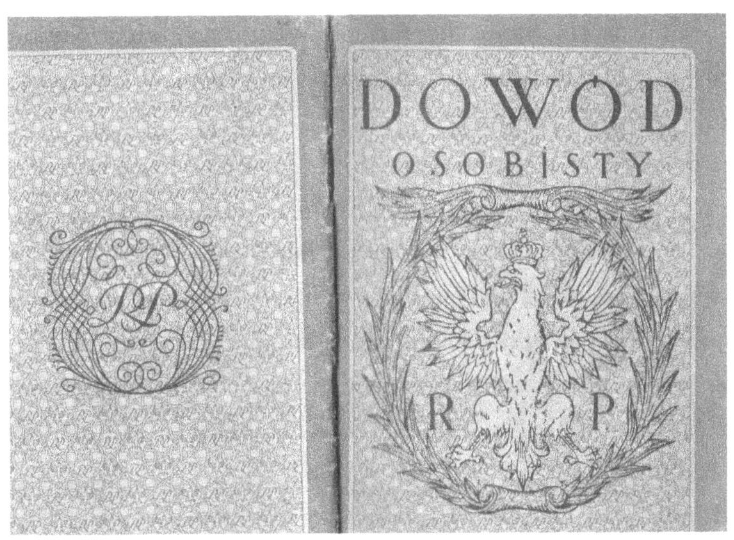

Tatjana's Polish passport photo, 1928. She was thirty-three years of age. And a Jew in hiding.

CHAPTER TWO

REVOLUTION AND ESCAPE (1917)

THE UNDERBELLY OF RUSSIAN SOCIETY had long simmered with unrest, a relentless wave of discontent that deepened as the Great War stretched on interminably. By the time the war had dragged into its third year, those domestic tensions had grown impossible to ignore.

Tsar Nicholas II's momentous abdication in early 1917 was a pivotal act that threw the nation into further turmoil. What began as a revolution soon spiraled into a brutal civil war, turning allies into enemies in a savage struggle for the very soul of Russia.

The first fires of rebellion sparked in the cities, where discontent was loudest. But they didn't stay there. The unrest spread outward—into the countryside, into quiet estates, into places like Białowieża.

Germany, too, was changing. Kaiser Wilhelm II's power was slipping. In Berlin, there was talk of a revolution, of a republic rising from the ashes of the German Empire—murmurs further energized by the Romanovs' fall in Russia. And now, whispers of Bolshevik forces closing in on the Białowieża Forest had turned into full-throated warnings.

Adi and Tatjana, like so many others, found themselves caught between divided loyalties and rising dangers. There would be no untouched corners, no safe neutrality. The world was shifting beneath them, and there could be no turning back. The specter of conflict threatened to engulf every nook of this restive domain. The inferno of revolution would spare no one.

Amid the chaos, Adi knew only one thing: Tatjana had to get out of Russia. Where they would go, how they would get there—he didn't have answers. But delay was no longer an option. Time was running out.

Acting fast, Adi secured forged travel papers for Tatjana. With the ink still damp, he roared into the expanse on his motorbike, pushing through the cold. When he finally reached the edge of the Białowieża Forest, night had fallen. Smoke curled up from beyond the trees, and the sky glowed with a sickly red hue.

Majestic Białowieża, a remnant of the primeval wilderness that once stretched across the European plain, was falling prey to an evil fire that tore through the undergrowth with agonizing force. Animals fled in panic, their anguished cries a mournful chorus haunting the forest.

Adi tightened his grip on the handlebars. Whatever came next, there would be no going back.

His motorbike broke through the smoke, its headlamp cutting a wavering path through the dark. Arriving at last to his destination, he cut the engine and leapt from the bike. The ground crunched beneath his boots: ash, ember, burnt earth. Smoke clung to him, streaking his uniform in soot and an orange glow—an artist's rendering of hope set against despair.

Tatjana stood framed in the doorway—still, silhouetted against the firelight, her presence both defiant and exposed. Her voice found him through the roar. "Where can we go?" she asked, her tone quiet but steady. "My family, my sisters—our roots entwine with this land."

Her words struck Adi. He didn't have an answer—only a promise. "We'll find a way to help them," he said, reaching for her hand. His grip was firm, comforting—an anchor in the tempest. "But right now, I must get you out. We'll head for the border. I won't let harm find you here."

Behind them, the fire surged higher, swallowing trees and sky. Tatjana turned once, her eyes lingering on the home she had known her whole life. Then she nodded.

They ran.

Adi lifted Tatjana onto the motorbike, positioning her securely behind him. Her arms encircled his waist without hesitation. There was no time to speak. With little more than two small wooden suitcases packed with their possessions, they fled into the tumultuous night.

They wove through burning trees and leaping flames with nature unleashing her fury all around them. As they broke free from the forest's choking edge, Adi's hands remained steady on the handlebars, his focus unshaken. The border to the Kingdom of Poland—and safety—was still leagues away.

Behind them, whole swaths of the forest collapsed into embers. Ahead, uncertainty loomed. Yet Adi held on to one small thread of hope: his reputation. He was still known within the government. His credentials as a structural engineer might carry weight, a fragile lifeline in a world upended.

They passed others along the way, on foot and in carts, faces pale with fear—a scattered procession of lives uprooted. Tatjana gripped Adi tighter as they passed a woman walking alone, shoeless, carrying only a child and a bundle wrapped in cloth.

At last, they reached the border—an invisible, unforgiving line that cleaved the known from the unknown. It was both an ending and a beginning.

Adi slowed as they neared the checkpoint, a jagged line of barrels and barbed wire lit by harsh floodlights. Soldiers stood along the barricade, rifles slung over shoulders, eyes sharp. Adi eased the bike to a stop, and dust rose around him and Tatjana like breath held too long. This was the line.

Behind them, everything was burning.

A soldier had stepped forward, his hand raised to stop them. The lines on his face spoke of the fatigue of ceaseless conflict, yet his eyes showed no malice.

Adi let the engine idle. "We seek passage," he declared, his voice steady and measured above the motorbike's muted growl. He masked his nervousness with calm clarity, knowing that fear could invite probing.

Tatjana said nothing. She didn't need to. Her stillness behind him was its own kind of force.

The soldier held their gazes for a long moment, then signaled to another guard. Adi reached into his pouch for the documents—his government credentials and the forged papers for Tatjana—and then handed them over without hesitation.

The second soldier scrutinized the papers, his eyes moving back and forth between the names, the stamps, the seal. No questions. No tells.

Then finally, a single nod. "Proceed," he said simply.

Adi nudged the bike onward and crossed into territory not yet marred by revolution's touch. Neither he nor Tatjana said anything. Gratitude lived quietly in the silence between them.

As the miles passed, the tension in Tatjana's shoulders eased. She leaned into Adi's back just slightly but enough to be felt. It was a gesture of trust, of shared survival.

"We'll find a place," Adi reassured her as they navigated roads that promised neither ease nor certainty. "There is talk that this whole area may be reclaimed as Poland, but as a republic this time."

"Poland?" The name escaped Tatjana in a weary sigh. The grip of fear and flight had finally sapped her energy. "Will it be safe?"

Adi pulled over on the side of the road, near a small clearing. Beneath a glowing moon, the quiet night was thick with expectation. Adi steadied the bike as Tatjana stepped off, then turned to her, eyes searching her face.

"Safer than anywhere in Russia. Safer than Berlin right now," he said. "And if a new government forms, there will be secure jobs with the state. They'll need engineers like me." He offered a small smile. "That's something I can do."

Tatjana didn't speak, just nodded.

Adi reached for her, and she let him hold her. It wasn't a dramatic embrace, just close enough to tell her she wasn't alone. "I'm with you," he said, "and I always will be. That hasn't changed."

Closing her eyes, Tatjana rested in Adi's arms, letting herself breathe at last. The road ahead was uncertain, but the fire was behind them. And in that quiet moment, she wasn't alone. Just for an instant, she allowed herself to feel what it was to be sheltered, to share the burden of fear she had carried alone for so long.

The calls of nightbirds and the whisper of wind through the trees surrounding their moonlit clearing stirred Tatjana from these thoughts. She withdrew slightly from Adi's arms, her eyes searching his in the silver light.

"Poland," she mused, the word a new concept. "I know little of this land, but I trust you. I'll go wherever we need to go."

Adi's smile was tender as he gently tucked a stray lock behind her ear. "You are brave, my love," he assured her, clasping her hands within his own. "In this new Poland, we shall begin anew. Marry, create a family, and yes, maybe even find peace."

Tatjana lifted his hand to her lips, her kiss a soft benediction. "This is the only path I want. And I'll walk it with you, whatever comes."

The quiet held them a moment longer. When the moment waned, Adi, with gentle reluctance, withdrew his hand. "It's time," he intoned, the words laden with both resolve and regret.

He guided her back to the motorbike and their few possessions. When he started the engine, it roared a defiant cry against the stillness as the bike carried them forward, to a place they hoped they could finally call home.

Adolf Dindinger on his motorcycle The Wanderer, 1916. As head of the Kaisergarde, he traveled frequently between Russia and Berlin even while the countries were at war.

Kaiser Wilhelm, with his famous white horses, being driven along the Polish Border Strip—part of a German imperial plan leading to the annexation of Polish territory that previously had been partitioned by Russia. *Witamy* (top left) means "Welcome."

CHAPTER THREE

BUILDING A LIFE IN BYDGOSZCZ (1918)

IN THE CITY OF BYDGOSZCZ, Poland, the young couple's promises of a new life became a tangible reality. Adi, true to his vow, secured a position as an engineer with the *Stadt*. His municipal work proved pivotal, helping rebuild the infrastructure of a young republic after the devastation of the Great War while also breathing life back into a city finding its footing and longing for renewal.

Tatjana, too, found her place in this rebirth. Her sharp mind and experience with numbers quickly made her indispensable in managing the city's growing financial recovery—a quiet but crucial force behind its resurgence.

Together, as husband and wife, Adi and Tatjana learned to navigate the rhythms of this unfamiliar life: new customs, foreign streets, moments of doubt. But day by day, what once felt fragile began to hold. Every sunrise drew them closer, through shared joys and challenges, as they built a life using equal parts grit and modest ambition.

In their newfound existence, Tatjana began to embrace the hybrid culture of Bydgoszcz, a city stitched together by German and Polish voices, each street corner echoing with layered histories. In the bustling market square, she bartered with vendors in fluent Polish for fresh produce and herbs, then effortlessly switched to German at the meat stalls for their choice cuts. Her fluidity with languages was remarkable—and it was vital for their seamless integration into this mosaic community.

Tatjana's transformation was profound yet necessarily discreet. She adopted her new identity with care, setting aside her Russian Jewish heritage for the outward appearance of an *Evangelisch* Christian woman with a Germanic name. It was more than a change in paperwork—it was a concealment designed for survival.

The decision to live in *Geheimnis*, in secrecy, carried deep significance. Tatjana's uncle was the renowned Rabbi Yitzhak Yaacov Reines, a towering figure in the Zionist movement. Hiding her lineage meant silencing a part of herself and the past that had shaped her. Tatjana's choice to veil her religious identity was not without risk—a prescient move that would carry untold consequences when the Nazis came to power.

Inside their apartment, daily life provided a respite from such looming fears. Their first year as husband and wife had the quality of something restored—like light returning to a painting long dulled by dust. There were struggles, of course, but in all the private daily rituals—meals, routines, stolen glances—they found their own rhythm.

When Adi arrived home and set his engineer's case by the door, its familiar *click* marking the end of another workday, the air would be thick with the rich aroma of freshly baked bread. Golden crusts would crackle softly as Tatjana slid the warm loaves from the oven, promising the shared comfort of a hearty meal. The late afternoon sunlight would slip through the curtains and pool on the floor, softening the edges of the world outside.

One such afternoon, Adi paused, inhaling deeply, a smile playing on his lips as he followed the fragrant trail to its source. "Something smells delicious," he remarked, his gaze settling on Tatjana as she brushed flour from her hands.

"It's your favorite—rye bread," she replied, her tone laced with affection. "And for dinner, bigos." A kind woman at work had shared her recipe for the German Polish dish known as "hunter's stew."

Adi stepped behind her, wrapping his arms around her waist. "You've made this place feel like home in every way."

In their kitchen, cultures merged in a culinary dance. Tatjana had a gift for balance: sauerkraut laced with caraway seeds, dumplings stuffed with mushrooms and minced meat. Each recipe was a celebration of their intertwined lives. Neighbors, drawn by the mouthwatering aromas wafting from under their door, were always welcomed into a home where the table was rich with flavors that honored both tradition and discovery.

"You've outdone yourself once again," the curt Frau Schmidt from upstairs remarked one evening as she savored a spoonful of *żurek*, the tangy rye soup that Tatjana had nearly perfected.

"It's all about the balance," Tatjana responded, her smile radiant. "In the blend of flavors, there is harmony."

That harmony extended far beyond their table, permeating every facet of their married life. Hand in hand, as they wandered through Planty Park, Adi would point out intricate cornices on old facades while Tatjana shared verses of poetry. Together, they mirrored the city itself: a quiet bridge between what had once been and what still could be.

One crisp autumn evening, as they nestled beside the hearth, hands wrapped around cups of steaming tea, Adi turned to Tatjana with a probing expression.

"Do you ever think about what stories we'll tell our children?" he asked quietly. "About your past?"

Tatjana's gaze drifted toward the fire. The flames offered no answers, only movement. "We'll tell them stories of courage," she said gently. "Of how to live with love. Of hope."

"But not about your family?" Adi's question hung in the air, tenacious despite his tender tone, seeking the truth that she kept so carefully hidden.

Her eyes, unflinching, met his. "Our children will be nurtured in love, raised in a home where their worth is measured by the strength of their character, the virtue of their deeds—not by bloodline or belief."

Adi nodded slowly. He understood. Some truths were too heavy for young hearts.

That winter, as snow blanketed the city in silence, they celebrated their first anniversary with a quiet meal at home. By candlelight, they spoke of the road they had traveled: its dangers, its joys, the delicate art of beginning again.

"You know," Adi mused between bites of pierogi glistening with butter and onions, "I never imagined life could be this full."

Tatjana's fingers reached across the table for his, a gentle pressure conveying unity. "We built this," she whispered.

Later, wrapped in blankets on the couch, they let the hush of night settle around them. Outside, the world spun on, full of noise and news. But within these walls, there was stillness and a shared promise, unspoken but understood: They would protect what they'd created, no matter what came.

Shadows did linger at the edges of their joy—whispers of Tatjana's past, and the fear that one day the truth might find its way in. But not tonight. This moment was for celebration—for companionship, for the life they were shaping together, and for their quiet rebellion against a world still emerging from darkness.

The chill of winter loosened its grip on Bydgoszcz, yielding to the lush blooms of spring. Adi and Tatjana welcomed the change with a stroll through the reawakening streets. The fragrance of damp soil and the hum of rebirth filled the air, signaling a fresh chapter in their lives and in the city they now called home.

Returning to the apartment, Tatjana paused at the threshold, a telltale tremor betraying her calm.

Adi, brow furrowed in concern, turned to her. "What is it, love? You've been quiet since we left the park."

A tentative smile tugged at Tatjana's lips as she sought the comfort of his hands. "Adi," she began, her voice a whisper woven with joy and wonder, "we're going to have a child."

"A child?" he echoed, his voice breaking with emotion.

She nodded, her eyes glistening. "A new life . . . our very own."

Without a word, Adi swept her into his arms, spinning her around as laughter burst from him, pure and unguarded, as if it belonged to some other version of him, before war and loss had carved him into something quieter. In that moment, the long shadows of winter fell away. What remained was something light and the beginning of something real.

"A father," he murmured into her hair. "I'm going to be a father."

Later, they curled into each other on the couch, a hush falling around them. Outside, the world continued. Inside, the apartment was quiet but for the tick of the wall clock and their synchronized breathing.

"We'll need to prepare a room," Adi mused aloud. "And there are so many things that we still don't know."

Tatjana leaned into him, her head resting softly on his shoulder. "We will learn," she assured him. "We have time, and we have each other."

In the ensuing days and weeks, their prosaic existence was infused with renewed vitality. The promise of new life became their daily dance, with dawn's light prompting musings over names and dusk's descent inviting dreams of familial bliss.

Adi threw himself into transforming one of the spare rooms into a nursery. In preparing to paint it, he chose soft hues of yellow and green that reminded Tatjana of the Białowieża Forest, whose peace and tranquility she rarely let herself dwell on.

As Tatjana's body changed with the growing life inside her, so too did the community around them. Neighbors began stopping by with warm congratulations and practical advice, and even stern Frau Schmidt from upstairs softened enough to knit a tiny pair of booties. Tatjana accepted each kindness with heartfelt gratitude, deeply touched by the way these small gestures wove a sturdy fabric of support for their growing family.

With each passing milestone, their home would burst anew with eager expectation. They envisioned the inquisitive eyes, the effervescent laughter, the captivating presence of a wonderful human being wrought from their deepest affection. They imagined the miracle that would soon fill their home with new meaning.

One evening, as the last golden stretch of summer unfolded, they reclined on their porch, the street across the way still pulsating with life. Adi's hand rested gently on Tatjana's rounded belly, feeling the steady kicks beneath his palm.

"This one has spirit," he commented, his voice tinged with a father's pride.

Tatjana laughed. "Clearly inherited from Papa."

Adi feigned offense, but his smile betrayed the pure delight that welled up inside of him. For a while, they let the sounds of the evening wrap around them: the clatter of a tram, the soft chime of dishes being cleared two floors above—life's little assurances that the world was still turning.

Yet beneath the gentle rhythms of domesticity was an undercurrent of concern. How long would this peace hold? They had found a haven in Poland, but history had already taught them the fragility of peace. How could they protect their growing family from life's cruel unpredictability?

Tatjana, her past veiled and her present unblemished, played her role flawlessly. But the nagging question remained: What if the veil lifted? What if they found themselves seeking refuge once more, struggling to make a new beginning in an unknown place?

In the relative calm—despite the ongoing Polish-Soviet War—the turmoil of the past already seemed like a distant storm, but their intimate knowledge of such chaos rendered the once improbable now frighteningly conceivable. They had witnessed the world's foundations shift abruptly beneath their feet. They knew that the future's script was yet unwritten.

But on that late summer night, all such worries were set adrift. Instead, Tatjana and Adi surrendered to the embrace of hopeful dreams, their touch gentle in twilight's tender glow.

"Tomorrow I'll start on a rocking chair," Adi said after a while, his voice low and thoughtful. "For you to sit in when you read stories or sing lullabies."

Tatjana tilted her head back to look at him, a hand resting over his. "I cannot wait to meet our little baby," she whispered.

"Nor can I." Adi leaned down to kiss her forehead.

Their conversation wandered easily, touching on lullabies and baby names, nursery curtains and neighbors who might help. As dusk folded into night, their words drifted off, replaced by the comfort of shared breath and the warmth of a world they had made together.

"We've come so far," Adi murmured into the darkness, his words almost a prayer. "But I think our real journey is just beginning."

"Yes," Tatjana agreed, quiet but certain. "And whatever comes, we face it side by side."

CHAPTER FOUR

NEW ARRIVALS (1920)

LIFE IN BYDGOSZCZ WAS SLOWLY rediscovering its rhythm after the Great War. Since Adi and Tatjana's arrival, a fragile but promising return to normalcy had begun to take hold. Though the residue of war and revolution lingered, the chaos that once defined the landscape was ebbing. Conflict still simmered along distant borders, but it no longer felt like the existential threat the Bolsheviks had once posed.

The war had stretched the bonds of family but had not severed them. Tatjana drew strength from rekindling connections with her sisters, reaching out across the divide with Manja—who, much like herself, lived discreetly veiled in Berlin—and with Fania, who practiced her faith quietly in Württemberg. Despite the miles between them and the differing ways they navigated the hidden truth of their identities, the sisters remained steadfast in their love. Every letter exchanged, every cautious visit, reminded Tatjana that they were still tethered, still a family—just learning to move forward and survive in a different world.

Outside, Bydgoszcz pulsed with the relentless rhythm of daily life, but within their home, a quietude prevailed, as if the entire city had paused here to mark the significance of a family milestone: the birth of their first child, Joachim.

Holding his newborn son for the first time, Adi was stunned by the fierce protectiveness that surged within him. Standing between the bed and bassinet, Adi brushed his fingers over Joachim's soft hair. Nothing could have prepared him for this primal rush of love. He was no longer only a husband or an engineer. He was someone's father.

Tatjana rested in bed, her body weary but her eyes alert as Adi hovered near the bassinet. "He's perfect," she murmured.

Adi nodded, unwilling to tear his gaze from his son's face. Cradling his newborn son, he discovered a gentleness that surprised even himself.

The peaceful hush was broken by a thin wail. Adi flinched—instinct more than fear—and then stepped toward the bed. His hands, more accustomed to steel and ink than soft flesh, moved with surprising care as he passed Joachim to Tatjana. She cuddled the baby against her chest with ease, and as he latched on, the cries faded.

"You're a natural," Adi said in admiration.

Tatjana smiled tiredly. "We'll see how natural I am at three in the morning when he's screaming, and I've had no sleep for days."

In a role reversal he hadn't anticipated, Adi soon found himself deciphering swaddling instructions instead of blueprints. His fingers, usually so certain with purpose, now seemed tentative on the curve of the infant's back.

Tatjana, watching her husband as he sat with their newborn son, broke the silence with a voice weary but sure. "He has your determination," she said softly—an observation weighted with quiet truth.

Adi chuckled, the sound warm and rich, filling their home with joy. "Let's hope he inherits your way with people." His thumb brushed the downy edge of Joachim's ear, and something in his posture shifted: less soldier, more sentinel. "Thank you," he whispered to his wife, his voice catching. "For this. For him."

Tatjana leaned over and kissed him tenderly. "You don't have to thank me. We're in this together."

Adi gazed at them both, a lump rising in his throat. He was a father now. And he would do everything in his power to keep them safe and give them the best life possible.

Joachim's first months passed in a haze of new discoveries for both child and parents. Each morning, light crept into the nursery as the city stirred awake. Tatjana, silhouetted against the pale dawn, would move quietly around the crib, adjusting the covers with practiced care. Waking up to the joys of motherhood every day was like encountering a beautiful flower blossoming anew.

Adi, ever the early riser, set out early for work each day, his thoughts lingering on his son's future even as he walked the familiar streets of Bydgoszcz. Evenings were his treasured time with Joachim. He would scoop the infant into his arms, narrating a world beyond the crib with a voice both proud and hopeful.

"This is our home," he would say, tapping gently on the walls. "And one day, you might build walls of your own."

From the kitchen, Tatjana would listen as she prepared dinner, her heart light yet also full.

After dinner, Adi often reached for his violin. With a gentle flourish, he would draw the bow across the strings, filling the room with a lilting strain. Tatjana would hold Joachim close and settle into her rocking chair, her body still tired but her soul content, as the melodies filled their apartment—sometimes lively, sometimes aching.

Joachim would fall silent, his small body relaxing as the music wrapped around him like a blanket. His tiny fists would unclench, and his eyelids would flutter. Then his eyes would lock on his father as if music were a language only the two of them could understand.

Adi's violin would sing of days past and whisper promises of days to come. Tatjana would hum along in quiet harmony, her voice low and steady—a duet of parental tenderness. The music would swell and dip, telling tales without words, weaving dreams into the evening air until the final notes faded into the hush of night.

Then, setting his violin aside, Adi would join Tatjana in tucking their son into his crib. They would pause together, watching the slow rise and fall of his breath beneath the flickering lamplight. Back in the living room, the world would narrow to two cups of tea and the quiet press of their shoulders against the sofa.

Tatjana would lean into Adi, her head resting against his, as they spoke in hushed tones of plans and dreams—a bigger home one day, travels to distant lands they had only read about in books. They envisioned a future for Joachim rich in education, experience, and perhaps music, if he took after his father.

One such evening, Adi traced the rim of his teacup, savoring the warmth seeping into his fingertips. Beside him, Tatjana nestled closer, her breaths syncing with his in silent regularity.

"Adi," she whispered, breaking the stillness, "there's something I need to tell you."

He turned toward her, his gaze immediate and intent. "What is it, my love?"

Drawing a deep breath, Tatjana said, "I'm pregnant again."

The revelation hung between them, delicate yet monumental.

"You're sure?" Adi's voice was an awed murmur.

Tatjana nodded as a half-smile crept in. "Yes. The doctor confirmed it this morning."

A wave of joy broke over him. "Another baby," he whispered, reveling in wonder.

Tatjana's soft laugh rang through the room. "Yes. We're doing this again."

Adi dropped to his knees beside her, pulling her into an embrace that spoke volumes. "How are you feeling?"

"Just tired," she replied, her shoulders sagging. "But happy. Very happy."

Back on the couch, Adi draped his arm protectively around her. Their quiet conversation, threaded with laughter and thoughtful pauses, flowed with names for the baby, small changes for the nursery, visions of Joachim becoming a big brother.

As the grandfather clock chimed the passing hour, Adi noticed Tatjana's fatigue. Her eyes were heavy with the day's end. "Time for sleep?" he whispered.

Together they moved through their nightly rituals—snuffing out candles, securing the home, retreating to their bedroom. Bathed in moonlight, Tatjana slipped into bed, her movements slow with exhaustion. Adi checked the room with a last glance before joining her, the rustle of sheets marking the close of another day.

As they lay there, side by side, sleep began its gentle descent. They were two bodies, one rhythm—and between them was the silent promise of what tomorrow might bring.

Hellmuth's arrival in 1921 brought a fresh surge of vitality to the family's apartment in Bydgoszcz, with his cries proclaiming life's relentless march forward. In welcoming his second son, Adi—whose hands were as adept with the bow of his violin as they had once been on the battlefield—confirmed that their greatest purpose was cradling his children. Of all his roles and accomplishments in life, *Papa* was the one that mattered most.

Tatjana—no longer the bold girl he had met in the forest but something stronger, steadier—moved through their home with quiet precision. Her beauty hadn't vanished, but it had changed, tempered into something more durable by motherhood, memory, and the blazing furnace of war. Her resolve was no longer born of youthful serenity but forged in the fires of a world that had asked too much of its keepers.

The conflicts of the past still hadn't disappeared entirely and were never far from thought. One late winter evening, over a dinner of pierogi and borscht, Adi broached the subject that had long been a silent guest at their table: the Great War's long shadow.

"The treaty," he began quietly, setting down his spoon and looking across the table at his wife. "Riga has been signed. It's official now."

His words hung in the air—not quite relief and not yet trust. Just the familiar shape of something like hope. Catching sight of Joachim, who was tugging himself upright in the crib with unsteady determination, Adi felt his expression soften.

"Poland and Russia," he added, as if repeating it might make it real. "They've made peace."

Tatjana cradled Hellmuth, bouncing him lightly to ease his evening fussiness. "Peace," she echoed, her voice heavy with both wariness and wonder. "But at what cost?"

"The borderlands," Adi replied. "They've drawn new lines. Some people are satisfied, but others . . ." His voice trailed off.

"Others will be dispossessed, just as I was," Tatjana added faintly, her eyes resting on their two boys.

Quiet fell between the two parents, broken only by Joachim's laughter as his little legs gave way beneath him once again. Soon those legs would grow strong enough for walking, then running, then racing toward a future neither Tatjana nor Adi could predict.

Their sons would grow up speaking Polish, enrolled in local schools—Adi's position with the Stadt made that inevitable. The Treaty of Riga had been signed, ending the undeclared war between Poland and Bolshevik Russia but also redrawing the European map once again—and splitting up national minorities among competing nation-states. The swift current of time still pulled them all forward, heedless of their precarious place in the new world order.

Both Adi and Tatjana knew their children would need to navigate an era fraught with new challenges and shifting borders. No matter how hard their parents tried to protect them, the two boys would face the same old question.

What kind of peace lasts?

CHAPTER FIVE

UNCERTAIN PEACE (1921)

EVEN IN THE WARMTH OF SUMMER, peace remained an uncertain thing.

Outside the cocoon of Adi and Tatjana's growing family, Bydgoszcz hummed with cautious hope. Market conversations carried threads of optimism, and neighbors exchanged guarded smiles beneath the sigh of collective uncertainty. The air itself seemed to ask, *Can the Riga treaty carve a path to lasting peace? Or is it only a temporary reprieve before the next upheaval?*

Adi, restless in the evenings, often sat on the balcony outside their apartment, speaking with passersby about the shifting political landscape. Each conversation brought its own shade of opinion—some painted with relief, others colored by doubt.

"We can breathe now," said Mr. Kowalski from next door as he stepped out for air one evening. "My son can grow up without fear of conscription."

From a window above came Mrs. Dąbrowska's warning voice: "Borders change," she cautioned, "but do hearts?"

In such moments, Adi's thoughts turned inward. His roots were still German—deep, familiar—yet his life now stretched into Polish soil. His sons, born of his German heritage and Tatjana's Russian Jewish lineage, were living symbols of worlds colliding, of cultures entwined.

As dusk deepened, so too did Adi's thoughts on identity, on belonging, on how his family would chart its course amid shifting borders, through a world in constant flux.

These thoughts were still swirling a few days later, as Adi tended their small garden in the afternoon. Tatjana joined him with Hellmuth cradled against her chest.

"Adi," she began hesitantly, adjusting the blanket around the baby, "do you think there will ever be true peace? Where Poles and Russians and Germans can coexist without all these grudges and endless disputes?"

Adi pressed the soil around a young plant before standing to face her. "Perhaps one day," he replied, his voice measured. "The treaty is a start. Poland is our home now, and we have a good life here. We've planted more than seeds in this soil. We've planted hope."

Tatjana looked down at Hellmuth's cherubic face. Joachim crawled over and tugged at her skirt until she lifted him, holding both boys together in her boundless embrace. The soft coos of their younger son and the innocent chatter of their older one combined in a comforting soundtrack. For a brief moment, framed by the fading light of day, Adi and Tatjana felt the fragile peace they had sown taking root.

The following week, an unexpected visitor appeared—a traveling salesman with bolts of fabric and a knack for weaving tales of news and rumor. "You folks are lucky," he declared as he unfurled cotton bolts across their kitchen table. "With this treaty signed, there'll be a lot less upheaval. Not so many border disputes."

Tatjana ran her fingers across the pale blue weave before looking up with quiet resolve. "And what about those who now find themselves on the wrong side of these new borders?"

The salesman shrugged as he packed away his goods. "Always winners and losers when lines get drawn."

After he had departed, Adi faced Tatjana, determination lighting his eyes. "We will write our own story," he said firmly, lifting Hellmuth and kissing his soft hair.

"And we'll start with these boys," Tatjana agreed, pulling Joachim close.

Outside, the world continued to shift, but within the walls of their home, an invisible pact held stronger than any treaty. Their bond of kinship and love fortified them against the tremors of an uncertain world. When neighbors gathered for tea, or when Tatjana visited with Frau Weiss for knitting advice and remedies for the boys' teething pains, the undercurrents of war and peace remained whispers, softened by the urgent tempo of family life.

Here, at least, peace had come—not as a grand idea, but as the quiet work of raising children amid the shifting sands of history.

Dawn bathed Bydgoszcz in gauzy light as Adi pulled his coat tighter, its wool a shield against the early morning chill. The city awoke, its streets bustling, as he walked to City Hall, where his expertise as a structural engineer kept him in constant demand.

The office of the Stadt buzzed with productivity. Draftsmen bent over their tables, clerks shuffled papers, and the air was thick with concentration. Adi slid into his chair, his gaze falling on blueprints for bridges and buildings that would shape the city's horizon.

"Adi!" Marek's call cut through the room. He was waving a newspaper, his face taut. "Have you seen this?"

Adi crossed the room to where other colleagues were clustering around Marek. The headline screamed, *UPRISINGS IN UPPER SILESIA*. Smaller subheadings spoke of German unrest and rising political tension.

Marek slapped the paper down. "It's getting worse by the day. These uprisings . . . they could spread here."

The tension in the murmurs of their colleagues was palpable, a collective unease felt by a nation that seemed forever on the precipice of change.

Adi sipped his coffee, shaking his head. "Germany isn't coming for Bydgoszcz. And even if it did, we've faced challenges before. We'll get through this too."

"But what about the war reparations?" asked Piotr, a fellow engineer. "The Germans say that it's too much—that it will cripple them."

"Then let them feel some of what they inflicted on the rest of us," Kasia muttered darkly.

Adi, walking the fine line of a German patriot in Polish employ, sought to temper the heated conversation with reason, advocating for stability over punitive measures. "Instability knows no borders," he reminded them. "If things collapse there, we'll feel it here too. All of us."

Silence settled over the group, heavy with the weight of unspoken fears. Each person in the office seemed to stare off at nothing, their thoughts drifting to their families and trying to imagine what might come next.

The spell broke abruptly when Director Kamiński burst through the door from his private office, his face flushed with urgency. "Adolf!" he called out breathlessly. "The bridge design for Wyspa Młyńska—we need to review it. Now."

The others quietly drifted back to their stations as Adi stepped into the director's office, its walls lined with shelves sagging under countless ledgers and parchments. The room exuded the scent of old paper and ink—a quiet monument to the city's layered history and the hopes for its future. Without preamble, the director unfurled a sprawling blueprint across his desk. It was a design for the new bridge, meant to be both a vital artery for commerce and a proud symbol of Bydgoszcz's resilience.

"We need your eyes on this," Kamiński said. "There's talk of pushing construction ahead of schedule."

In the dimming light of the drafting room, Adi's dedication was palpable, his presence united as one with the blueprint before him. He pored over the intricate web of lines and calculations, his finger pausing on a critical juncture.

"This requires reinforcement," he said, tapping the paper lightly as if to feel the stress point. "It's the spine of the bridge. We strengthen this, and the whole structure holds."

The director, brow furrowed in deep contemplation, scribbled furiously as Adi continued to explain, his analytical gaze never wavering from the skeletal outlines of future skylines. For the next few hours, they toiled in a bubble where time's passage was marked only by the waning light and the rhythmic scratch of pencil on paper.

Finally, as dusk deepened, the director closed his notebook with a decisive snap. "Enough for today," he said, giving Adi a respectful nod. "We'll resume with fresh eyes at sunrise."

As Adi gathered his things from his desk and prepared to leave for home, Piotr stopped him. "Do you really believe our work will hold, no matter what happens?"

Adi's answer came without hesitation. "We're building more than bridges, Piotr. We're building hope—something tangible that people can see and trust when everything else feels uncertain."

Piotr nodded slowly, as though absorbing not just Adi's words but the deeper strength behind them.

Outside, Adi stepped into streets now veiled in twilight. Lights blinked on in the windows of Bydgoszcz as the city surrendered to the hush of nightfall. Adi's daily walk back to the apartment was more than a mere return home; it was an intentional crossing from a world of lines and measurements to one where his children's laughter and the solemn toll of church bells spoke of life's simpler constructs.

Tatjana's silhouette framed the doorway as she balanced little Hellmuth in her arms while Joachim toddled beside her, clutching his wooden motorcycle. "Dinner's almost ready," she said, smiling as Joachim dropped the toy and reached for his father with small, grasping hands.

Scooping the boy into his arms, Adi kissed Tatjana's forehead and then little Hellmuth's. Looking into his older son's bright eyes full of innocence and wonder, he saw the duty that lay beyond the drafting table—the duty to forge a legacy not only of stone and steel but also of endurance, something strong enough to withstand the harshest gales of history.

Yet as the seasons turned, the winds of change did not subside as Adi had hoped, and he often wondered where in this shifting landscape his family truly belonged. The Dindinger home continued to serve as a refuge, where time marked its passage through the milestones of the family's youngest members: Joachim learned new words each day in German, Russian, and Polish. Hellmuth began to crawl with determined curiosity across the worn wooden floors.

Through it all, Adi kept a close eye on the erratic social and political situation in his homeland. The tumultuous events of the 1920s lingered like a shadow at the edge of his consciousness—especially after the failed ambitions of young Adolf Hitler in the 1923 Beer Hall Putsch. As Germany grappled with hyperinflation and violence, Adi found his sanctuary in Bydgoszcz and their home there. Within the walls of the Dindinger apartment, amid the quiet strength of his family, he did not retreat from history. He built against it.

CHAPTER SIX

HOLDING CLOSE
(1925-1932)

IN THE EARLY SPRING OF 1925, Adi and Tatjana stood outside the modest frame of the local Polish schoolhouse. The building, humble in its purpose, released a swarm of exuberant children into the crisp afternoon air, their laughter and bright chatter painting joy across the somber canvas of the postwar world.

Among the throng of small bodies and eager voices was Joachim, just five years old but already growing tall. His dark hair was tousled, and his eyes were bright with curiosity and quiet intelligence, soaking in every detail of his new school life. Nearby, four-year-old Hellmuth's voice rang out, calling for his older brother to join the games underway.

Meanwhile, Adi and Tatjana cradled two new babies in their arms: one-year-old Erika and newborn Christa. Their two beautiful daughters rounded out a family that felt truly complete.

Homeward bound, the Dindingers walked as a unit, a serene tableau set against a backdrop of gathering unease. Adi, ever attuned to sinister rumblings beneath the surface, sensed the dissonance growing between the public calm and private concern in their adopted country. But he refused to allow their household, ever a fortress of laughter and love, to be stifled by the creeping shadows stretching across the land.

Ever since Poland had regained its independence, the fledgling government had staggered from one crisis to the next. Cabinets collapsed almost as quickly as they formed. Whispers of fleeting alliances and ill-gotten gains echoed in the grand halls of power, while outside those walls, ordinary people shouldered the true burden—rebuilding their lives, brick by brick, from the rubble of ongoing conflict.

Calls for a more inclusive Poland clashed with louder voices demanding a more Catholic, pro-Western, explicitly anti-German nation. The fact that the postwar Polish economy largely catered to German interests only stoked the fires of resentment.

Later that night, as the stars blinked awake in the expansive sky, Adi sat at the dining table, combing through the day's newspapers by the glow of the lamp. From the wireless came the crackle of distant unrest: industrial strikes, political speeches, and skirmishes bearing names he barely recognized.

Tatjana quietly cleared and washed the last of the dishes, then draped a hand over her husband's shoulder. Each broadcast report was a droplet in the rising tide of apprehension that lapped at the edges of her awareness. "It's late," she whispered. "Come to bed, Adi. The world will wait."

Adi's gaze, heavy with concern, lifted to meet hers. "I know," he sighed, the contours of his face softening under the lamplight. "But it's the *waiting*, Tatjana. The feeling that any moment . . ."

She said nothing more, only rested her hand over his. In the hush that followed, they sat together, listening to the murmuring wireless. The news from abroad only heightened their unease. And as the night deepened, so too did the sense of a nation—and a family—poised on the brink of an uncertain dawn.

Indeed, the following day brought no relief. In the town squares, in the shops, and behind the closed doors of residences, the fervor of unity and division invigorated definitions of the "true Pole" and the "outsider."

Tatjana tended to Erika and Christa in the garden while listening to Joachim and Hellmuth discuss their lessons from school. In those tender, fleeting moments, when her family was gathered around her, Tatjana could almost believe they were insulated from the storm clouds amassing at the borders of their world.

But each day's sunset lengthened the shadows at their threshold. Dinnertime became sacred—an hour of togetherness. Yet even here, conflict and instability sometimes intruded.

"Some people are starting to organize," Adi said one evening, laying down his spoon. "Claiming they need to defend Poland."

"Defend it from what?" Joachim asked innocently as he passed the bread to Hellmuth.

"From change," Adi said carefully. "Some fear the loss of the familiar, the comfort of the known. But the world doesn't stay still; it changes. We can only teach you how to meet those changes."

As they sat there, a family at the crossroads of history, the dialogue unfurled—a delicate balance of guarding their children's innocence while gently lifting the veil on the realities beyond their garden's embrace.

Later, after the children had drifted to sleep, Adi and Tatjana sat on the balcony, the stars above them sharp and still.

"We could always return to Germany," Adi ventured, the words coming out faster than he meant them to, as if trying to outrun his own doubt.

Tatjana didn't answer right away but fixed her eyes on the sky. "Germany, too, is far from a haven," she murmured, her voice the softest of laments. "Here, we've planted something real. We've made a life."

The years passed quickly, but the uncertainty remained. By the end of 1931, headlines told of markets collapsing, families scraping by, countries slipping further into crisis. The Empire of Japan seized Manchuria from China, claiming to liberate it—but in truth, it was conquest. In the West, most people were far too preoccupied with the daily struggle to survive and provide for their families during the Great Depression. There was no room left for outrage.

The League of Nations, that grand experiment in collective security born from the ashes of the Great War, offered little more than words in response to Japan's ham-fisted invasion of Manchuria. A world already bowed beneath many sorrows could muster little more than a weak exhalation in response.

Unbeknownst to the citizens of Europe and America, who were wrapped in concerns about their own survival, the bold maneuver in the Far East sowed the seeds of far greater conflict. Lacking consequences from the international community, Japan's imperialist stride in Manchuria created ripples, which soon expanded into waves that would, in time, swell into the torrents of global war.

As the world around them slid faster and faster into the grip of madness, the Dindinger family remained mostly untouched for the moment. Adi and Tatjana poured their energy into raising their children with unwavering devotion, anchoring them in the steadying forces of education and faith, even as the world outside threatened to unravel.

Joachim was eleven and Hellmuth right behind him at ten years old. Though close in age, their differences had begun to show. Joachim was gentle, thoughtful, and introspective, with a keen interest in science—chemistry in particular. Joachim's protective embrace of his role as the elder *Bruder* meant he often shouldered responsibility for the mischiefs and mishaps of his younger siblings. Hellmuth, by contrast, was filled with energy and confidence, his charm already catching the shy smiles of girls at an age when he was only just starting to notice.

Their younger sisters were no less distinct. Erika and Christa, ages seven and six, had taken to ice skating with an ease that surprised even Tatjana. Their coordination, their shared rhythm was more than talent; it was instinctual, hinting at a strength still forming. Though they shared a love for skating, the girls had begun to branch out in their own ways: Erika was the fearless one—thriving on pushing boundaries and inspiring those around her to do the same. Christa, by contrast, moved with quiet focus. When skating, her grace was unmistakable. At the piano, her hands mirrored the precision and elegance that propelled her across the ice.

Evenings at the Dindinger home were sacred as ever—a time when twilight's hush enveloped their apartment, and the soft glow of lamps and candles transformed their space into a haven of warmth and belonging. After supper, Adi would open his violin case with care as Christa—the youngest maestro in their midst—approached the piano with a fervor that belied her tender years. Her progress in music had been nothing short of remarkable, and she now possessed the skill to accompany her father.

As Adi tuned, the first pure notes filled the apartment. Christa listened for her cue, watching him closely. He gave the smallest nod. She began slowly—a few quiet notes, followed by the simple beauty of her playing, growing bolder with every bar. Adi soon joined in with a harmony line, the violin's rich tone entwining delicately with the higher registers of the piano.

The music wound through the apartment, folding into the tranquility of the evening like something remembered and beloved. Joachim and Hellmuth quietly set aside their card game, captivated. Erika and Tatjana fell silent mid-conversation. All were equally mesmerized by the heartwarming duet.

As Christa's fingers danced to the end of the lively tune, her grin was wide, and her hands dramatically lifted from the keys. Warm applause filled the room, and Christa turned to Adi, eyes sparkling with anticipation. "What do we play next, Papa?"

Adi chuckled at her eagerness. "Let's try something a little slower this time." He raised his bow again and began a familiar church hymn.

Christa, after a tentative start, soon found the rhythm. Erika and Hellmuth added their voices. Joachim and Tatjana joined one verse later, the family singing together as one. Their apartment swelled with love and music, and their spirits soared upon the beauty of shared creativity.

When the final note dwindled to silence, Tatjana delicately brushed a tear from her cheek. Adi set down his violin and crossed the room to plant a tender kiss on her forehead.

"One more?" he asked Christa, who was still perched on the piano bench.

She nodded excitedly.

Adi picked up his violin again, meeting his daughter's expectant scrutiny. "How about your favorite lullaby?"

Christa's face lit up instantly, and she positioned her fingers over the starting chord. Adi cued her in with a subtle dip of his bow, and once more their instruments filled the room with a heartfelt melody, weaving together an intimate nocturne that spoke to the soul.

The family sat enraptured. Christa seemed to be playing with more passion than ever before. As the final notes faded into the night, she turned to beam at her parents.

"That was beautiful, mein goldenes Tita," Tatjana whispered tenderly, opening her arms as Christa, beaming, ran into her cherished embrace.

Adi set down his violin and squeezed his daughter's shoulder affectionately, his eyes shining. "We're so proud of you," he said.

Under their praise, Christa glowed.

When Tatjana released her from the hug, Adi moved to stand behind his wife's chair, hands resting gently on her shoulders. He looked out over the warm scene before him: music lingering, children safe, home whole. It was a scene to hold close, a memory to savor.

Later that summer, after the elections of July 1932, the Nazi Party—with Adolf Hitler as its leader—rose to become the largest political force in the German parliament. While much of the world looked away, Polish intelligence was already deeply involved in clandestine work. In Bydgoszcz that same year, cryptologists made a vital breakthrough that began the process of cracking the Nazi Enigma code—a discovery that would be crucial to winning the next world war.

No one in the Dindinger home could have known, but the world beyond their walls had already begun to shift again—and the quiet resistance had begun.

Beloved Papa with Erika on the left and Christa on the right, on their way to strawberries and whipped cream after their weekly Sunday skating practice in Bydgoszcz, 1932.

Joachim, Hellmuth, and Erika with their *Schlittschuhe*, "ice skates,"
speeding down a hill in Bydgoszcz, 1933.

PART II

Heading Toward War

CHAPTER SEVEN

THE RISE OF HITLER (1933)

ON THE MORNING OF JANUARY 30, 1933, under a sky that gave no hint of the earth-shattering geopolitical storm to come, President von Hindenburg reluctantly appointed Adolf Hitler as Chancellor of Germany. The news rippled outward into the greater European region and beyond, carried through hushed conversations and crackling radios. Despite no immediate signs of the impending upheaval, that moment ignited a far-reaching catastrophe. The course of millions of lives shifted irrevocably.

When Adi arrived at City Hall that day, his footsteps echoed down the unusually quiet marble corridors, where colleagues clustered in tight, uneasy knots. Faces pale and drawn, they exchanged whispers, newspapers clutched in hand. With the troubling events in Germany, the entire region had taken a dangerous step into the unknown.

Nearing his office, Adi overheard snippets—*Chancellor, Nazi Party, Hitler*—breaking through the uneasy murmurs.

"Have you heard?" someone muttered darkly, adjusting his spectacles. "Hitler has been appointed."

"I don't like it," another replied, his voice a low growl. "The man is a powder keg."

Adi paused by his desk. The gathering unease of recent years was no longer abstract. It had taken form—shared, contagious, heavy in the chest.

"Morning, Adi," came the greeting from a colleague, his voice lined with the same strain gripping the entire building.

"Morning, Franz," Adi replied under his breath. "I see everyone's read the papers already."

Franz nodded. He always had a keen sense for politics, attuned to the undercurrents now swelling into a tidal wave. "Indeed. This is too close to home to ignore."

Adi settled into his chair and began sifting through the blueprints scattered across his desk. Their measured lines offered a fragile semblance of control, transforming his office into an island of peace in the middle of the turmoil. But even there, within those familiar walls, foreboding seeped in, curling into corners and threading into his bones.

Colleagues came and went as the morning wore on, each visit another verse in the day's litany of apprehension. The refrain was always the same: tremulous fear over what tomorrow might bring.

Near noon, Adi stepped out for air. The streets still moved—children laughed, vendors hawked, trams clanged. At a small café near City Hall, he ordered coffee and watched the mundane ballet of life continue: people purposeful, weary, seemingly indifferent to the headlines. But beneath the city's hum, he felt a tremor.

Not everything was the same. The heavy steps of policemen patrolling the streets cut through the gentleness like a warning—a reminder that the peace they took for granted was as breakable as the porcelain mug in his hand. The powers that upheld order today could just as easily wield oppression tomorrow.

Indeed, within weeks, the German parliament in the Reichstag passed the Enabling Act with shocking speed and near-total consensus, effectively dismantling Germany's democratic framework. The flimsy Weimar Republic gave way to something darker, harder, more unyielding in the face of dissent. Overnight, the machinery of Nazi power began to lock in place.

At his desk over the next few weeks, Adi tried to focus on blueprints and calculations, but outside his office, history seemed to be rewriting itself by the hour. Day after day, journeying to and from City Hall, he carried no more answers than before. If anything, his concerns had deepened.

One day at the end of February, Franz burst into the room, face taut. "Adi! The Reichstag. Have you heard?"

Adi shook his head.

"They've torched it—the Reichstag is in flames."

"What?" The word barely escaped.

"It's all over the radio."

They joined a cluster of colleagues huddled around a console set atop a filing cabinet, listening in shock to the reports surfacing amid static on the airwaves: . . . *devastating fire at the Reichstag building last night . . . President Hindenburg . . . emergency decree . . .*

Low murmurs rose.

"We're on a dangerous path," someone whispered.

"It's an excuse for more control," another said bitterly through clenched teeth.

"They're blaming communists," Franz murmured, eyes wide. "But who really knows?"

Adi felt every muscle tense against an invisible weight. He stepped away from the swirl of conjecture and the radio's hollow voice forecasting doom.

As afternoon waned, he paced the riverbank, where stray leaves drifted onto dark water—a gentle descent at odds with the uproar tearing through his mind. How would life look in a year? A month? He tried to summon hope, but the image dissolved against the backdrop of his beloved, unraveling Germany.

At home that evening, Tatjana greeted Adi with an embrace before returning to the sofa, where she and the girls were mending shirts and socks. When he barely spoke, she looked up, reading him as easily as a favorite novel.

"What is it?" she asked softly.

Adi shook his head. How could he explain the feeling that everything was about to unravel? "We need to be careful," he said at last. "Things are changing quickly."

Tatjana nodded and took his hand—a silent vow that whatever the world might bring, they would face it together.

Adi was right. The coming year would unfurl with insistent momentum, stoked by the signing of the Concordat with the Vatican—a diplomatic coup that granted Hitler an early sheen of legitimacy, especially given the large percentage of Catholic Germans. The ink was barely dry before the propaganda machine wielded the agreement as proof: If the Pope recognized and bowed to the Nazi Party, who could object?

In October, Hitler withdrew Germany from the League of Nations. It was more than a diplomatic rupture; it was a symbolic rejection of global cooperation and a bold declaration of nationalist isolation. With that single act, Germany turned inward. The world watched as the tenuous threads of peace began to fray.

Moreover, 1933 ushered in another chilling milestone: the birth of the Gestapo—the Geheime Staatspolizei—a secret state police apparatus fueled by the ambition of prominent Hitler ally Hermann Göring. Within two short years, the deft maneuvering of Holocaust architect Heinrich Himmler would elevate the Gestapo into a ruthless force, striking fear into the souls of the German people.

Hitler had swept into power fueled by anger and resentment following Germany's loss in World War I, but Germany's transformation did not happen in a vacuum. Across Europe, governments were rising and falling as ancient kingdoms dissolved into tentative republics. The old world was slipping, and few had the power to stop it. Some believed Hitler would restore order and prosperity; others thought that at least he could not make things worse.

The night after the Reichstag fire, Adi still did not know what to think or what the future held. But deep in his gut, something ominous took root.

Sunlight danced across the frozen pond, scattering diamond twinkles as Erika laced her skates and began bouncing on her heels.

"Patience, Eka," Adi chided gently. "You'll be flying soon enough."

Tatjana knelt by Christa, winding a scarf around her neck. "Let this be your armor against the cold," she whispered.

The two sisters took to the ice. Erika launched forward like a spark—wild, joyous—carving playful arcs across the glassy surface. Christa followed in her wake, graceful and composed, quiet poetry in motion. At the edge, Adi and Tatjana stood hand in hand, pride warming them against the chill. They stepped onto the ice together, sharing a slow, measured glide that spoke of years spent finding balance.

"Look at them go," Tatjana murmured. "Fearless."

"Our girls," Adi agreed. "Strong in all the ways that matter."

Erika circled back with a spray of ice. "You're too slow!" she teased.

"Is that so?" Adi laughed, letting her pull him into her orbit, cautious strides giving way to bolder sweeps.

Christa paused, then turned to Tatjana. "Will you skate with me, too?"

"Always."

Mother and daughter pushed off side by side. For a little while, beneath a pale winter sun, the world felt steady enough for joy.

As the sun dipped lower, shadows stretched. "Race you to the other side?" Erika grinned.

"You're on," Christa answered.

"Three . . . two . . . one!" Adi called.

The girls launched like twin meteors, laughter trailing as blades bit into ice. Around the pond, bundled spectators formed a corridor of cheers. Near the far end, Joachim and Hellmuth waited by the finish, eyes fixed, clapping for pride and warmth alike.

Erika leaned forward with practiced drive. Christa matched her stride for stride, each push narrowing the distance. The clamor swelled, then hushed as the sisters surged toward the line—and crossed together, a plume of ice crystals sparkling like confetti.

"Who won?" Erika gasped.

"Too close to call," Christa panted.

Hellmuth shrugged. "Couldn't tell."

"Same here," Joachim said. "Too fast."

Inside the changing shack, Adi wrapped an arm around each daughter. "In my eyes, you're both champions."

Tatjana's smile glowed. "Your joy is victory enough."

Laughter buzzed as the family peeled off skates, warmth still clinging to wool and cheeks. Properly bundled, they started home beneath the low sun, teasing and telling tall tales as the twilight fell.

"They're growing so fast," Tatjana murmured, looping her arm through Adi's. "Soon they'll be too old for family skating days."

Adi's hand rested over hers. Time would move forward as it always did. But days like this—laughter, camaraderie, simple joy—would hold.

At home, coats were shed, and boots thudded to the floor. Joachim headed to the kitchen to make cocoa, the sweet scent soon filling the room. Hellmuth coaxed the fire; Erika and Christa curled onto the sofa, cheeks rosy.

"Did you have fun today?" Tatjana asked, spreading a blanket over each girl.

"It was wonderful! Eka is so fast—but I almost beat her," Christa beamed.

Tatjana laughed. "My little speed skaters! Just don't push yourselves too hard."

"We're careful," Erika insisted. "But you should see me jump—not at the pond. In the evenings, at the rink. I can go so high!"

"She taught me, too," Christa added proudly.

From the armchair Adi raised his hands in mock protest. "Don't look at me. I've no idea where all that boldness came from."

"From their dear *Mama*, of course," Tatjana said, eyes twinkling.

Joachim returned with a tray of steaming mugs and passed them around. For a moment they sipped in contented silence.

"Eka is right," Hellmuth said at last. "She jumps so high—and Tita moves like she's dancing on air. You should see them. They're really good."

"My little swans . . ." Tatjana studied her daughters. "Perhaps it's time your Papa and I see those talents for ourselves."

"You'll come watch us practice? At the rink?" Erika sat up, vibrating with excitement.

"Of course," Adi said warmly. "It seems our daughters have hidden gifts. We should see them properly."

Christa bit her lip. "But I still have so much to learn."

"Then learn," Tatjana said gently. "For now—will you show us?"

Christa nodded. "Yes!"

"Prepare for awe," Erika declared. "We will present wonders!"

"It's settled," Tatjana said, meeting Adi's eye. "Next weekend—a family outing."

The girls erupted in cheers, talking costumes and routines. Over their heads, Tatjana and Adi shared a look—pride threaded with the soft ache of time's quickening pace. Their daughters were beginning to soar. The realization was both wondrous and bittersweet.

Days fell like snow. At the rink, the girls' dedication turned each evening into a ballet of perseverance. Coaches watched them spin and leap—mirrors of determination, chasing perfection's elusive edge.

At last, the big day arrived—clear and cold, crisp with promise. Christa nudged her breakfast, appetite fleeing.

"You'll need your strength," Tatjana reminded, hand warm on her daughter's shoulder.

Across the table, her face pale, Christa picked at her bread.

"Nervous?" Joachim asked kindly.

Christa nodded.

Erika clasped her hand. "Tita, we can do this. Pretend it's any other practice."

Color crept back into Christa's cheeks. "You're right. We can do this."

On the walk to the rink, passersby smiled at the sight of two girls skipping with anticipation, Adi and Tatjana arm in arm behind them.

At the rink, Erika and Christa laced their skates in practiced silence. Around them, other skaters laughed and chased one another, but the sisters were already hearing the music, already preparing for the dance. When the first bar sounded, they shared a glance—and launched.

In perfect sync they carved the ice: sit spins, toe loops, lutzes, axels—each movement clean and fluid, repetition transmuted into grace. They were not merely skating. They were *flying*.

When the final notes faded, the girls came to a stop, chests heaving, cheeks flushed. Silence held for a heartbeat—then applause erupted, echoing off the boards. Adi and Tatjana stood among the cheering crowd, their faces lit with awe.

"You were magnificent," Tatjana said, fighting emotion, as they approached.

"Beyond delight, my children," Adi said, gathering the girls close. "The very essence of grace and beauty."

Christa's eyes gleamed. "You must come again. Coach says if we work hard, we could make the national team!"

"Is that so?" Tatjana kissed each forehead. "Then work you shall. The future is yours."

On the walk home, the girls chattered about costumes and steps.

"Our little swans have taken flight," Tatjana murmured.

"Indeed," Adi said. "And I suspect this is just the beginning."

CHAPTER EIGHT

ORDER INSIDE CHAOS (1936)

IN THE SERENE WARMTH OF the living room, sixteen-year-old Joachim traced a finger along a page in his chemistry textbook, his brow furrowed in focused curiosity. Diagrams of atomic structures danced beneath his fingertip, and his eyes gleamed with the thrill of discovery. Perched next to him on the worn sofa, Erika, just twelve but already showing an impressive understanding of science and basic chemistry, mirrored her brother's intensity.

Joachim tapped the page. "See this, Eka? This is how atoms come together, how new compounds are formed. It's like"—he paused, searching for the right word—"like alchemy, almost."

Erika leaned in closer, taking in the wonder of the diagrams printed on the page. "But it's not magic, Joachimchen. It's the science of the universe. No tricks or illusions, just the language of science."

Joachim's smile broadened with pride in his sister's insight. "True. But isn't it still a kind of miracle? How everything we know—the air, the stars— all follows the same hidden logic?"

Erika gave a thoughtful nod. "Order inside chaos," she murmured.

From the other room, the windup Victrola played a fast-paced tune. Hellmuth and Christa had cleared a space amid the furniture and now twirled in time with the music. Christa's laughter chimed through the air as Hellmuth led her in an improvised dance, their movements fluid and carefree.

The scraping of a chair drew the family's attention toward Adi, seated by the radio console, adjusting the wireless dial with steady fingers. The amber hue from the set highlighted the concern on his face. Reports from abroad filled the living room, each word laden with the gravity of a world teetering once more on the brink of upheaval.

Adi shook his head, his sotto voce mutterings lost to all but himself. "First the Luftwaffe. Now this." His hand rested on the dial as if he might turn back time.

Across the room, Joachim and Erika exchanged a glance. "Let's join Papa," Joachim whispered, just as the announcer's voice surged through the wireless, firm and urgent.

"In direct violation of the Versailles Treaty," the radio boomed, "Hitler has ordered German troops into the Rhineland."

Hellmuth froze midstep, his playful demeanor fading as he, too, caught the news. Christa stopped beside him, her smile faltering.

"Is that . . . dangerous?" Erika's voice was barely audible over the droning report.

Joachim nodded slowly. "It could mean war," he said quietly. "Again."

Hellmuth stepped toward their father. "Papa? What will this mean for us?"

Adi turned off the radio and, in the sudden silence, tried to summon reassurance. He forced a smile, but it didn't quite reach his eyes. "History, my children, is often a cycle," he said after a pause. "Today, we read it in books. But sometimes"—he glanced toward the silent radio—"sometimes the lessons find us. This is one of those moments."

He gazed from one child to the next.

"We're far from the Rhineland. That matters. Still, it's time to stay aware—but not afraid. We must not surrender to fears that have yet to knock upon our door."

Erika intertwined her fingers with Joachim's, her grasp a silent plea for the reassurance her brother's presence always provided.

As Christa reached to halt the Victrola, Adi stayed her hand softly. "No, let the music play, goldenes Tita. Music is something we hold on to. Especially now."

The Victrola continued its song, a melody unchanged even as their lives had imperceptibly, irrevocably shifted beneath their feet. And the kitchen murmured as usual with the final touches of dinner, the warm, savory scent of roasted vegetables and broth drifting through the apartment.

Then came Tatjana's voice, bright and sure. "Dinner is ready!"

Drawn by her call, they each found their place at the dining room table, lovingly and meticulously arranged as always. Every utensil, every plate had been placed with muted intention—a bulwark against the reality outside their walls.

"Let's eat while it's hot," Tatjana smiled as she carried in plates heaped with food.

Hellmuth tried to inject some levity back into the evening. "Remember when Joachim tried to cook dinner and nearly blew up the kitchen?" Laughter broke out, cautiously at first but then boisterously, a release valve for tension that had no place at this table.

Joachim, offering a playful scowl in Hellmuth's direction, joined in the jest. "My experiments are best suited to a laboratory, I'll admit."

Erika giggled, and Christa started humming absent-mindedly to the tune playing in the background. Tatjana leaned over and touched Adi's hand briefly—a silent exchange. The tension hadn't vanished, but it had softened, thinned enough to make room for appetite and small talk.

Conversation that night wandered through harmless territory: school projects, skating practice, a teacher's classroom joke. As dishes were passed and emptied, the apartment returned to a warmer, steadier feeling. The family moved through the meal like a ritual, familiar, rhythmic, grounding.

When plates were cleared and dessert was brought to the table—steamed apples with cinnamon and cream—Adi rose slightly from his chair, one hand resting on its back.

"We've faced uncertainty before," he said, his voice low but even. "And we hold fast to what we know. This family. This table." He paused, glancing at each of them. "As long as we have each other, we have something stronger than fear."

No one replied, but heads nodded, and hands reached for one another across the table. Everyone lingered over dessert, savoring the sweetness on their tongues, letting hope linger, too, amid laughter and unspoken plans for tomorrow.

Early the next morning, noises that typically filled the City Hall offices—the buzz of chatter, the ding of typewriters, the shuffling of papers—were noticeably absent. A somber mood infiltrated the room. Engineers and draftsmen sat motionless at their desks, each one lost in apprehension, their eyes downcast or staring blankly ahead.

Adi let his gaze fall back to the unfolded newspaper on his desk and released a long, weary sigh. The headline glared up at him, its bold black letters mocking his hopes for peace: *GERMANY'S WEHRMACHT MARCHES INTO RHINELAND.*

The Versailles Treaty, once touted as a safeguard against war's return, had been eroding for years. Now it lay fully undone, stripped of authority by the tread of German boots crossing into forbidden territory. Over the years in Bydgoszcz, Adi had sensed the tremors of change, the gradual shifting, the normalization of aggression. But reading it here, in ink and certainty, felt like crossing a line. There would be no turning back. The world was stepping once more into the long shadow of conflict.

Adi sighed again—a sound heavy with foresight and resignation. More than just tremors, these were the stirrings of a geopolitical earthquake. The cracks were spreading beneath the very foundations of the nations he loved and the life he knew. Looking around at his colleagues, Adi knew they all felt as he did: afraid, betrayed, lost. The future seemed suddenly unpredictable. Would there be war again? Would families be torn apart and homes destroyed once more?

Years ago, in the aftermath of the Great War, the resurgence of Germany's might would have stirred a sense of pride in him. He had once worn the uniform, served his Kaiser, and basked in the glory of the Fatherland. He remembered that feeling: order, honor, purpose. But time, and the mantle of fatherhood, had softened the edges of his nationalism. Now, strength looked different. It wasn't found in flags or marches but in keeping your children fed, your family safe. And in that light, the headline could not inspire. It could only warn.

Rising from his desk, Adi approached the window, seeking solace in the familiar view of Bydgoszcz below. The comforting rhythms of the city streets, the golden spill of light from storefronts, the footsteps pitter-pattering over cobblestones . . . it all whispered of a simpler life—a life of peace he had helped construct from the ruins of conflict. These were his people, undeserving of the storm threatening to consume them.

The soft creak of a chair pulled Adi from his thoughts. He turned to see Pavel, one of the senior engineers and a mentor to Adi ever since he'd joined the office—an older man who had seen promise in the eager young engineer and had taken him under his wing. Now Pavel came and stood beside Adi at the window, looking out over their city with tired eyes.

"So," Pavel said at last, his voice grave with resignation, "Germany rises again, it seems."

"All the restrictions placed after the war . . ." Adi's words trailed off as he shook his head, bitterness lacing the thought. "They mean nothing now."

"Yes," Pavel sighed. "The mighty Versailles Treaty—undone by a single march."

The two men stood without speaking for some time, both lost in thought as they watched scenes of everyday life unfolding below: a street vendor calling out his wares, an old woman shuffling along with her cane, two schoolboys laughing and jostling each other as they hurried past.

Finally, Pavel turned to Adi. "What will you do?" he asked quietly.

Adi kept his eyes on the view. "What can I do? I have a family here. A job. A life." He hesitated, then added, "Germany is my homeland. But this is my home now, too."

Pavel nodded slowly. "Yes. Many of us feel the same." He placed a hand on the younger man's shoulder. "For now, we keep our heads down. We do our work. And we pray."

Adi managed a faint smile. Pavel had a talent for knowing just what to say.

The office door creaked open, and Director Kamiński entered, his usual energy muted. The room seemed to hold its breath as the director stood in the doorway, solemnly surveying his staff.

"Gentlemen," Kamiński began heavily, "I'm sure you have all seen the news." A murmur of assent rippled through the room. "Right. Well, there's no sense dwelling on it. We still have deadlines. Obligations. We're here to do the work of the people." His hands came together with a crisp clap. "Let's get to work, shall we?"

Adi did his best to absorb and emulate Kamiński's resilience as he turned back to his blueprints—lines and angles, that comforting familiarity amid the chaos. The other engineers gradually shuffled back to their own desks, the earlier silence replaced by the familiar sounds of a day's work beginning. But a heaviness still hung in the air—a question no one dared to speak: *What does the future hold?*

Pavel caught Adi's eye from across the room and gave an encouraging nod. They would carry on, Adi realized—keep moving forward, whatever came. For now, the best response to the drumbeats of war would be to engage in the battles they could win: those fought on paper, with pencil and scale, creating structures that aspired to outlast the destructive ambitions of men.

With a resolute motion, Adi folded the newspaper, its black-and-white headlines disappearing in the creases, and dropped it into the wastebasket. It was a symbolic act, an unvoiced declaration that fear would not paralyze him.

As the day unfurled, the pulse of the office steadied. Each engineer gladly became lost in a world they could shape—one of steel and stone, of structures that would stand defiant, resisting the march of time and turmoil. In their shared purpose, Adi and his colleagues found an answer to that silent question hovering in the air.

The future was a landscape yet to be drawn, and they held the tools to build it.

Adolf, left, designing a layout for a new bridge in Bydgoszcz, circa 1933. *Tief und hoch,* "deep and high," tunnels and bridges were Adolf's engineering specialty.

CHAPTER NINE

THE STRANGLING ANGEL (1937)

THE MORNING SUN SCATTERED A soft light across the bedroom floor, faintly illuminating Christa as she lay curled beneath her blankets. Tatjana tiptoed quietly into the room, her footsteps muffled by the rug. Her eyes were fixed on the unnatural pallor of her daughter's face and the ominous swelling of her neck. Christa's breathing came in uneven rasps, shallow and wheezing.

"Goldenes Tita," she whispered, her fingers brushing a damp lock of hair from Christa's forehead. The words carried more comfort than explanation—a mother's plea folded into affection.

Christa stirred, her voice a dry whisper. "Mama," she managed, her words followed by a rattling cough. She tried to sit up, but the effort left her winded. Tatjana's hand was already at her back, steadying her.

Adi appeared in the doorway, his face drawn tight. "How was your night, Tita?" he asked, though the question held its own answer. His voice was calm, but the undercurrent of fear was unmistakable.

Christa smiled faintly. "I dreamed of music," she said softly, "but . . . it turned into coughing."

At breakfast, the usual sound of her spoon chiming inside her bowl was missing. The porridge, usually a welcome start to her mornings, sat untouched, stirred only enough to make it look like she'd tried.

Adi watched his younger daughter quietly, his eyes narrowing in concern. "You've scarcely eaten a thing," he said tenderly.

Her reply was lost in a sudden outburst of coughs, the effort bringing tears to her eyes. "I'm not hungry," she managed, her voice hoarse.

After a silent exchange of worried looks with her husband, Tatjana returned her attention to Christa. "Liebchen, I know how hard you've worked for the skating competition. But you need your strength now." Her voice was gentle, coaxing. "Just a few bites?"

Christa gave a faint nod, her smile weak. "I don't want to miss it," she said. "But . . . I can't eat much."

Throughout the day, Christa's energy faded. She drifted from the piano bench to the couch, her limbs heavy, her usual grace dulled. Every step seemed to cost her something. The music she played was thin and uneven, her fingers missing notes they usually landed without a thought.

By late afternoon, with the sun casting long, golden slants across the parlor, Christa had nestled into the folds of a blanket on the couch. The room was warm, but she couldn't stop shivering. Tatjana folded the blanket close around her daughter's shoulders. No one spoke.

The whole family had heard the stories of swelling throat and high fever. The so-called strangling angel had been sweeping through the city. In another time, another place, it might have been treatable. But in Bydgoszcz in 1937, it was still a threat that arrived stealthily, stealing breath and voice alike.

What little Adi and Tatjana could do, they did—gathering close to their daughter, anchoring themselves in routine and affection. Their love could not cure her, but it wrapped around her like a second blanket, a wordless reassurance that she was not alone.

Watching Tita closely, Tatjana pressed a hand to her forehead. The heat rose hungrily from her skin, and her pulse was unsettlingly rapid. "Adi," Tatjana called, urgency rising in her voice.

He appeared a moment later, kneeling beside the couch as Tatjana dipped a cloth in cool water and laid it across Christa's forehead. "What is it, Liebchen?"

Tatjana did not look away from Christa, brushing a thumb across her temple. "She's burning up," she murmured. "And her heart is racing. I think this might be the same illness everyone is talking about."

Her words rooted Adi to the spot, immobilized by the fear growing inside him.

Christa tried to rise, but the effort triggered another coughing fit that left her gasping for air. Her eyes, wide and frightened, searched her parents' faces. "Mama? Papa? What's happening to me?"

Tatjana caressed her daughter's cheek, her voice calm but edged with the same fear Adi felt. "We'll go see Dr. Weiss, mein Kind. He will help us."

The sky was painted in dusky hues by the time they reached the doctor's office, a modest brick building that had become all too familiar in Bydgoszcz as the diphtheria epidemic tightened its grip on the community.

Dr. Weiss greeted them with a quiet nod as they entered his examination room—a sterile space that smelled of antiseptic and fear. "Tell me what's been happening," he inquired, motioning for Christa to sit on the exam table.

Christa's voice was barely audible between fits of coughing, but she described her symptoms as best she could. Tatjana filled in the gaps: the fever and fatigue, the loss of appetite, the labored breathing.

Dr. Weiss listened without interruption. When Christa finished, he examined her throat, moving with a care that belied the tension in his expression. He adjusted the light, peered into her mouth again, and finally leaned back.

Adi gripped Tatjana's hand as they awaited the verdict.

"I'm afraid it looks like diphtheria," Dr. Weiss finally said. "Her throat is inflamed, and there's a characteristic gray membrane forming. It's typical of what we have been seeing lately."

Tatjana's breath caught as Adi's arm came to rest around her waist. "What can be done?" she asked, barely above a whisper. "She's only twelve years old."

Adi's voice, tight with fear, sought a sliver of hope. "There must be something—some new treatment? Don't they have it in America?"

Dr. Weiss's expression grew grave as he met Adi's gaze. "They do. But it's experimental, and we don't have access to the antitoxin here in Poland—not even in Germany." He paused, watching their faces. "You've probably heard of the dogsled team saving lives in Alaska."

They had heard of it: the Great Race of Mercy in January 1925, when the dogsled carried the serum across the frozen wilderness to save dying children during a diphtheria outbreak.

"But here, unfortunately," the doctor continued, "we have no such miracle."

Tatjana's hand flew to her chest, her breaths coming fast and shallow. Adi tightened his hold on her, steadying them both.

"So we'll have to manage this ourselves," Dr. Weiss said. "Careful rest. Isolation from your other children. It's the only way to reduce the risk and give her a chance."

Adi's jaw tightened. "Then we'll do whatever it takes."

He looked at Christa, small and pale against the white paper on the table. A lone tear wandered down the curve of her cheek. "Will I ever skate again?" she asked, her voice no more than a breath.

Dr. Weiss's kind smile held more melancholy than reassurance. "You need to rest now," he said softly. "Healing takes time, Christa. But yes—there's still hope."

That evening Christa was tucked into her own bed, her room transformed into a careful quarantine. As night fell, her coughing returned with force.

Tatjana remained at her post by her daughter's bedside. The lamp's faint glow flickered against the walls, casting a frail light by which she prayed. Between doling out sips of water and whispering reassurances, she kept a steadfast vigil, her voice calm even as her own heart raced.

The days slipped into a slow, hushed rhythm. Tatjana became the keeper of cleanliness, wiping down surfaces and washing hands, her every motion a strike against the unseen foe. Adi kept the other children busy, encouraging walks and errands to give their sister the quiet isolation she needed.

Meanwhile, Christa lay swaddled in blankets, fevered and weak. New chest pain added to her burden—each breath sharp, each movement a struggle. No cloth could cool the heat. No warmth could chase away the cold creeping in from within.

In the sanctum of the dimly lit bedroom, Tatjana read aloud from Christa's favorite books, the familiar stories offering a link to steadier times. She conjured distant forests, brave girls, clever foxes—anything to ease the dread and fill the stillness.

Adi, too, kept watch, bringing his own kind of comfort. His narratives were of bridges and towers, of problems solved and designs made strong enough to last. "In my eyes," he told her once, brushing hair back from her damp forehead, "you're stronger than anything I've ever built."

And so they fought—the days stretching into nights and back again—battles marked by small victories: a breath less labored, a moment more lucid. Christa clung to their words. When she couldn't speak, she listened, her fingers twitching under the covers with each remembered story. In her mother's fables and in her father's chronicles, she found fragments of strength she feared had slipped away.

At night, Tatjana leaned in close and whispered what she dared not say aloud in daylight: The music would return. Papa's violin would sing again. Christa's fingers would dance over the piano keys.

"Come back to us," Tatjana murmured. "The music awaits our goldenes Tita."

When the chest pain worsened, Dr. Weiss came to the apartment. One look, and the strain deepened in his brow. The pain had an unsettling name—*diphtheria myocarditis*—a potentially disastrous complication of the infection. Again, he explained, there was no treatment for this.

Tatjana's breath caught. Adi reached for her hand. They didn't fall apart. They couldn't afford to. Instead, they held the line—one stationed by Christa's bed, one in the hallway—switching places like sentinels. They spoke little. They didn't need to. The silence said everything.

One morning, as the first light of dawn slipped through the tightly drawn curtains, Christa's eyelids opened wider than they had in weeks. The harsh rasp that had haunted her breathing had eased. The feverish haze that had dimmed her gaze was gone.

"Mama?" Christa's voice carried new strength, the fragile spark of recovery.

Tatjana leaned in, her face alight with hope. "Yes, meine Liebe?"

"I think I can sit up today," Christa said, her small voice marked with determination.

Tatjana nodded, holding back tears. That simple wish felt monumental. The dark clouds had parted—they could see the horizon at last.

She moved quickly, rearranging pillows to prop her daughter up. Christa winced as she sat, but the triumph on her face made the effort worth it. Sunlight streaked across her cheeks, and Tatjana took it as a sign—the world offering its own encouragement.

"You're doing wonderfully," she said, smoothing Christa's hair with a tender touch born of weeks of worry.

Christa looked at her, eyes clear. "Mama, when can I skate again?"

Tatjana smiled. "You've made it through the worst, Tita, but your body isn't ready yet. Strength needs time to grow back fully. The ice will wait. For now, it's rest and healing. Let's not rush what is just beginning."

A shadow crossed Christa's face. "But Mama," she whispered, defiant and hopeful, "today I feel stronger."

Seeing the struggle on Christa's face, Tatjana offered a gentle compromise. "Your fingers still remember," she said softly. "Would you like us to bring the piano to you?"

Christa hesitated. The piano didn't offer flight or speed like the ice rink—but it was familiar, a partial release from the anchor of confinement. Her fingers ached for something to do, some expression of movement, of life. "Yes," she whispered. "That would help."

With careful movements, Adi transformed the room, shifting furniture to make space for the piano beside Christa's bed. Tatjana worried at first that all the restrictive measures—isolation, stillness, restraint—might have stifled the spirit they were trying to protect. Soon, however, Christa's hands found the keys, and her notes filled the space between worry and waiting. The melodies she played were a bit hesitant, unsure, but they warmed the somber room.

Adi lingered in the doorway, radiating pride in his daughter's resilience but also sorrow that this was where her music had to live for now. As the final chords dissipated, he found his voice. "You play beautifully."

Christa gave a small, tired smile. "Thank you, Papa," she said, her eyes drifting back to the keys. "But it's not the same. It's not the ice."

"No," Adi agreed. "But what you create here . . . it's part of your strength, too. Every note helps carry you forward."

Christa nodded, knowing he was right.

Day after day, her fingertips danced upon the keys. Often, drawing out the night's farewell, Tatjana would pause outside Christa's bedroom door, captivated by the delightful notes of another song. The music guided her through the hush of the evening, steadying her heart as it had steadied her daughter's.

Christa was determined to recover fully, to skate again. It was only a matter of time. But for now, the touch of her hands on the piano was enough—a recognition of dreams deferred but not abandoned.

Late one evening, as the sky darkened and the bustling day gave way to stillness, Adi arrived home to find Christa surrounded by cascades of blank music sheets, mastering a complex melody. "What are you creating here?" he asked, setting aside the remnants of his workday as he stepped into her world.

"A piece of my own," Christa answered, intent on composing a concerto from her imagination. Her concentration unbroken, she kept her pencil moving, sketching out harmonies on the manuscript.

She hummed a phrase, and Adi listened, nodding slowly. "It already sounds enchanting," he said warmly. "Like you're finding your way forward."

Christa beamed up at him. "I hope so," she whispered.

In those tender moments, father and daughter shared dreams built on notes and harmonies rather than leaps and spins or lines and angles. Serenity filled the room, revealing life's capacity for beauty even within the confines of necessity. The house found its rhythm again—a delicate dance of creativity and caution, of nurture and hope. And the family renewed their unswerving focus on safety and freedom.

CHAPTER TEN

A WORLD GONE MAD
(1938)

ANSCHLUSS. THE WORD REVERBERATED THROUGH the living room of the Dindinger household. Adi's fingers tightened around Tatjana's hand, their knuckles blanching. The announcer's voice crackled through the radio static, delivering news that would stop people in their tracks throughout Europe: "Austria has been annexed by Nazi Germany."

It was a chilly evening in March. Joachim sat rigid on the sofa, his posture braced against an invisible force. Erika instinctively leaned closer to him. Hellmuth's eyes narrowed as he studied the faces of his family. Christa's fingers paused above the piano keys, her last note suspended in air.

Erika broke the silence. "Do you think he'll stop there? With Austria? What about Poland?" Her voice was calm but heavy with the fear they all shared.

Joachim looked at her, his expression solemn. "Hitler's appetite seems insatiable."

Hellmuth scoffed lightly, trying to shake off the fear. "Some say that he'll be satisfied now—that he just wanted to bring Germans back into the fold."

Adi's sigh was thick with doubt. "To believe that is to forget the lessons of history. We must brace ourselves for what may follow."

Tatjana remained motionless, though every part of her longed to pull her children close, to wrap them in the safety of her arms. "We are together. That is our strength."

As the months passed, the Dindinger family carried on with their daily lives beneath a sky that grew heavier by the day, filled with the dread of what might come. September arrived with its golden hues and crisp air, but with the final day of the month came new unease as word of the Munich Agreement spread like wildfire.

"The Sudetenland," murmured Adi one evening at dinner, shaking his head as he folded the newspaper again. "Ceded to Hitler. And the rest of Czechoslovakia will be next."

Joachim's jaw clenched. "See? He isn't stopping. He isn't backing down. Every concession is fuel for his fire."

"What about Poland?" Erika asked, worry piercing her voice. "What about us?"

At the piano, Christa's melody wove delicately beneath the mounting tension—a soft counterpoint to the growing angst.

Across the table, Adi and Tatjana exchanged a glance of unspoken resolve. "We stay informed and vigilant," Adi said firmly, knowing they would do everything they could to shield their family from the storm on the horizon. "We keep our heads down and our spirits up. For now, that's all we can do."

As days stretched into weeks, Christa continued to play, her music a steady heartbeat in a world slipping into madness. Joachim and Erika found refuge in the immutable laws of chemistry—a world where formulae followed rules, unlike the one unraveling outside their door.

"Look at this compound," Erika said one afternoon in their makeshift home lab, her eyes bright with excitement.

Joachim leaned over her shoulder, admiring her work. "Stable bonds," he noted with a nod of approval.

"Just like us," Erika replied with a smile.

In quieter moments, Joachim confided his deeper worries to Erika. "Hitler won't stop," he insisted, staring out the window at the darkening sky.

"Don't borrow trouble, Joachimchen," Erika murmured, resting her head against his shoulder. "Papa would say to focus on today. We can't predict what will happen tomorrow."

"No," Joachim replied, his voice low. "But Papa knows more than he is willing to say out loud. There is a shadow in his silence."

The following morning, light filtered through the curtains as the aromas of freshly baked bread and strong coffee filled the kitchen. Adi sat at the head of the table, buttering a slice of bread while Tatjana poured coffee into his cup, the steam curling upward between them. The light banter between Joachim and Hellmuth over the final dollop of jam sketched an illusion of normalcy across the breakfast table.

"Boys, remember to eat your eggs," Tatjana chided, nudging their plates forward. "You need your strength."

The boys, nearly grown, obeyed their mother's instructions. Joachim was always reverential toward his parents, even at eighteen. Hellmuth was a little rowdier, but quick to follow his older brother's lead.

Adi looked at Tatjana and offered a reassuring smile. But the heaviness in his gaze betrayed what they both knew: The news from Germany, the whispers of violence were always waiting—just outside the edges of their careful peace. Though Tatjana smiled back as she set down the coffeepot and took her seat, Adi knew her stomach churned with the same dread that gripped his own.

A knock at the door shattered the morning calm. Adi and Tatjana exchanged a nervous glance. It was rare to have visitors this early. Rising from his chair, Adi moved toward the door, his pulse quickening.

A neighbor from their building stood in the doorway, her face ashen, apron wrung tight between trembling hands. "Adolf," she began, her voice quivering. "I'm sorry to trouble you and your family so early, but . . . with my husband out of town, I didn't know where else to go. Have you heard?"

"Heard what?" Adi's stomach tightened. "Please come in," he gestured, remembering hospitality amid his concern. Tatjana appeared beside him, worry written clearly in the lines of her face.

But the neighbor didn't step inside. Her next words came in a whisper, each one carefully drawn. "It's all over the radio," she whispered. "Last night . . . all of Germany has gone mad."

Hellmuth dropped his spoon with a clatter onto the floor. Joachim's fork paused mid-air, the bite of egg forgotten.

"What happened?" Adi asked, quiet but firm.

The neighbor swallowed. "The Jews . . . shop windows shattered . . . synagogues desecrated. Many have been taken away. Others . . . killed . . ." Her voice broke.

Tatjana's hand flew to her mouth, as if to hold back a cry—or the thoughts she dared not voice.

Already they were calling it Kristallnacht, the Night of Broken Glass. The Nazi regime had orchestrated and encouraged public rioting, the smashing of storefronts, setting fire to synagogues—a pogrom fueled by propaganda and rage, designed to target Jewish businesses, homes, and people.

Tatjana's children still didn't know about her Jewish roots, but her sister Fania in Württemberg wore her Jewish identity openly. And Manja, in the very heart of Berlin, Tatjana realized in terror, was at the epicenter of the nationwide violence.

The neighbor's report tumbled out like stones in an avalanche. "They say it's happening everywhere—Berlin, Frankfurt, Vienna."

Joachim set down his fork slowly as understanding took shape in his young eyes. Beside him, Hellmuth's face was a mixture of confusion and alarm.

Adi drew a deep breath before responding, his voice measured and calm. "We are grateful to you for this news. Please, stay for coffee or tea." He spoke with the muted steadiness of someone used to steering through storms. When she politely declined, he continued. "Well, if you hear anything before your husband returns, let us know. It must be frightening to face such times alone. Let's hope the madness doesn't reach our city."

The neighbor nodded faintly, stepping back with hesitation before turning and shuffling down the hall, leaving shock and fear in her wake.

Adi closed the door softly and returned to the table. "Tatjana," he began, trying to temper the urgency in his voice, "we must check on Fania. As soon as possible."

She nodded slowly. Her eyes found his—steel meeting steel—and in that look, he saw her resolve harden beneath the fear.

Hellmuth's voice broke through the dense, sorrowful silence. "Papa? What is . . . Kristallnacht?"

Adi leaned forward, his hands clasped, his expression grave. What clarity could he give to his children about this sudden descent into humanity's darkest corners? "The leaders of Germany seek to gain power through hatred, by turning neighbors against each other. People were harmed simply because they were different—because they were Jewish."

"But why?" Hellmuth asked, the innocence in his voice a stark contrast to the grim truth pressing around them.

"Fear," Adi said simply. "Driven by ignorance, it can lead to terrible things."

Tatjana reached across the table to clasp Hellmuth's hand. "But remember," she added, softly yet firmly, "our duty is to stand for what's right and to reach out to those in need."

"What will happen now?" Joachim's voice barely rose above a whisper. He looked from his parents to Hellmuth, tension clear in his hunched shoulders.

Adi's eyes met Tatjana's again, drawing strength from her resolve before replying. "We will move forward with caution. And we will continue to live with courage."

The rest of breakfast passed in near silence, the only sound the rhythmic clink of cutlery against plates—measured, mechanical, reassuringly ordinary despite a world outside that had become far less certain than it had been at dawn.

CHAPTER ELEVEN

INVASION (1939)

SEPTEMBER 1, 1939, DAWNED WITH an eerie silence over Bydgoszcz. The streets, usually alive with the clatter of daily life, lay in unnatural calm. Adi's first instinct was to embrace the tranquility as a brief reprieve from the undercurrent of tension that had been accumulating with each passing day.

Tatjana was already awake, standing at the kitchen window, her figure outlined against the gray light. She cradled a mug of tea in both hands, her gaze fixed on the empty street. "It's too quiet," she whispered into the hush that cloaked their home.

Adi crossed the room to join her. "Even the birds aren't singing."

They stood in silence, side by side, listening. No footsteps. No bicycle bells. No dogs barking. Only the slow, steady tick of the grandfather clock in the hallway—an ominous metronome counting down to an unknown fate.

At precisely 4:45 a.m., the world shattered. The German invasion of Poland had begun.

Airplane engines roared through the darkness over Bydgoszcz, tearing away the last shreds of calm—the first brutal notes of war, rattling the city with such force that its very bones seemed to shake. Bydgoszcz, straddling the Vistula and Brda Rivers, had long been a strategic prize. Its location between Pomerania and East Prussia and its large population of ethnic Germans, some sympathetic to Hitler's Reich, made it an early target of air raids, and for the tanks, motorcycles, and artillery that would soon follow.

Adi's pulse raced as he clutched Tatjana's hand. Her fingers were cold and rigid in his grasp. Joachim and Hellmuth scrambled from their beds, startled awake by the commotion, and hurried to join their parents in the living room. Adi rushed to Erika and Christa, pulling them away from their bedroom window just as the first explosions began to rock the city.

"The Germans . . . they are here," Adi murmured, a stark acknowledgment for himself as much as for his family. "The war . . . it has come to us."

They huddled together in the living room, clinging tightly to each other as the madness outside crept closer. The tightly drawn curtains did little to muffle the staccato of gunfire that encroached upon them.

"What do we do?" Tatjana's voice trembled against the din.

"We stay put," Adi replied with a steadiness he did not feel. "It's too dangerous outside."

And so they waited. Each hour stretched impossibly long, each minute an eternity. The foundations of their home seemed to quiver with the concussions from outside. The clock refused to move.

When Adi finally peered through a narrow sliver in the curtains, the once familiar streets were now an alien landscape of smoke and fire. Soldiers—mere silhouettes against the inferno—advanced, methodical and impersonal, as they orchestrated the destruction. Behind him, the radio's static-filled voice offered fragmented updates, none of which were reassuring. Bydgoszcz, it said, had been a strategic target. The rivers that once fed the city were fated to become clogged arteries of war.

In the corner, the children asked questions no parent should have to answer. "Why are they doing this?" Erika's eyes were wide with terror.

"Are we going to die?" Christa's voice was barely audible.

Tatjana wrapped her arms around them both. "No," she said, her voice firm but low. "We're staying together. We're keeping each other safe. That's what matters."

Adi joined them on the floor. Together they built a fragile refuge—not from bricks or walls but from whispered songs and half-remembered bed-time stories, repeated like prayers. The sound of gunfire outside turned the walls into drums, but inside they all clung to each other like castaways in a storm.

Night fell and darkness swallowed Bydgoszcz, but no respite came. Adi and Tatjana took turns resting while the other stayed awake and listened, alert to noises they couldn't hope to stop. And still the fighting didn't let up.

By the following morning, Saturday, September 2, Adi and Tatjana had created a precarious order from the chaos. Tatjana inventoried their supplies, rationing food and water with practiced efficiency. Adi reinforced the windows with scavenged wood and metal, turning their modest home into a makeshift fortress.

Joachim took charge of his siblings' morale, inventing games to distract them from the terror beyond their walls. Hellmuth's usual exuberance was dulled, but he still managed to make jokes that elicited weak smiles from Erika and Christa. Erika clung to her older brother's words, finding comfort in his steady, reassuring presence.

Christa found peace at the piano. She played softly, her fingers tentative at first, then more sure, weaving small threads of melody through the heavy atmosphere of dread. Her music became an invisible shield of grace against the noise of war.

Sunday, September 3, dawned with unexpected calm. The gunfire could still be heard in distant parts of the city, but the Dindingers' neighborhood had fallen silent overnight. The family, too exhausted to question it, allowed themselves the comfort of believing they'd been granted a reprieve.

Adi peered through a narrow gap in the boarded window. The streets lay eerily still once more. No movement. No figures. Only the hollow quiet of a city holding its breath.

He gathered his family around him. "It looks safe to go outside," he murmured, his tone a mix of caution and hope. "If we hear the church bells, that will be our sign." The power of their faith was what the family needed, he thought—a tether to something real, something enduring.

Tatjana gave a slow, resolute nod. "Yes, we need to pray."

Quickly, quietly, they dressed, every movement deliberate. Then they waited, ears straining for the distant peal of the church bells. If they rang, it would mean that all was not lost—that one thread of their old life still held.

When Adi finally opened the door, the cold morning light spilled in with the ringing bells. The air was sharp with the tang of smoke and a pervasive sense of fear. They moved as one, footsteps soft on the cobblestones, eyes darting between shadowed doorways and broken windows. The silence around them was not peace—it was suspense.

They flinched at every sound—the creaking of a loose shutter, the roars and cracks of a burning building, the distant bark of a dog—expecting the violence to resume at any moment. Each footstep's echo betrayed their presence. Each breath might carry weight.

Finally, the Uniert Church—unified by its dedication to both St. Peter and St. Paul—loomed ahead, its spire puncturing a sky streaked with dark plumes and gray smudges. Its doors stood open, like arms outstretched to welcome its lost children home. Inside, they found others like themselves, neighbors whose haggard faces were marked by sleepless nights on the raw edge of survival. The congregation was sparse, however, with many pews empty where friends and family had once filled them.

Adi and his family slipped into a pew near the back, heads bowed in exhaustion as much as reverence. Tatjana clasped her hands tightly in her lap, knuckles pale with prayer. Adi draped an arm around her shoulders, pulling her close.

The minister stepped behind the pulpit, his suit rumpled but his eyes alight with a spirit no terror could extinguish. He began the service without preamble or procession but with a direct summons to faith for those who had congregated—for those who, somehow, still hoped. His words, rich and earnest, filled the empty space with something solid: hope amid despair, faith when all seemed lost.

From the pulpit, the sermon seemed to wrap around the chilled worshippers, protection against the harsh reality they now faced. Hellmuth listened intently to every word, as if answers might be found in scripture that could not be found in the streets outside. Erika and Christa prayed fervently on either side of Joachim, hands clasped tight. Their prayers were whispered and urgent—pleas for peace and for something to hold on to. In a world where bombs could fall at any moment, prayer became a kind of gravity, keeping them tethered to reality and reason.

Tatjana's voice joined in the hymns, a subtle defiance against the dissonance of war. The old melodies, clear and poignant, rose and fell in the cold air.

As the final echoes of the service faded, the Dindingers stepped out of their temporary sanctuary. For a fleeting moment, the world outside felt a touch gentler than it had a few hours before. Maybe it was the collective strength of fellowship, the simple, shared human need to grasp for light in the darkest of times.

Adi led his family through the streets with constant vigilance, his pace steady but pressed forward by unease. He was a father shepherding his flock through dangers seen and unseen. He couldn't have known they were being followed from a distance.

They made it home carrying food, firewood, and hope—and the naïve relief of having made it through another day. The whole family—though still tired and scared—was eager to put aside their worries about the future for just a little longer. It was Sunday, after all. The cozy habits of an ordinary afternoon beckoned: a shared meal, Adi playing the violin, Christa joining him on the piano. Maybe, for a while, the war would feel far away.

But war is a cunning beast, with calm often the precursor to a fiercer tempest. Indeed, this lull was but the eye of the hurricane. The beleaguered government in Warsaw had just given a directive that would shatter the Dindingers' lives.

Still basking in the residual peace from the church service, Adi was about to secure the door when an uproar clawed its way toward them from the street. The commotion grew louder—a series of angry shouts, the clomp of boots pounding on the pavement, the ominous percussion of fists hammering on doors. The sound moved like a wave up the street, fast and deliberate.

Then their door shook. Once. Twice. And then it shattered inward with a resounding crash.

Adi froze for a half second, then turned instinctively to shield his family. He never got the chance to speak.

Uniformed Poles swarmed into their home, their eyes cold, their movements practiced. Their faces betrayed no emotion—only cold, insensitive purpose. These men were the executioners of Order 59, a proscription decree, a purge. These men carried lists—lists of names. And Tatjana's name was on one of them.

Tatjana stood defiantly in front of her children, her petite frame trembling with outrage. "What is the meaning of this?" she demanded, her voice taut with fury.

One of the men stepped forward, his expression unreadable as he scanned the list in his hand. "Tatjana Dindinger?"

Her chin lifted slightly. "Yes?"

"You are to come with us."

The room erupted in chaos. Adi lunged forward, only to be seized by two guards. Joachim's protests were muffled as he, too, was restrained. Hellmuth tried to dodge past a guard but was caught midstride and shoved aside.

"No! You can't take her!" Erika screamed, tears streaming down her face as she clung desperately to Tatjana's arm.

Christa stood paralyzed, horror etched across her features as she watched her mother being pulled away from the family.

"Please!" Tatjana's cry rose above the turmoil as she struggled against the grip of the men dragging her toward the door. "My children need me!"

But her pleas fell on deaf ears. The decree had been issued, and there was no room for mercy or reason in its execution.

The same terrible scene was playing out not just in Bydgoszcz but also in German communities throughout Poland. Any ethnic German deemed sufficiently prominent or respected—or anyone who could possibly be a threat to the Polish government during the German invasion—was to be rounded up. Those not executed on the spot were dragged from their families, torn from their homes, and marched away into an abyss.

As Tatjana was forced outside, Adi caught one last, chaotic look at his wife. Her eyes were afraid not for herself but for the family she was leaving behind. And then she was gone.

The silence left in her absence rang louder than the chaos.

PART III

The War Begins

CHAPTER TWELVE

RECLAIMING THE LIGHT (1939)

IN THE AFTERMATH OF TATJANA'S abduction, a dense silence settled over the Dindinger household. It clung to the walls, broken only by the ticking hallway clock, each second already a quiet reminder of her absence.

Outside their battered door lay an altered world. Freedom had been stripped away overnight. A mother could be torn from her children without warning. Yet inside that door was the same strength, the same love as ever: a father set on protecting his children and children determined to survive and reclaim what had been stolen from them—their mother's light. That light was needed now amid the growing darkness enveloping all of Poland—indeed, all of Europe.

Tears carved clear paths down Erika's dirt-streaked face, her sobs a piercing counterpoint to Christa's quiet weeping. The girls clung to each other, their world unraveling in the space of heartbeats.

Joachim, nineteen and with the fire of youth blazing in his eyes, clenched his fists. Hellmuth, a year younger but no less determined, mirrored his brother's stance. The brothers exchanged a glance, then moved as one toward the splintered threshold.

Adi caught them by their shoulders, his grip iron despite the tremor that shook his frame. "No," he said, voice ragged with emotion. "You cannot."

"We have to do something!" Joachim's voice cracked. "They took her!"

"We can't let them take Mama!" Hellmuth exclaimed, urgency taut in his cry.

Adi yanked them back, his heart breaking. "And what would you do? Run into the street and demand her return? You think they will listen? They have guns. They have orders. They will not hesitate to shoot you down. And how will that help your mother?"

Joachim's face twisted in anguish as he glanced back at his sisters. "Then what? We just sit here? Do nothing while they—"

"No," Adi interrupted, tightening his grip to emphasize each word. "We endure. For her. For all of us. Don't you see? We must be here when she returns." He released his sons and turned away, his shoulders sagging.

Despair clung to the room, thick and suffocating. But someone had to stay standing. It was the only way to make the family whole again.

Adi's gaze swept over the fragments of his family. Their unity was their strongest defense in a suddenly hostile world. "We'll find her," he said, his tone resolute, though it cost him everything to muster that assurance. "But not like this. Not through recklessness."

He knelt in front of his daughters, taking their hands.

"Your mother is strong," he said gently, searching their faces for understanding. "She would want us to be strong too. To think before we act."

Erika sniffled and nodded slowly, while Christa leaned into Adi's embrace.

He pulled them closer. "We'll find a way to help her. We just have to believe she can endure until then."

"But how could they just turn on us?" Joachim's voice cracked. "After all these years, we've been nothing but good citizens."

Adi, weighed down by a heavy heart, observed his son's struggle. "It's complicated, Joachim," he said, his words cloaked in grief. "Our roots run deeper than the soil we stand on. Our bonds to Poland are strong, but our German blood still defines us."

Joachim turned from the window, confusion knitting his brow. "Can't we tell someone we aren't like the other Germans? Surely, they would believe you, after all the years you've spent working for the government."

Adi straightened, his eyes locking with Joachim's. "Being German is part of who I am. I can't shed my heritage like an old coat, even if I wanted to. It's woven into the fabric of my soul, my memories, and the way I see the world."

The room was silent then except for the occasional distant gunshot, a chilling reminder of the danger just beyond their walls. With a father's instinct to protect and a leader's drive to act, Adi stood firm, locking his gaze with Joachim's and Hellmuth's.

"Listen." Adi's voice was a low rumble of controlled urgency. "We need a plan. We must wait and gather information. And when the time is right, we act. We cannot end up sharing your mother's fate—or worse."

Joachim met his father's gaze squarely. "So what do we do?"

Adi exhaled. "First, we stay together. We talk to friends, neighbors, people we can trust—anyone who might know where your mother and the others were taken."

"And then?" Joachim pressed.

"We wait," Adi replied, "for a moment that doesn't put you or anyone else in danger."

Hellmuth looked at his father and then his brother. "And if that moment doesn't come?"

Adi placed a guiding hand on Hellmuth's shoulder. "Then we make our own moment. But not blindly."

The boys nodded. It wasn't a plan—not yet. But it was a beginning.

As the light of day waned, the conversation settled into a strategic session: names, places, messages to send, questions to ask. The children, gathered around Adi, began to shed the last traces of their innocence, understanding that the road ahead would demand strength they had yet to summon. Each move had to be taken carefully to avoid the direst consequences.

"We start with what we know," Adi continued, low and firm, "but secrecy is essential. We don't know who might be watching or listening."

His words were a call to arms, a promise spoken with the steady resolve of a man who could not and would not yield.

Erika nodded, a cascade of tears marking her cheeks. She understood, and she would not back down. After all, she was her mother's daughter.

Joachim hugged his sister. "We'll each have a role in bringing Mama home," he said, his analytical mind already mapping their next steps.

"Yes, we will do this as a family." Adi turned to Erika and Christa, their youthful faces lifted to him, wide with fear yet shining with faith. "United, as your mother would expect. With courage and with hope."

As the hours passed under the oppressive burden of the new curfew—its silence punctuated by the distant crack of gunfire—the children drew closer under Adi's watch, a broken circle clinging to its remaining links.

That day, the Dindingers became warriors in a battle for their family and for their very souls. That day—September 3, 1939—was also the beginning of World War II.

In the trying days that followed, despite the strength of their mission and his resolve, Adi drifted without Tatjana. His routines frayed; his sense of time dulled. Joachim found himself in the unexpected role of both son and makeshift patriarch. He didn't say much about it. He just did what needed to be done.

Joachim would rise with the sun, his footsteps echoing down the hallway as he made his way to the kitchen. The scent of brewing coffee wafting through the house would rouse his father from another restless night. Adi would shuffle in to find breakfast laid out neatly: bread buttered and cut into precise triangles, soft-boiled eggs resting in their cups, porridge steaming on the stove.

"You need to eat something, Papa," Joachim would urge, pushing a plate toward his father.

Adi's eyes would lift to meet his son's, gratitude in their depths as he took a bite. Joachim's presence of mind brought a semblance of normalcy and continuity to their lives.

After breakfast, Joachim would sit with Hellmuth at the old oak desk in the study. Hellmuth was nearing the end of his schooling but found it hard to focus with their mother gone.

"Just think of it like an equation," Joachim encouraged, pointing to the math problem in Hellmuth's workbook. "Balance each side. That's all it is."

Hellmuth would nod slowly, determination setting in as he picked up his pencil and began to work through the problem under Joachim's guidance.

Outside their window, clashes erupted in the streets between Poles, underground Nazi sympathizers, and the Wehrmacht troops. The lines blurred: Who was soldier? Who was bystander? Who was simply unlucky?

From the living room, fourteen-year-old Christa stared through the curtains, her hands pressed to the glass. She saw people fall in the town square, their lives stolen by the snap of a rifle. "They're killing people," she whispered. "I saw them. Lined up. Then—" Her voice caught. "I want Mama to come home."

The gunfire had started on September 1, when the German offensive began. By the time the Wehrmacht occupation had taken hold, on September 5, Bydgoszcz was already breaking. The last of the Polish troops pulled out under cover of night on September 4, leaving the city to the mercy of the Third Panzer Division. The civilian militia held what territory they could. But by the end of that week, Polish civilians were fighting from basements and back stairwells.

The gunshots would continue for another five weeks.

Meanwhile, inside the Dindinger house, schoolwork lost its meaning. Erika, normally sharp and driven, struggled to care. Reading assignments and skating practice felt ridiculous when people were dying in the streets.

But Joachim found a way to reach her. He brought out his chemistry set and proposed experiments like puzzles. Rather than try to distract her with play, he offered her purpose. As they worked together, he saw something flicker back into her expression—not happiness exactly but wonder. It was the only kind of light he could give in place of their mother's smile.

Christa clung to her music, but every note seemed muted without Mama's voice singing under her breath nearby. Still, she played, because playing meant she hadn't given up. And Joachim never missed a performance. He sat nearby and listened attentively, offering applause and encouragement to bolster her spirits. He kept up the calming routines Mama had established, too—especially important after Christa's bout with myocarditis.

Even amid the German occupation, the rhythm of daily life was maintained by shared responsibilities. Adi managed the bills and repairs, while Joachim oversaw cooking and cleaning with help from his siblings. Their teamwork was seamless—unspoken yet synchronized. They moved as one unit, even though each soul was aching.

The grief was there for each of them, just beneath the surface, but it had no room to breathe, no opportunity to take over. Purpose was the balm. And purpose, for now, was family.

CHAPTER THIRTEEN

DEATH MARCH (1939)

AUTUMN'S CHILL BIT INTO TATJANA'S flesh as she trudged along a path strewn with dirt and debris. The relentless rhythm of marching boots melded with the moans of the weary and the cries of the wounded. Her once luminous blue eyes, now dulled by days of anguish and fatigue, searched the horizon, where a blood-orange sun cast elongated shadows over a column of broken souls.

Tatjana's heart hammered against her ribcage, a staccato beat mirroring the tempo of their forced march. Around her, ethnic Germans staggered forward under the sharp gaze of their Polish captors. She clutched her thin coat tighter, though it did little to warm the chill seeping into her bones.

A scream shattered the air, followed by a dull thud just ahead—a body hitting the ground. Tatjana's gaze darted to see a man crumple under the butt of a rifle, his plea for mercy cut short by a boot to his face. She swallowed hard, forcing herself to look away, knowing pity was dangerous. Here, empathy was treason.

She had learned quickly that kindness was a luxury none of them could afford. The guards treated them like cattle, not people—prodded and culled and shoved forward without rest. Bayonets gleamed in the waning light, silent warnings that each step might be their last.

As night fell, their pace slowed, but it never stopped. Darkness brought no mercy but rather new horrors. Each step sent a jolt of pain from Tatjana's blistered feet and aching legs, but she dared not slow down. Weakness was punished. Hesitation was fatal.

In their march south from Bydgoszcz, they had passed through towns where anger and hatred met them like a physical force. Villagers emerged from their homes and shops, not with food or water but with stones and spit. They hurled insults and objects with equal fervor, their faces twisted into masks of rage. The German prisoners endured it all—each blow, each cruel word. They had no other choice.

In these moments, Tatjana's secret lay heavy in her chest. No one could know she was Jewish. Silence was her only protection. If her true heritage were discovered—whether by captors or by comrades—there would be no defense. The Poles loathed her German surname, but the Nazis would kill her because of her blood.

As she marched on, her thoughts drifted to her children, to Adi. Would they know what became of her? Would they understand that every agonizing step she took was for them? Each breath she drew was a prayer wrapped in silence.

A sharp command cut through Tatjana's daze. She lifted her head to see that they were approaching an open field, where the captives were ordered to lie down in rows, their bodies aligned like crops beneath a cold and indifferent sky. There was no cover in sight should bombing commence with dawn's light. Daylight always meant risk—not just from within but from above, where the Luftwaffe droned like distant thunder. At least the skies stayed empty at night. But fear never slept.

As Tatjana lowered herself onto the cold earth, bruises flared against the pressure. Around her, others collapsed. She didn't know their names, only the shape of their suffering—bone-tired bodies curled in the dirt, breath whispering into the dark. Here and there, someone murmured a word, a prayer, a soft curse—small sounds that flickered like candlelight before sleep claimed them. She turned her face upward, where the stars hung still, and allowed herself a moment's respite.

In this fragile space between wakefulness and dreams, Tatjana gripped hope like a lifeline. The memory of her family became her breath, her warmth, her prayer. In the silent darkness, she conjured the feel of Adi's arms, the laughter of her children, the music of home. That love—impossible to silence—carried her through another night.

And when dawn finally crept across the field, painting the earth in muted gold, it was not just the light that rose. Tatjana rose too. Bruised, blistered, hollow—but unbroken—she stood with the others.

And so they marched on.

Each town they reached along this death march brought new eyes to witness their suffering. Crowds gathered in hatred, not pity. The people of Poland spat, jeered, and hurled stones at their German neighbors. It was a world stripped bare of humanity, where even children pointed with contempt, mimicking the cruelty of adults. Town squares were patrolled by Polish guards with eyes as cold as the steel of their rifles.

The faces around Tatjana blurred into one collective expression of despair. Some she recognized: neighbors from Bydgoszcz, women who had once smiled at her in the bakery line yet were now skeletal and silent. They had become strangers, shuffling forward in torn coats too thin to matter.

Life on the march was a daily battle against dehumanization. Tatjana whispered her name under her breath like a talisman: "Tatjana Dindinger. Tatjana Dindinger." Her mantra was a defiant reminder that she was still someone, not a number. Not yet a corpse.

She learned quickly that the weak fell first. Food remained scarce, doled out in meager portions that left stomachs crying in protest. The water was often tainted, bringing illness and suffering. Tatjana watched fellow prisoners wither day by day—cheeks hollowing, eyes receding, bodies collapsing with the solemn finality of surrender.

Yet in this hellscape, she found purpose. Survival, she realized, was not enough. She must be a lifeline for others as well. She had been raised among forests, schooled in the secrets of bark and leaf. That knowledge became her currency. Along the road, she foraged like a ghost, unseen and tormented—gathering dandelions, plantain leaves, anything with a hint of nutritional or medicinal value.

"Chew on this," she would whisper to a fellow prisoner wracked with coughs. "It will help ease your throat."

The latrines were hellholes, rank with disease. People avoided them until desperation clawed at their insides. Tatjana tied scraps of cloth into makeshift masks, slipping peppermint leaves inside to soften the stench—a small mercy in a place that offered few.

Each night, Tatjana lay awake on the hard soil or on wooden planks, listening to the chorus of human pain: a man moaning through fevered dreams, a woman reciting prayers in a language Tatjana barely understood. Each voice imprinted in her memory like a tally mark on the scorecard of suffering, with every sound, every life, every breath still clinging to hope.

The march had its own hierarchy. Tatjana kept her distance from collaborators who bartered scraps of humanity for a crust of bread or a minute of rest. Trust was a luxury she could not afford. Neither warmth nor mercy flowed freely in this desolate world.

Her body bore witness to the endless cruelty. Bruises blossomed across her skin, marks left by splintered wood, twisted sleep, and the sharp bark of commands not obeyed quickly enough. Yet Tatjana's strength wasn't just in physical endurance. It was in her resolve to see her family once more. Images of Adi and their children were talismans she held close in moments when death seemed like the easier path.

One evening, as dusk settled on their slow approach to the beleaguered town of Łowicz, Tatjana found herself near a small group of women huddled around a clandestine fire. It was rare, this quiet moment. The fire offered not just warmth but a semblance of humanity.

"You have children?" asked an older woman, her voice cracked and frail, her eyes unable to meet Tatjana's.

"Yes," Tatjana replied softly, allowing herself a moment to picture them—Joachim's earnest face bent over his chemistry problems, Erika's graceful figure gliding across the ice, Christa's fingers coaxing songs from the piano, Hellmuth's laughter filling their home.

"They must be missing you terribly," another whispered.

Tatjana nodded but said nothing more. She couldn't afford to let thoughts of them consume her here. To dwell on her family could undermine the strength she had built like armor around her. Others, she knew, drew quiet courage from her composure—not because she grieved, but because she still stood.

The dawn sky over Łowicz bled the colors of fire and ash. In the distance, artillery split the silence with ruthless precision. German howitzers roared, the Luftwaffe shrieked overhead, and the ground quaked beneath it all. Beneath that cacophony, chaos would soon erupt.

Tatjana's heart pounded to the rhythm of war. She had lost count of the days since her capture, each one blurring into the next in a haze of fear and uncertainty. Artillery fire had grown closer and closer, and with it came whispers of what horrors might come next.

Yet nothing had prepared her for the sudden eruption of Nazi uniforms swarming the town—or the growl of the Panzers rolling through the fields beyond.

CHAPTER FOURTEEN

LEARNING THE TRUTH (1939)

THE GERMAN INVASION OF POLAND brought brutal innovations in warfare—blitzkrieg tactics that tore through cities and farmlands with terrifying speed. Yet it wasn't just bombs and bullets that redefined the battlefield. The most corrosive force was ideological.

With the rise of National Socialism came poisonous divisions, new racial hierarchies that seeped into every corner of life. In Bydgoszcz—now referred to by the German name Bromberg—tensions mounted by the hour. Neighbors eyed one another with suspicion. Whispered rumors carried more weight than facts.

And then, as if Poland's suffering wasn't already complete, the next blow fell: On September 17, the Soviet Union invaded from the east. A nation already bleeding from one border now bled from another.

Without Tatjana, time had warped for the Dindinger family. Days stretched too long. The silence was too heavy. In the evenings, Adi often sat at the kitchen table surrounded not by the living hum of his children but by ghostly echoes of laughter that had once filled the room.

Joachim paced the floor, his mind restless, footsteps creaking across the worn boards like a metronome of worry. "Why should it matter that you and Mama are German?" he insisted, frustration hardening his voice as his feet came to a stop. "We live *here*. We contribute to society. We sat in Polish classrooms and learned Polish history."

Adi's response was steeped in hard-earned wisdom. "Heritage," he said gently, "can be a double-edged sword. It can be the pride that lifts you high or the mark that singles you out. It's a complicated puzzle, my son, one we cannot rework simply because we wish it so."

Joachim resumed his pacing, the floorboards groaning under the weight of his restlessness. "And what good is that heritage now?" he said, voice tight with grief. "Look where it's gotten us. Mama has been taken away. Our neighbors are eyeing us with suspicion. I hate what Hitler is doing. I hate that, because of him, we're seen as tainted, as the enemy."

Adi's fingers drummed on the wooden table. "That hatred, Joachim, is proof of our moral compass, pointing true north away from the madness. You carry our history but not his stain. There's honor in where we come from—poets, thinkers, builders. That is the legacy we must separate from the tyranny that seeks to claim it."

Joachim halted and leaned against the wall, his shoulders slumping as he exhaled a heavy sigh. "But if being German makes us targets here in Poland, then what?"

"There's strength in owning who you are," Adi said, his voice rising with conviction. "I won't deny my heritage simply because a madman has hijacked it for his own purposes. That doesn't mean I support him—I despise everything he stands for—but I can't stop being German. I wouldn't, even if I could."

He paused, eyes drifting to a family portrait—happier times captured in a frame.

"Maybe that's why they took your mother," he went on, softer now. "She was an easy target for their cruelty—a woman with a hidden past living in occupied Poland. Maybe someone was trying to send me a message or take revenge over some perceived slight. Your sweet mama might have been pulled into someone else's vengeance."

Joachim edged closer, worry palpable. "But the Poles could have taken *you* as well—you're as German as she is."

Adi let out a weary sigh and shrugged. "Perhaps my job with the Stadt offers some protection. Maybe someone intervened. Maybe I was just lucky." He shook his head slowly. "But don't mistake that luck for safety, my dear boy. I am under no illusion. None of us are safe."

A heavy silence followed as Joachim absorbed his father's words.

"There's more," Adi continued quietly. "Your mother . . . was born into the Jewish faith. In Russia, not Germany."

Joachim stared at him, stunned. "But Papa, why keep such secrets? Why was I left in the dark?"

"You were just a child," Adi explained. "Why fill your head with things you couldn't possibly understand? But you're grown now. You deserve to know. And this must remain between us." His voice lowered. "Knowledge can be dangerous in times like these. I don't want your siblings to carry the burden of this secret."

Joachim looked down, struggling with the revelation. "What do we do now? How do we go on knowing they could come for any one of us—at any time?"

"We stay alert," Adi replied, standing from the table to face his son squarely. "We keep our heads down when we must. We stand tall when it matters—when it *really* matters. We protect one another. We hold on to hope that your mother will come back."

"And if she doesn't?" Joachim asked, fear lacing his voice.

Adi placed a hand on his son's shoulder. "If that day comes, we live in her honor—with the courage she has taught us, the warmth she has given. We stay brave and never forget who we are or where we came from."

A long silence filled the room before Adi spoke again.

"Keep this safe within you, Joachim," he said, the command firm but fatherly. "It isn't from fear or shame that I ask this of you. It is for survival."

"I will," Joachim whispered, his voice hoarse, his mind heavy with what had been entrusted to him.

"And know this," Adi added, gathering strength. "I would never wish our heritage away, even though we must keep your mother's birthright a secret for now. Have no doubt, our heritage has shaped us—all of us. It has made you who you are. We must keep it hidden. But never let it be erased."

Joachim exhaled slowly. "I understand," he said at last. "And if it comes to the worst . . ."

Adi held up a hand, shaking his head. "We won't speak of that now. We will carry on as we have always done—with hope."

One brisk afternoon, Joachim returned from town with his cheeks flushed from the wind. Behind him stood a lanky boy with keen eyes and a quiet, thoughtful expression.

"Stefan has a mind for molecules!" Joachim announced proudly, ushering the boy inside as leaves skittered across the pavement behind them. "You should hear him talk about covalent bonds. He makes chemistry sound like poetry."

Adi looked up from where he sat near the fireplace, documents strewn around him. He mustered a smile for his son's friend, a welcome distraction. "Glad you could join us, Stefan," he said, his voice warm though a bit hoarse from disuse.

Stefan nodded politely before turning his gaze toward Erika. "Your brother told me about your love of chemistry as well. Perhaps we are kindred spirits."

Erika blushed but met Stefan's gaze head-on. "Maybe so," she replied, quieter than usual but unable to hide her curiosity.

Within moments, the two were deep in discussion about catalysts and reaction rates. Stefan's enthusiasm met Erika's growing confidence, and Joachim couldn't help but smile. It had been too long since Erika looked so engaged, so alive.

That night, over a modest dinner of cabbage and potatoes, Stefan regaled them with stories from *Gymnasium*—quirky teachers, harmless pranks, whispered jokes passed between desks. His laughter came easily and was contagious, a rare gust of brightness that swept through the Dindinger home like fresh air through a sealed room.

Later, while drying dishes side by side, Stefan turned to Joachim. "You're holding up better than expected," he said quietly. "As well as anyone could . . . given everything."

Joachim shrugged off the compliment with a tight smile. "We do what we must." There was no pride in the reply, only endurance. Stefan placed a hand on his friend's shoulder, a silent acknowledgment of the burden he carried.

When they joined the others in the living room, music finally pushed back the fog. Adi drew his bow across the strings of his violin, Christa's fingers found the keys, and soothing harmonies rose like breath into the air. The house, long quiet, exhaled. Something shifted that day—not everything, but something.

CHAPTER FIFTEEN

A BOND IS FORGED
(1939)

ADI STOOD IN THE DOORWAY, unnoticed, watching Stefan and Erika bent over a clutter of beakers and flasks on the kitchen table. Laughter rose between them, a sound so pure and unburdened that it momentarily broke through the dark clouds that had settled over the house since Tatjana's abduction. Adi could see a connection between these two young people that surpassed their shared love for chemistry.

"Careful! Adding too much will turn our experiment into a disaster," Stefan warned, reaching out to correct Erika's motion with a teasing look. "We'll have a kitchen full of foam."

Erika's cheeks flushed as a grin tugged at the corner of her mouth. "I would've caught that, you know," she countered with mock indignation. "I'm not always in need of rescue."

Stefan's hand lingered a moment longer than necessary before he withdrew it. "I've no doubt," he replied. "But sometimes it's nice to have someone looking out for you, isn't it?"

Silently, Adi stepped back, leaving them to their moment.

It was a relief to see Erika more like herself again, especially after recent events at school. Just days earlier, she had burst through the door, her face streaked with tears. "Papa! At the Copernicus Gymnasium . . . my friends . . ."

She choked on her words. "A student—he shot a German soldier, and now . . . They've executed fifty students! My friends, Papa! My friends!"

Adi rose swiftly, the color draining from his face as he crossed the room and took her by the shoulders, steadying her. "These are dark days, Eka," he lamented, keeping his voice steady as though it might soothe the chaos of fear. "I know you're frightened. I am too."

"I'm . . . I'm terrified, Papa!" she replied, falling against him, wracked with sobs.

Adi drew a breath. "The Einsatzkommandos . . . They are ruthless. This is part of a larger plan to erase our Polish and Jewish friends from existence." Weeks of gathering information, trying to understand what had happened to Tatjana, had left him even better informed. His eyes hardened at the thought of Reinhard Heydrich, the orchestrator of such atrocities. "This is the horror we are up against—the calculated cruelty of a regime that knows no limits."

Erika's sobs had filled the room, a haunting reminder of the peril that lurked beyond the fragile safety of their home.

Now, Adi mused over the evolving landscape of his family's life—the gaping hole left by Tatjana's abduction, but also Stefan's seamless integration into their household. Joachim's best friend often came bringing levity, curiosity, and even joy. For a moment, watching him and Erika, Adi allowed himself to believe that not everything was collapsing, that life was still reaching forward.

The sound of the front door opening pulled Adi from his thoughts. Joachim stepped inside, his face weary from the long hours at his after-school job at the detergent lab but brightening at the sound of laughter from the kitchen.

"Sounds like I'm missing all the fun," Joachim remarked, draping his coat over a chair and making his way toward the voices.

In the kitchen, Erika had just added the final reagent to their bubbling mixture. The solution shimmered into a vibrant shade of blue. "Perfect," she beamed. "See? We make quite the team."

Joachim entered, his eyes flitting between his sister and his best friend. "Seems I've been replaced as your favorite lab partner."

Erika glanced up at her brother, her expression softening. "No one could ever replace you, Joachimchen. I always miss you."

Stefan turned to greet Joachim with a warm smile. "We're just keeping your seat warm. Care to join us?"

"I wouldn't dream of interrupting such progress," Joachim replied with a chuckle, though a hint of something else flickered and faded in his tone.

Erika slipped off her apron and came to greet him. "How was work today? Anything new at Persil?"

Joachim nodded, pleased to be asked. "We're testing a new soap formula—something that works better in hard water. It's early but promising."

Stefan jumped in before Erika could reply. "That's funny—Erika and I were just talking about mixing oils with alkaline bases, trying to mimic soap ourselves. You'll have to show us how it's really done."

Joachim raised an eyebrow, intrigued.

Across the room, Adi watched them with quiet pride. Their curiosity, their hunger for knowledge, was a light that refused to dim, even as the world outside darkened.

That evening, dinner came together amid lively exchanges on chemical bonds and molecular structures. Christa had prepared stew, its rich aroma permeating the household. As they gathered round the table, Hellmuth recounted tales from school while Christa teased him about his newest girlfriend. Joachim offered workplace anecdotes, carefully curated to keep the mood light. Stefan listened attentively, laughing in the right places, occasionally sneaking glances at Erika when he thought no one would notice.

When the time came to depart, Stefan hesitated at the doorstep, turning to Erika with an earnestness that stilled her breath. "I've been meaning to ask you—would you be interested in a university lecture next week? Industrial chemistry. I thought it might be right up your alley."

Erika's eyes lit up. "I'd love that. Thank you for thinking of me."

Their gazes held a beat too long before Stefan nodded and stepped into the cool evening air.

Stefan's presence had grown constant. He often arrived before Joachim got home and stayed late into the quiet hours after dinner. Adi, always watchful, noted the subtle dynamics—the way Stefan sought Erika's opinion first, the exchanged glances sharing unspoken jokes. It was clear to everyone, except perhaps to Erika and Stefan, that their bond had grown beyond shared curiosity. They moved in an orbit all their own.

One evening, while Joachim labored late at his other job at the Tysler lab, trying to perfect a new chocolate recipe, Stefan lingered to help Erika clean up after an experiment gone awry. The mess was impressive. Still, they moved through the kitchen with practiced ease, a dance mastered after spending so many evenings side by side.

"I'm sorry about the mess," Erika apologized for the tenth time as their failed experiment's frothy overflow receded.

Stefan chuckled, wiping down the table with a damp cloth. "It's nothing we haven't seen before." He paused. "Besides, I can't think of many better ways to spend an evening."

Erika's hands, still damp from the cleanup, grew still as his words settled between them. Her eyes flickered with a maturity that belied her fifteen years. "I'm glad you're here, Stefan," she said, keeping her voice composed. "But we both know that—"

"That you're young, and I'm not so much," he finished, a soft smile touching his lips. His tone was sincere, not dismissive. "I know, Erika. I'm not here expecting anything. I just enjoy your company. Your mind. The way you light up a room."

She nodded, grateful for his understanding and respect. Both knew the boundaries set by age and circumstance. She leaned against the counter and let out a slow breath. "It's just . . . so senseless, isn't it? The fighting, the losses." Her gaze drifted to the window. "We're trying to use science to make life better, and out there"—she gestured vaguely—"it's all being torn apart."

Stefan set aside the cloth and stepped closer. "I know. My mother's Polish and my father is German. Families like ours get caught in the middle. Every day is a balancing act of identities and loyalties." He hesitated, then reached for Erika's hand. "The Wehrmacht is here to stay, I believe. And the Nazis too. Judging by what I see, this invasion will end quickly. Poland doesn't stand a chance against the German military."

Erika sighed, recalling friends from school—bright, eager faces disappearing one by one through conscriptions and casualties. "Leonard from my class . . . he was sixteen," she whispered, her voice cracking. "He wanted to be an architect—dreamed of building bridges, not destroying them."

Stefan squeezed her hand.

"And Liesel . . . her entire family vanished overnight," Erika went on, anger rising. "No warning. Just gone. Because someone decided they didn't belong."

Names poured out like overflow from a breached dam: friends spirited away, classmates who left and never returned. Her grief was laced with fury at the injustice that made their absence possible.

"They were just kids like me," Erika choked out. She couldn't bring herself to speak of her own loss. Her mother's arrest was never far from her mind, but hope that Tatjana still lived dimmed with each passing day.

Stefan pulled up a chair; Erika sank into it gratefully. He crouched beside her, eyes glistening with shared pain. "We've all lost someone," he said softly. "That's what war does. They say it doesn't discriminate, but it does."

Adi's tireless research had discovered that the German Reich started making "kill lists" two years ago, under the codename Operation Tannenberg—and that the Poles had made lists too.

"No one's hands are clean. It's all so cruel." Stefan paused. "Even so, we must hold on to something. If we cannot have peace, then we must have purpose."

Erika brushed away tears and met his gaze. Fire returned to her eyes. "You're right. We will make it matter. What we know, what we do—it has to count for something."

Stefan gave a solemn nod. "We'll get through this," he promised. "Not apart. Together."

For a long moment, nothing moved but their heartbeats. In that stillness, they weren't just friends caught between forces they couldn't control; they were allies choosing, in their own small way, to fight for a different future.

In the living room, overhearing his daughter's passionate words of loss and hope, Adi felt a wave of profound affection—and a pang of sorrow—sweep through him. He knew she had grown too fast, that he was witnessing the premature end of innocence. Yet he found comfort in knowing Stefan stood by her side—a dear friend who understood the complexity of lives caught between two worlds at war.

In the hallway, the clock ticked steadily, indifferent to the burden of the two young people, its rhythm a reminder that time doesn't stop, even when the heart begs it to.

Stefan rose and offered Erika his hand again. "Let's turn this grief into something useful," he said with a weary smile. "Let's create."

Erika clasped his hand in hers and nodded, brushing away the last of her tears and turning back to their makeshift lab. Together they pored over notes and diagrams once more—a subtle act of defiance against the chaos outside and a renewal of their commitment to building knowledge in a world bent on destruction and ignorance.

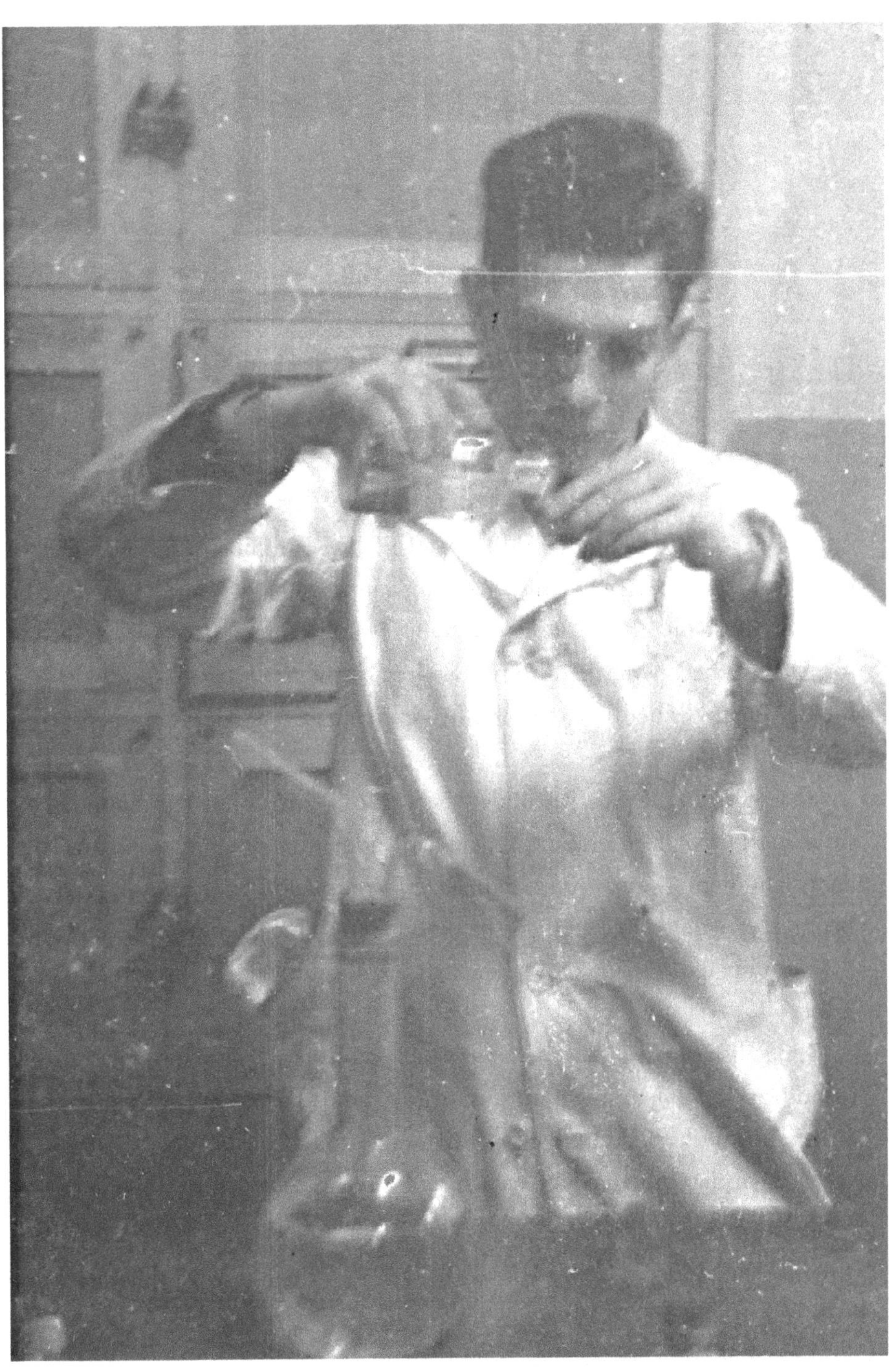

Joachim, the elder *Bruder*, experimenting with his chemistry set at home in Bromberg, 1937.

CHAPTER SIXTEEN

UNBROKEN (1939)

ARRIVING ON THE OUTSKIRTS OF Bromberg, Tatjana's feet touched the soil of her dreams. A tremor ran through her, a tidal wave of emotion breaching the walls she had built to survive these past weeks of terror. She had been wrenched from this place by the machinery of war. Now she returned, her body marked but her spirit intact—a living testament to endurance.

That morning in Łowicz, under the roar of German howitzers and the shrieking Luftwaffe, German soldiers had suddenly poured into the town, boots hammering stone, voices clipped and commanding. The Battle of the Bzura, they would later say, was the bloodiest and most bitter of the entire Polish campaign. Tatjana only knew that it had sounded like the end of the world.

The Polish guards, once stern with their captives and sure in their commands, now stood stunned and disarmed. Hands raised. Faces drained of color. Their authority crumbled like the walls around them.

In their place now stood German soldiers, shouting orders. Tatjana felt adrift amid a sea of faces as bewildered as her own.

"Line up! Schnell! Alle Deutschen hierher!" one of the soldiers commanded. "All Germans, come here!"

Tatjana froze.

Around her, the Germans from Bromberg who were once outcasts under

Polish guard—exhausted, emaciated, and facing doom—suddenly found themselves thrust into privileged limelight. They gathered quickly, seeking safety under the wings of their perceived protectors.

After the barest of hesitations, Tatjana took a step forward.

Then another.

Each movement was laced with dread. Her breath caught as her eyes scanned the chaos. Would they question her? Would someone know she wasn't truly one of them? Her heart beat a desperate rhythm as she tried not to falter.

A soldier approached, his gaze sweeping over her like a gust of cold wind. "Name?" he demanded.

"Tatjana Dindinger," she replied, voice steady despite the tremor within.

He checked his list, then nodded curtly. "Move with the others."

She moved forward, feet propelling her toward a group united by the arbitrary grace of heritage—a heritage that was hers only on paper. Her fate now hung upon the slender thread of that long-ago forgery, the one that had already saved her life once. Survival no longer hinged on justice. It was a negotiation with destiny.

The haunting truth would later reach her: The Jewish men and boys of Łowicz—those whose blood matched hers—were herded into the town's central synagogue. For two days they were tortured. Then they were executed by the newly formed infantry regiment Leibstandarte SS Adolf Hitler. This was the grim epilogue to her chapter of suffering. It was genocide in its infancy. It was the end of innocence.

But Tatjana was spared that knowledge for now and on the march once again. The hours moved on, and night began to fall, measured by the stars blinking overhead. Finally, they reached an encampment set up by their "liberators"—a word that soured on Tatjana's tongue even as she spat it out in a whisper—where temporary tents stood like ghosts against the twilight sky.

"We'll process you here," a German officer explained, ushering them into an area cordoned off with barbed wire. "You will be given food and shelter until we can transport you back to Bromberg."

Bromberg.

Bydgoszcz.

Freedom.

Family.

The thoughts flickered in Tatjana's mind like beacons of hope as she found herself sitting on a rough cot inside one of the tents, surrounded by strangers speaking softly of home and families they hadn't seen for weeks. Her thoughts turned to images, of Adi and their children, of the time she'd missed and the warm laughter and embraces she remembered so vividly.

A bowl of thin soup appeared before her, handed off by a young German soldier whose voice lacked the bark of his uniform. "Es ist nicht viel," he said apologetically. "It's not much, but it will get better."

She nodded in thanks but found she had little appetite. Instead, she cradled the bowl for its warmth, as if it might reach somewhere deeper than her stomach—as if heat could stir hope back to life.

The journey back to Bromberg was a long blur of faces and silence. Weariness carved deep into every expression. No one needed to speak. Anticipation sat thick in the air.

Tatjana took a seat near the window of the rickety transport, the landscape passing in a smear of greens and browns. With each mile along the road, the knot in her chest pulled tighter. Her hands lay gently in her lap, the skin mapped with hardship. They trembled slightly, holding the fragile belief that soon—after everything—she would be home.

Back with Adi.

Back with their children.

In Bromberg at last, she walked the familiar streets stretching before her, altered but still known. Buildings wore bullet holes like open wounds. Windows were shattered, their jagged edges glinting in the sunlight. The town bore its scars as she bore hers—both survivors of a war they hadn't asked for.

Yet as Tatjana approached her home, the pallor of her face gave way to a faint glow, as if the color were returning not just to her skin but to her life. Beneath every mark of what she had suffered, her eyes still burned—with clarity, with courage.

Finally, she reached the familiar door that stood like a threshold to the world she had lost. With a hand that belied her nervousness, she knocked.

Silence greeted her at first, a prolonged pause where time held its breath. Then came footsteps—cautious at first, quicker with each second—until the door swung open.

Adi stood there, his face a portrait of shock and disbelief that melted into unbridled joy. His voice broke as he uttered her name, the sound full of love barely contained.

"Tatjana!"

Then came the children—Joachim, Hellmuth, Erika, Christa—beautiful, beloved faces she had feared she would never see again. Eyes widened, mouths opened, but no words came. Language seemed too small for the moment.

Without hesitation or decorum, Tatjana stepped into Adi's arms. He pulled her close, his frame shaking with sobs. The children rushed in, surrounding her in warmth and movement, tears and touch. Each hand steadied her. Each embrace rewrote a piece of the pain.

Joachim's sturdy grip on her shoulder steadied her even as he trembled. Erika's soft hands cupped her face with gentle reverence. Hellmuth's eager embrace nearly lifted her from the floor. Christa clung to her tightly, head buried against her mother's shoulder as if proximity alone might undo the distance they had survived.

Tatjana held them all close. She kissed each head tenderly before pulling back just enough to see their faces. Their features told stories of worry and waiting but also tales of strength.

"We thought . . ." Adi began, then trailed off. The words were unnecessary. Everything was written on his face.

"I know," Tatjana replied softly, tears brimming. "But I'm here now."

She crossed the threshold and re-entered the space that once held their joys and struggles—their ordinary, precious life. The walls still stood, but everything inside bore the weight of what had passed. Photographs looked older now, touched by more than time. Furniture, worn and familiar, seemed to hum with echoes of laughter from a different world—from before the axis of life shifted.

Their home had endured this storm. And so had she.

They gathered around the kitchen table—the heart of it all—where they had shared countless meals and laughter before the war's long shadow fell over them. The table still held the last signs of living: a half-eaten crust of bread Joachim had abandoned at lunch, Erika's books spread across one corner like wildflowers, Christa's sheet music fluttering gently in the breeze from an open window.

Tatjana stood in the kitchen doorway, absorbing it—this unbroken thread of home.

Voices rose in eager disarray, stories tumbling out: schoolwork continued despite uncertainty, dance steps practiced in living rooms instead of studios, makeshift chemistry labs, melodies whispered after curfew. All defiant acts of normalcy in frighteningly abnormal times.

Tatjana listened to it all, letting each moment stitch her back into the fabric of a life paused. Her own story—a chronicle of shadows and survival—remained untold for now, its darkness too stark for the tender light of homecoming. In time, she knew it would spill forth, shared and faced together. But only when the family was ready to trace the outlines of past pain without the sting of fresh wounds.

For now, joy was enough. The sheer fact of being together again—alive and intact—was its own miracle. It filled the room like an extra presence at the table. Tatjana allowed herself to surrender to the peace, however fragile, and to breathe freely among those she loved. The world outside still burned, but within these walls, a moment of stillness was carved from the chaos.

Of the thousands rounded up in the Bromberg Death March, only 212 returned. The rest disappeared into the smoke of war. On September 21,

Bromberg's newspaper, the *Deutsche Rundschau*, Nr. 212, published the names of those who had come back.

Tatjana Dindinger's name was on that list.

Though history's lens may be clouded by narratives shaped by victors and vanquished alike, the core truth remains immutable. Tatjana's journey through the Death March—her confrontation with the visceral cruelty at humanity's nadir—is an indelible part of her story.

It is a story of survival. Of endurance. And of returning, against all odds, to the hearth and heart of family.

By the end of November 1939, the entire Jewish population of Bydgoszcz had been destroyed.

...tſche Rundſchau.   **Nr. 212.**

...omberg, Donnerstag, 21. September 1939.

...ie Liſte der in Lowicz geretteten Volksdeutſchen,
die an dem Höllenmarſch von Bromberg nach Lowicz teilnahmen.

Wir ſind in der Lage, im folgenden eine Zuſammenſtel-
... derjenigen Volksdeutſchen zu veröffentlichen, die nach
... Befreiung durch die deutſchen Truppen als gerettet feſt-
...ellt werden konnten. Unterdeſſen iſt ja bereits ein großer
... der Geretteten in die Heimat zurückgekehrt. Um aber
... Angehörigen der vielleicht noch in Lodzer Heimen und
...kenhäuſern Erholung ſuchenden Perſonen Gelegenheit
...eben, ſich über das Schickſal der Ihrigen zu vergewiſſern,
...n wir die nachſtehende Liſte folgen. Betont werden muß
... jedoch, daß die Liſte nicht Anſpruch auf Voll-
...ndigkeit erheben kann.

Hilde Lorner
Dorothea Lange
Gertrud Kretſchmann
Helene Drews
Ingrid Detlow
Gertrud Detlow
Irmgard Detlow
Emil Dams
Emil Hinz
Kurt Tarnow
Franz Drews
Armin Stöckmann
Paul Schulz
Karl Droß
Anaſtaſie Leszczow
Arthur Plum
Ferdinand Lang
Guſtav Paſchke
Waldemar Paſchke
Auguſt Hener
Friedrich Wertheimer
Edmund Himke
Auguſt Kojente
Max Brüſchke
Hermann Wieſe
Arthur Breittwieſer
Max Ziehſack
Alois Groß
Otto Müller
Walter Huſe
Emil Reef
Reinhard Reſſe
Albert Reltner
Oswald Wernicke
Richard Bötcher
Egon Krauſe
Günther Borrmann
Willi Mietz
Margarete Bromberger
Helmut Bertram
Willy Tornow
Rittler
Walter Gabriel
Otto Gabriel
Lüttmann
Heinz Eckert
Arthur Pankrat
Willy Kramer
Hoffmann
Siegfried Guttemeyer
Gertrud Müller
Luiſe Kroſt
Anna Werner
Wanda Eſſef
Eliſabeth Hilbig
Charlotte George
Gertrud Schmidt

58. Anna Schröder
59. Margot Frohwert
60. Erna Dirlam
61. Eliſabeth Dirlam
62. Charlotte Grabowſki
63. Eliſabeth Kelm
64. W. Stein
65. O. Mirus
66. Frieda Schimmelpfennig
67. Herrmann Dittmann, Bromberg
68. Guſtav Brauer, Bromberg
69. Otto Brauer, Bromberg
70. Leo Machalinſki, Bromb.
71. Rudolf Gehrke, Bromberg
72. Paul Hoffmann, Weichſelhorſt
73. Fritz Sonnenberg, Lochowo
74. Hermann Kern, Bromberg
75. Richard Weiß, Bromberg
76. Arthur Fiſch, Bromberg
77. Bruno Stabke, Bromberg
78. Heinrich Franz, Friedingen
79. Line Innenfeldt, Sienno
80. Heinrich Kruſe, Friedingen
81. Stanislaus Swiatel, Weichſelhorſt
82. Siegmund Korzewſki, Bromberg
83. Felix Seydowſki, Bromb.
84. Johann Wollmann, Bromberg
85. Paul Riemer, Bromberg
86. Florian Orylſki, Bromb.
87. Ernſt Marquardt, Bromb.
88. Richard Voigt, Schulitz
89. Guſtav Scheive, Weichſelhorſt
90. Paul Wirth, Goldfeld
91. Werner Ebeling, Triſchin
92. Ernſt Höhn, Fordon
93. Robert Wolf, Triſchin
94. Otto Becker, Triſchin
95. Rohlfing, Weichſelhorſt
96. Julius Küchel, Fordon
97. Hertha Küchel, Fordon
98. Bruno Schwarz, Crone
99. Martha Schwarz, Crone
100. Urſel Schwarz, Crone
101. Helmut Rinke, Zempelburg
102. Jendrike, Bromberg
103. Eddy Popitz, Bromberg
104. Gilliſch, Bromberg

105. Liebtke, Crone
106. Liefke, Crone
107. Holz, Hoheneiche
108. Karl Tonn, Nakel
109. Riſtau, Otteran
110. Wendland, Schulitz
111. Möller, Fallenburg
112. Kloſſ, Nimtſch
113. Behnke, Czarnowke
114. Stach, Czarnowke
115. Knuth, Triſchin
116. Kolonder, Samſeczno
117. Jordan, Nakel
118. Reiß, Bromberg
119. Zimmermann, Bromb.
120. Wichmann Bromberg
121. Hertha Wagner, Bromb.
122. Hinz, Bromberg
123. Keßler, Wtelno
124. Hackbarth, Lochowo
125. „   „
126. Stricke, Zempelburg
127. Flatau, Schulitz
128. Lübtke, Lochowo
129. Kitzmann, Großendorf
130. Dubolz, Großendorf
131. Teske, Großendorf
132. Rofenfeld, Großendorf
133. Meyer, Großendorf
134. Schmidt, Großendorf
135. Wegner, Damrau
136. Mirus, Bromberg
137. Zittlau, Bromberg
138. Rudolf, Bromberg
139. Steit, Bromberg
140. B. Eckert, Bromberg
141. Lüneberg, Bromberg
142. Müller, Bromberg
143. Jekaſſon, Bromberg
144. Hübſcher, Bromberg
145. Ilinſki, Tonin
146. Kluge, Trzemiętowo
147. Kottke, Lindenwald
148. Krauſe, Siebenbergen
149. Demuth, Nakel
150. Demuth, Schubin
151. Becker, Bromberg
152. Rofenberg, Bromberg
153. Hübſcher, Bromberg
154. Becker, Bromberg
155. Schmidt, Bromberg
156. Böttcher, Nakel
157. Martini, Schönfee
158. Lehr, Neuhof
159. Krummerli, Birken
160. König, Waltersruh
161. Seefeld, Pawlowke

162. Bettin, Lochowo
163. Beck, Hoheneiche
164. Liefke, Nakel
165. Huth, Kulm
166. Böttcher, Nakel
167. Seehafer, Kruſchin
168. Sikorſki, Schulitz
169. Bruno Junchen, Schulitz
170. Lipke, Schulitz
171. Bettinger, Damrau
172. Walter Otto, Kolomierz
173. Rasmus, Bromberg
174. Gizinſki, Bromberg
175. Willy Becker, Bromberg
176. v. Behrens, Bromberg
177. Januſchewſki, Bromberg
178. Marks, Neuhof
179. Benkendorf, Neuhof
180. Schwarzrock, Crone
181. Swiefke, Crone
182. Martha Swiefke, Crone
183. Krenz, Lochowo
184. Hoffmann, Schulitz
185. Hoffmann, Kulm
186. Beni-Schulz, Bromberg
187. Klaus Steller, Bromberg
188. Tiehlke, Bromberg
189. Ernſt Müller, Bromberg
190. Herbert Zimmermann, Bromberg
191. Gertrud Czarnecki, Bromberg
192. F. C. Büge, Bromberg
193. Turczyl, Bromberg
194. Havemann, Bromberg
195. Kubitz, Bromberg
196. Wilczynſki, Bromberg
197. Klaus Neubert, Fordon
198. Frau Neubert, Fordon
199. Heinz Neubert, Fordon
200. Hugo Hinrichſen, Paulinen
201. Friebe, Pyſzczyn
202. von Born-Fallois, Sienno
203. Köhn, Nakel
204. Job, Nakel
205. Baumgart, Bromberg
206. Anna Kaſſner, Bromberg
207. Dindinger, Bromberg
208. Tabiane Dindinger, Bromberg
209. Erich Dietrich, Bromberg
210. Groß, Bromberg
211. Gotthold Starke, Bromb.
212. Georg Büttner, Bromb.

Gewähr für die Richtigkeit und Vollſtändigkeit der Liſte
kann nicht übernommen werden.

*

Ihre Heimattreue mit dem Tode befiegelt

haben aus dem Kreiſe Schwetz folgende deutſche Volks-
genoſſen, die verſchleppt und von polniſchen Mördern erſchoſ-
ſen bezw. erſchlagen wurden:
Schröder-Bratwin,   Bitzer-Lont,   Nickel-Lubien,
Brunk-Neuenburg,   Kohl-Neuenburg,   Nehlipp-Schönau.

CHAPTER SEVENTEEN

CHANGES AT HOME (1940)

LEAVES, TINGED WITH THE LAST breath of autumn, skittered across the cobblestones of Bromberg as Joachim paused in the doorway of his family home. His gaze lingered on the sturdy oak door, its grain worn smooth by years of comings and goings—joys and sorrows alike. Around the Dindinger house, a hush had fallen where life had once pulsed with laughter and music.

Adi's hand came to rest gently on Joachim's shoulder, a gesture of solidarity in the face of unspoken doubts. "It's a big step, Joachimchen. But you're ready. You've been an excellent student. And your manager at Persil wrote a very thoughtful letter of commendation."

Joachim turned to meet his father's gaze, his expression a blend of determination and doubt. "It's not just the university, Papa," he admitted, the confession spilling out in hushed tones. "It's . . . everything that comes with it."

Adi met his son's eyes squarely. "I know," he said simply, with a gravity that deepened as the solemn looks passed between them. "Berlin is . . . complicated."

It was the gentlest truth they could speak aloud, an understatement—a soft drop of honesty, given the rising tide of madness overtaking Germany.

Still, Joachim nodded, grateful for his father's gift of insight, for not pretending everything was fine.

From the doorway, Erika stepped forward—Joachim's constant companion and coconspirator in everything from schoolwork to quiet acts of resistance. Her fingers laced with his, a gesture as natural as breathing, forged through years of shared dreams and whispered strategies. "We'll keep things going from here," she assured him, her eyes steady despite the shimmer of unshed tears.

Joachim answered with a tender squeeze of her hand, sealing the promise between them.

The train station offered no pause for a proper farewell—just noise and motion, the rhythm of departure indifferent to what it carried away. The hum of passengers, the hiss of steam, and the metallic breath of locomotives set a backdrop of impermanence as Joachim shouldered the weight of his luggage and his family secret.

Hellmuth ruffled his brother's hair, grinning with mock bravado. "You'll write to us about all the crazy parties you attend, won't you?"

"Every detail," Joachim replied, managing a half-smile.

Christa's embrace was fierce, as if she could hold him fast, keep him from joining the tides of the unknown. "Promise you'll come back soon," she murmured, her voice muffled against his coat.

"I promise," he replied, though the words felt brittle. Promises were fragile things in times like these, easily broken when everyone knew tomorrow was no longer guaranteed.

Then came Tatjana. She folded Joachim into her arms, her embrace powered by worry and maternal love. "Take care of yourself, my boy," she whispered into his ear.

"I will, Mama." But he could not shake the heaviness that clung to him like a second skin.

Joachim boarded the train and found his seat by the window. The whistle sounded; the carriage lurched. His sigh fogged the glass as faces blurred and receded. He watched Bromberg shrink away, feeling the strings of connection stretch and strain with each clack of the wheels beneath him.

His thoughts unfurled along the journey—memories tangled with uneasy hopes and anticipation. He envisioned the Chemotechnikerschule der Reichshauptstadt Berlin, a place once shaped by ambition, now shadowed by the Reich's oppressive symbols—looming swastikas and iron-fisted salutes. The pursuit of knowledge was no longer neutral; it was tainted by ideology.

When the city finally clawed its way into view, Joachim felt as if he had entered another world entirely. This was not the Berlin of his childhood visits to Aunt Manja. Its buildings loomed like sentries, watchful and gray. Power and peril walked hand in hand. Every surface seemed to whisper of surveillance. Every movement felt monitored.

Joachim's exit from the train was a step into this new reality, his feet finding the platform where the march of military boots resonated with a chilling cadence. With each step through Berlin's heart, he felt an invisible heft settle on him. Landmarks scrutinized him with the Reich's silent, omnipresent watchfulness. Slogans proclaimed national pride, but they read more like warnings than welcome.

And then the school appeared: the Chemotechnikerschule, stone and steel polished to austere perfection. Its entrance beckoned not in greeting, but in austere judgment.

Joachim paused, bag in hand, breath held. He stared up at the grand structure that once represented his future—and now held his uncertain fate.

Back in Bromberg, Tatjana moved through her home in measured silence. Her footsteps lingered in corners that still held echoes of Joachim's laughter. She paused at the back of his chair, remembering the tilt of his head as he explained his latest experiment, forehead furrowed in concentration. Now there was only the memory of his voice, a ghostly whisper suspended in the stillness.

From the doorway, Erika watched, her own heart aching with the absence of her brother. "Mama," she said softly.

Tatjana turned, a tender smile touching her lips despite the sorrow in her eyes. "Yes, Eka?"

"Would you like me to make some tea?" Erika asked, stepping into the room.

"That would be nice," Tatjana replied, her smile turning wistful.

Erika set water to boil, her movements practiced but hollow without Joachim's banter filling the kitchen. The whistle of the kettle sliced through the quiet, a single, sharp note. She poured hot water over the leaves and watched the steam rise.

When she returned, tray in hand, Tatjana was perched on the edge of Joachim's favorite armchair, her fingers tracing patterns in the fabric as if she could read a message left behind. The aroma of tea filled the space with warmth in a room gone cold.

"Here we are," Erika said, setting down the tray and taking a seat opposite her mother.

Tatjana wrapped her hands around the porcelain. The heat seeped into her skin but did little to chase away the chill in her heart. What might Berlin hold for her son?

"He'll do well there," Erika murmured, as if reading her thoughts. "Joachim is strong."

"Yes," Tatjana sighed. "He is."

Elsewhere in the house that day, the steady thud of Hellmuth's ball striking the wall marked time in a rhythm that spoke of more than mere play. With each bounce, he seemed to challenge an unseen adversary—perhaps fate itself.

Christa leaned against the doorframe, arms crossed. "You're going to scuff the wall if you keep that up," she said.

Hellmuth caught the ball and faced her. "It's just paint."

Christa walked over and plucked the ball from his hands. "Joachim would've already distracted you with something less destructive."

"You're right." He ran a hand through his hair. "I miss him."

"We all do," Christa said quietly, handing back the ball.

In the days following Joachim's departure, each member of the Dindinger family adjusted in their own way. Erika—buoyed by her steadfast companion, Stefan—felt most acutely the silence left behind. Chemistry, once a shared dialogue, became a monologue, each discovery a little dimmer without Joachim to marvel beside her.

For Hellmuth, at age eighteen, the cusp of adulthood no longer hovered at a distance. It stood before him now, demanding he step out of childhood's shadow and meet the responsibilities waiting in the light.

Months later, the front door creaked open and the house fell still. A heartbeat later, Joachim bounded across the threshold. His eyes scanned the room until they found one face: Tatjana's. Time seemed to collapse between them. The worry lines etched into her face softened, and a radiant smile broke through.

"Joachimchen!" she cried, rushing forward, arms already open.

He returned her fierce hug, inhaling the comforting scent of home that clung to her. "Mama, I've missed you so much," he murmured, his voice catching.

"And we've missed you, son," Adi said, placing a firm hand on his son's shoulder.

The others gathered around, wrapping Joachim in the warmth of the family circle.

Erika beamed. "Well, look what the cat dragged in! Did they at least teach you some manners at that fancy school?"

Joachim laughed, the sound rich and full. "Maybe one or two. But I'm still your same old Joachimchen—just with a few more books rattling around in my head."

Hellmuth gave him a solid thump on the back. "We wouldn't want it any other way. How's Berlin treating you? Met anyone interesting, or is it all Nazis and notebooks?"

Joachim's smile faltered. "It's . . . different," he said carefully. "Busy. But my studies keep me occupied. It's a city full of contrasts—energy mixed with tension." He turned to Erika. "And you? Still chasing down atoms with Stefan?"

Erika rolled her eyes good-naturedly. "Someone has to keep pushing the boundaries of science while you're off playing scholar."

Tatjana's brow creased with motherly concern. "And what of your Aunt Manja? Have you had a chance to visit her?"

"Of course, Mama. She's doing well." His grin warmed. "UFA, the big German film company, loves her design work. She has even become friends with Ingrid Bergman!"

Tatjana gave a small sigh of relief. "I'm glad. It's comforting to know you have family there. She's always been gifted. I must visit her soon—it's been much too long."

Adi nodded, eyes twinkling. "Your aunt has been too kind. No wonder you've put on a few pounds since leaving home." He gave Joachim's arm a playful squeeze.

As they moved to the kitchen to prepare a celebratory meal, the house came alive with familiar music: the clatter of pots, the sizzle of pans, and laughter rising like steam. For a few precious hours, they let themselves believe that the world outside had paused—that the storm gathering on the horizon might still pass them by.

But the war, like time, did not pause.

Erika practicing her sit spin in Bromberg, 1940. The love and practice of figure skating continued throughout the war even when ponds were bombed.

Christa skating on a pond in Bromberg, 1941.

CHAPTER EIGHTEEN

CONSCRIPTION (1941)

MORNING LIGHT FILTERED INTO THE dining room, casting long shafts of gold across a table draped in silence. The warmth of the sun felt cruel in contrast to the cold, oppressive stillness inside the Dindinger home.

Adi sat at the head of the table, unmoving, his hands clasped tightly around a cup of coffee that had long gone cold. He stared into the middle distance, as if the silence might answer a question he didn't yet know how to ask.

Across the room, Tatjana moved in slow, practiced motions—setting the table, straightening a napkin—not that any of it was needed. It gave her something to do besides cry. Her eyes were already red and swollen, her face pale and drawn, her eyes careful to meet no one's.

At the window, Erika stood still as a statue, her gaze pinned to the familiar cobblestones below. Outside, life moved in its customary rhythm, ignorant of the upheaval within the walls of the Dindinger home. The bakery down the street had opened. A tram passed. But the rhythm of ordinary life only deepened the wrongness inside their house. Erika's posture, usually upright with the pride of her academic and athletic accomplishments, was now stooped. Her reflection in the glass was unfamiliar—not yet broken but getting close.

Christa sat curled in her chair, legs tucked beneath her, eyes wide and silent. The piano keys sat untouched, the absence of her music leaving an empty space for the family's heartache.

Hellmuth's chair scraped loudly against the floor as he pushed back from the table. He muttered something about needing air but didn't wait for a response. His tall frame moved slowly, already rebelling against the uniform that would soon claim him.

Joachim sat motionless, his own call-up papers spread out before him like a sentence already passed. For a long time, he said nothing. The confidence that once marked his every argument—every plan for the future—seemed to have drained from him. His features, always so animated with discussion and debate, now bore the gravity of the moment, the hard set of his jaw a barricade against fear and uncertainty.

In the hush that had settled over them, each member of the Dindinger family was ensnared by private torments—united by love yet divided by the cruel march of history's unyielding advance. The war hadn't just come for Joachim and Hellmuth; it had reached them all, sealing not just their fates but that of the entire family.

After the door clicked shut behind Hellmuth, Adi finally spoke, his voice barely more than a whisper. "We must be strong for them."

Tatjana sat down and reached across the table, finding Joachim's hand. Her touch was tender, but it trembled with unspoken dread.

"I never thought I'd wear their uniform," Joachim muttered, glancing down at his hands—imagining them stained not with chemicals from his beloved experiments but with dirt and blood from battles he never asked to fight.

"You're not alone in that," Erika replied softly from her place by the window. "Hellmuth doesn't believe in it either. None of us do."

"But what choice do we have?" Joachim's voice cracked. "Say no—and risk everything? Risk all of you?"

Adi stood and crossed to the table, placing a hand on his son's shoulder. "Our family has survived worse," he said, not as comfort but as fact. "And we'll survive this, too."

Joachim finally looked up. In his father's eyes, he saw more than history—he saw the understanding of war and its aftermath. And he saw a plea for resilience.

The wind gave a howl, and Hellmuth stepped back inside, his face flushed from the cold. He rejoined them without a word, leaning against the wall, wrestling with his own thoughts.

Christa rose quietly and approached the table, eyes brimming with tears she fought to hold back. She placed a hand on each of her brothers' arms—a touch meant to convey love and solidarity when words had failed.

The clock ticked on, loud and deliberate, its rhythm marking moments they wished they could halt.

"Too bad we can't go together," Hellmuth said at last. "At least then we would have each other."

Joachim gave a small nod. Nothing needed explaining. The bond between them wasn't just blood anymore; it was fear, loyalty, and the knowledge of what they might lose. "We'll stay with each other," he insisted quietly. "In our heads. That's how we get through this."

With conscription cleaving their paths in two different directions—Joachim to the Wehrmacht and Hellmuth to the Luftwaffe—the brothers faced the harrowing prospect that this goodbye might be their last. There was no promise of return.

Tatjana wiped away a tear as she set down plates of food no one touched. She paused beside each of her sons, pressing kisses to their brows, silent prayers to guard them against the unknown—a mother's blessing.

The following days passed in slow motion, each hour punctuated by mundane tasks performed with heavy hearts. Duffel bags sat half-zipped on the floor, filled with the barest pieces of comfort: shirts, socks, folded photographs. Each item was tucked into place like a question no one dared to ask.

As dusk settled over their last evening together, dinner passed in near silence. They ate mechanically, minds elsewhere—on unspoken fears and unfulfilled dreams.

Later that night, Adi found Joachim alone in his bedroom, surrounded by chemistry books and scribbled notes—relics of a dream deferred. The scent of ink and old paper clung to the space. It was a room that belonged to a boy, though the world was calling for a soldier.

"Promise me something," Adi said quietly as he sat beside Joachim on the bed.

Joachim looked up, sensing the enormity of his father's words.

"Even there," Adi continued, gesturing toward the window and the horizon beyond, "look for something beautiful. Don't let the darkness erase it. Not from you."

Joachim nodded, then pulled his father into an embrace. There were no words—just the warmth of memory and the fervor of all the things they hadn't said. Adi, who had once borne the mantle of a soldier and whose weathered youth was lost to war, saw his son standing on the edge of the same path, shouldering a legacy steeped in sacrifice.

Tatjana entered Hellmuth's room in much the same way to find him sitting listlessly on the bed, bouncing a soccer ball off his foot in slow, rhythmic motions. The sound was hollow and distant, like a childhood slipping out of reach.

"Remember who you are," she said softly, perching on the end of his bed. She reached out and stilled the ball. "Your uniform doesn't define you. It's not what you wear that matters; it's what you believe."

For a moment, he looked like the boy she had raised—the one who hoped time might still stretch a little longer. But the uniform said otherwise.

Morning arrived too quickly, their final moments ticking away as they gathered at dawn to see the boys off. They stood in the yard huddled close, all arms and silence. When it came time to part, there were no grand speeches, only tight hugs trying desperately to bridge the coming days apart—and whispers of love meant to linger long after goodbyes were said.

Joachim turned first, walking toward the train bound for unknown trials with the Wehrmacht. Hellmuth followed moments later for the Luftwaffe transport. Their stoic faces hid sorrow in the seams. Beneath each man's exterior beat a heart loyal not to war but to one another—and to the family they were leaving behind.

PART IV

Purpose

CHAPTER NINETEEN

PART OF THE MACHINE (1941)

GRAVEL CRUNCHED BENEATH JOACHIM'S BOOTS as he stepped onto the base and into a world dictated by orders and precision. Every motion had a purpose, every breath a tempo set by discipline and urgency. The noon sun cast little warmth on his back as he tightened the straps of his pack, each buckle snapping shut with a promise of the day's toil. He squared his shoulders and made his way to where a sergeant was organizing new arrivals.

The sergeant's voice cut through the air, clear and authoritative. "Line up! Shoulder to shoulder! Eyes front!"

They fell into formation—a patchwork of young men, now unified by the rigidity of training. Joachim stood among them, outwardly composed, turmoil contained. His heart was a silent drumbeat echoing the love and fear that accompany every soldier into the fray.

"You are now part of a machine," the sergeant barked. "A machine does not question. It acts! Your actions will lead us to victory!"

Joachim flinched inwardly. He didn't believe in any of it—not the victory, not the cause—but he kept his eyes forward. Adaptability would serve him now. It wasn't acceptance; it was survival.

Hours blurred into weeks—drills, exercises, endless briefings. Joachim absorbed every detail, committing instructions to memory. The rumble of tanks became a constant soundtrack as the troops prepared for what lay ahead.

In the mess tent, men spoke quietly of homes and what they'd left behind. Different stories, a single prayer: a swift end to the war and a safe return. There were few illusions about glory.

"Attention!" an officer's voice rang out as he entered the tent.

Trays stilled. Postures straightened. Tension thickened.

"The Führer has set our course," the officer declared. "We will invade Russia. We will eliminate those subhuman Slavs. We will advance with the might of our military. We will win and win quickly!"

A ripple moved through the ranks like an electric current. The sound of *Russia* steeled some and drained others. Joachim stood among them, the words still echoing in his mind. He wasn't there for rhetoric or symbols. His motivation lay in the simple, primal instinct to guard his family and country—and to survive whatever awaited.

He'd been assigned to the Third Panzer Division—Second Company, Third Armored Battalion, Army Group Center. The Third Panzer was a storied unit, forged during the resurgence after Hitler's rise. Their tanks bore the insignia of the Berlin Bear, and their reputation had been hardened in Poland during those first days of war—in Bromberg.

They called themselves the Armored Bears, and now Joachim wore the patch too. It would soon carry him to the Eastern Front.

That night, under the flicker of a barrack lamp, he wrote home. Each word was measured—not quite the truth, not quite a lie.

MAY 20, 1941

Liebe Eltern und Eka und Tita,
Life here is strict and regimented, but it suits me well. I find comfort in routine in these uncertain times. Please don't let my absence bring sorrow into the house. I will have more to write as we prepare for battle.

Viele Grüße und Küsse,
Joachim

Sealing the letter, Joachim let his gaze drift into the night. The stars were gone, hidden behind clouds as thick as the unknown ahead.

By dawn, the camp stirred with electric urgency. The clarion call of duty sent soldiers rushing to their stations, the ground itself shaking under the armored weight of the Panzer columns. Joachim, too, was swept up in the flurry, his instincts guiding his hands over motorcycles and Kübelwagen. Bolts were checked and components tightened in a dance of precision, where man and machine intertwined in anticipation of war.

"Joachim!" The familiar voice cut through the din: a fellow soldier who had come to respect Joachim's steady nature and adept hands.

Joachim turned, offering a brief, calm smile. "Ready when you are."

They climbed into their Kübelwagen, the engine rattling to life, and rolled out across the packed dirt, heading into whatever awaited them.

Hours later, as the convoy pushed through scarred countryside, preparation gave way. The bumps in the road jarred more than their bodies. The war wasn't coming—it was here.

By dusk, the battalion halted at the edge of a wooded ridge—their last stop before crossing into Ukraine. In the waning light, officers hunched over maps lit by red lanterns, their discussions a muted hum against the soldiers' silent routines. Oil was checked. Weapons were reassembled. Letters were tucked away. Each man was an island of contemplation yet tethered by one binding truth: Tomorrow everything would change.

As Joachim settled in for the night, his thoughts drifted to what lay ahead. What challenges would they face? What would victory—or defeat— mean? Who would they become?

There were no answers in the darkness. Only silence—thick and still— like a breath held before everything breaks.

Disembarking in the Harz Mountains near Nordhausen, Germany, Hellmuth was met by a gust of frigid air, the mountain's chill slicing through his jacket. Around him, the platform swarmed with fresh recruits—a mix of high-spirited and solemn young men, some laughing too loudly, others stone-faced and unreadable. Each boy, like Hellmuth, had been summoned from the warmth of home into the unknown.

A stern voice barked orders, directing them to line up with military precision. Hellmuth scrambled to comply, his breath like a ghost in the mountain air.

Over the past few weeks, he had surrendered to the rigor of military training. Endless drills, inspections, marches, and physical tests pushed him to his limits, mentally and physically. In the mess hall and barracks, he kept mostly to himself, his natural exuberance buried beneath the daily grind.

As he fell into formation now, he risked a glance at the faces around him—nervous, eager, already molded into masks of resolve. No one looked back at him. He felt out of place: These boys looked ready. He did not feel ready. He kept his eyes forward and tried to quiet the churn in his stomach.

The drill sergeant kept shouting commands as the line of recruits marched toward the barracks, their synchronized footfalls ricocheting across the compound. Hellmuth focused on the cadence—each step, each breath—anything to steady his nerves. He thought of his family back home in Bromberg, picturing his mother's warm smile and the solidity of his father's presence. Their expectations lay heavy on his shoulders, even though he knew they didn't want him to be there.

Months passed before the monotony gave way to the challenge of flight school, and with it came a subtle shift. Hellmuth found a new friend in Urs, another boy from Bromberg, whose familiar dialect and solid camaraderie eased the sharp edges of his loneliness. At night, drained from the day and curled in his bunk, Hellmuth would scribble letters to Joachim and then talk with Urs—about their old lives, about sports and dances and girls. Those memories belonged to another life, but remembering helped him hold on to the person he used to be.

Then came the day of his first flight. Strapped into a Klemm 35, with the engine growling beneath him and the ground crew's final checks fading into silence, anticipation surged within him. From the terror of takeoff to the majesty of open skies, the transition left Hellmuth spellbound. Once airborne, his fears melted into awe and wonder at the sensational view. He grinned from ear to ear, thinking maybe he could do this after all.

The weeks went by in a blur of classroom lectures on aerodynamics, aeronautical engineering, meteorology, and training in the reception of Morse code. Then came additional flight hours on heavier equipment. Hellmuth slowly gained confidence in his abilities, learning to trust his instincts and handle the aircraft with finesse. His earlier landings, which had jarred bones and ego alike, evolved into seamless reunions with the earth, each attempt demonstrating his growing prowess.

In the boundless theater of the sky, Hellmuth danced among the clouds, perfecting rolls and loops, every maneuver a step toward mastery. He wasn't fearless; doubt still followed him back to the ground. But up there, in those fleeting, fluid moments, Hellmuth was not a soldier in training or a cog in the war machine. He was just . . . free.

On a clear, crisp morning in August, Hellmuth passed his final check ride and was awarded his pilot's license. That afternoon, standing tall as his commander pinned the coveted silver wings to his chest, Hellmuth allowed himself a flicker of pride. His hard work had paid off, and he was now an officer and a pilot in the Luftwaffe.

He was assigned to the Junkers-52, a transport aircraft used primarily for supply drops and troop movement. Occasionally this type of aircraft ferried high-ranking officials—even Hitler himself—but more often, it shuttled paratroopers into hostile territory. The work was dangerous. Still, Hellmuth felt a grim relief: Unlike his friend Urs, now training for fighter missions, he would not be tasked with raining destruction from above. His goal was survival, not conquest.

One morning later that month, Hellmuth awoke before dawn to the familiar sound of the bugle call. But as he dressed for the day's duties, his thoughts turned to the visit he would receive that afternoon. It was the first time he would see Papa and Christa since he'd left home. How much had changed?

The morning dragged by slowly. Hellmuth tried to focus during briefings and weather reports, but his mind kept wandering: Were they doing well? Would they bring letters from Joachim? He hoped they would arrive with some small comforts from Bromberg—a home-baked pastry, perhaps, or maybe a good book. Mostly, he just wanted to see them and to unload the burden of responsibility for an hour, maybe two. To feel, if only for a little while, like someone's son and brother again.

Finally released for the afternoon, Hellmuth's stride quickened as he made his way toward the base's visitor center. Amid the crowd, a spark of anticipation flared. Christa's joyful waves erased the gray routines of the day. Beside her, Adi stood in quiet conversation with another guest but turned the moment he spotted his son.

Hellmuth rushed over and folded his sister into a tight hug. Then he turned and grasped his father's hand, holding it a moment longer than formality required.

As they strolled through the nearby village together, Adi and Christa spoke of news from home. Mama was keeping busy with community duties. Erika was close to graduating, and Stefan continued to be a frequent dinner guest. Hellmuth smiled, picturing home moving along as best it could.

They stopped to rest beneath a sprawling oak tree. Christa pulled out a tin of sugar cookies that Mama had made—his favorite kind. Hellmuth eagerly helped himself as Christa and Adi filled him in on neighborhood happenings and anecdotes. The cookies tasted like childhood, transporting him back to better days. For the first time in weeks, Hellmuth felt himself relaxing.

But eventually, the sun dropped lower, and it was time. Christa hugged Hellmuth fiercely, whispering for him to take care.

Adi gripped Hellmuth's shoulder and looked him straight in the eye. "We're proud of you, son."

Then, with final farewells, his family left, leaving Hellmuth standing alone, watching until they were out of sight.

The walk back to the base felt longer and colder than before. Hellmuth replayed the day's conversations in his mind, extracting every last detail. He knew the loneliness would creep back in as soon as he returned to the barracks. Still, his family's presence had cast a light, pushing back the shadows of isolation that so often filled the spaces between the walls. Those few treasured hours with Papa and Christa had bolstered Hellmuth's spirits and given him renewed strength to face his duties.

Their visit had filled something in him, though he hadn't realized it was empty. It reminded him what he was trying to survive for.

As he entered the barracks, his friend Urs from the bomber squadron called out, "Hellmuth! A letter arrived for you. Looks like it's from your brother."

Surprised, Hellmuth took the envelope. He recognized Joachim's handwriting, but the postmark was May. Delayed three months—not really a surprise. He tore it open, hungry for any news from his brother.

MAY 1941

Lieber Bruder,

I am writing this letter by lantern light as the days here are long. They are filled with marches and weapons instruction. We begin our movement east soon. We will be heading to Russia. The officers speak of honor and duty. I try to listen, but my heart isn't always in it.

I think of you and our family every day. Stay focused. Survive one day at a time. Don't dwell on what was or what may come. Just stay present. It's the only way I have made it through these long days.

Write to me often. Let me know if you need anything to make your days more comfortable. I know Mama would hardly disapprove of a soldier requesting cigarettes or a bottle of something strong!

Stay strong and safe,
Joachim

Hellmuth read the letter twice, then folded it neatly and slipped it into his pocket.

By now, he knew exactly what Joachim was heading into. Germany had invaded Russia on June 22. Operation Barbarossa was a three-pronged assault launched just after 3 a.m., preceded by an artillery barrage, followed by motorized infantry, and supported by Luftwaffe bombers. Hellmuth knew Joachim had been deployed with Army Group Center, positioned at the very heart of the Eastern Front.

But optimism was high that Germany could be victorious quickly. Joseph Goebbels saturated the airwaves with his propaganda, and the country believed him. Hellmuth wasn't so sure.

He thought about Joachim's comment on alcohol and cigarettes and felt a faint ache. Hellmuth had not touched either one since training. The military had ended his childhood rebellion months ago. No more adventures with friends, no more lazy days by the river. All those memories felt like relics of another life, someone else's life. His brother didn't know him anymore.

But he shook off the weight of such memories. He wouldn't dwell on them—not today.

Anyway, he was grateful for the connection the letter provided. His brother was out there somewhere, facing worse hardships. To get through this ordeal, they would both need to rely on their inner strength and the love of their family—until the day came when they could return home.

CHAPTER TWENTY

COME WHAT MAY (1942)

EVEN IN THE DARKEST HOURS, life finds a way to persist. The human spirit, stubborn and resilient, reaches for joy in the most unlikely places. For young couples like Erika and Stefan, now in Berlin—Erika studying chemical engineering and Stefan in medical college—stolen moments of normalcy became a precious lifeline anchoring them to hope and to each other.

The weight of their circumstances—the constant propaganda, the whispered dissent, the ongoing war—could easily have crushed their spirits. Yet they, like so many others, found ways to carve out spaces of light in the engulfing darkness. These moments, fragile and fleeting, served as reminders of what they were fighting for: the simple, profound joy of living and loving freely.

In the bustling streets of Berlin in early springtime, life marched on with a strange, steady rhythm. The city was a paradox, where modernity mingled with old-world charm, and uncertainty pulsed beneath every solid cobblestone. Cafés along Unter den Linden remained lively, their windows gleaming with warm light as patrons sipped coffee and engaged in hushed conversations. The aroma of fresh pretzels wafted from bakeries, a comforting constant in uncertain times. And in the evenings, couples like Erika and Stefan would emerge from their daily routines, daring to dream of a future beyond the current political climate.

Their date nights became sacred rituals, carefully planned and eagerly anticipated. Sometimes, it was a simple candlelit dinner in Stefan's modest student apartment, made meaningful by laughter and love. Other nights, they slipped into the velvet shadows of a theater or cabaret, letting the music and lights transport them far from the looming storm of war.

In those precious hours, they allowed themselves to be just Erika and Stefan. Not a medical student grappling with the growing moral compromises of his profession. Not a young woman caught in the machinery of a regime she neither supported nor trusted. Just two young people, deeply in love. Their conversations drifted away from the grim realities of everyday life and filled instead with playful banter, shared ambitions, and the light-hearted flirtation that comes so naturally to the young and enamored.

These evenings served as more than mere distractions. They were affirmations of life, of love, of the indomitable human capacity for joy even in a crumbling world. Each smile, each laugh, each tender touch was another act of defiance, rejecting the forces that sought to control every aspect of their lives.

As the sun dipped below Berlin's skyline, Stefan waited at the entrance to the Tiergarten. He smiled as he saw Erika approaching, her hair catching the last rays of sunlight, and the weight of their circumstances momentarily lifted. Tonight, they would allow themselves to forget the uncertainties on the horizon, if only for a few hours. Tonight, they would remind themselves of the beauty that still existed in the world, and of the future they hoped to build together.

"There's my future doctor," Erika called out, her eyes bright with expectation. "I hope you haven't been waiting long."

Stefan grinned, pulling her close. "For you? I'd wait all night if I had to."

Erika playfully swatted his arm. "Flatterer. So, what's the plan for tonight, Herr Doktor?"

"Well, Fräulein," Stefan said, offering his arm, "I thought we might take a stroll through the park, then perhaps catch a show at the Wintergarten. I hear they have a new jazz band playing."

Erika's eyes lit up. "Jazz? How scandalous! Are you sure your delicate medical student sensibilities can handle such excitement?"

Stefan laughed, a rich, warm sound that pushed back any threat of darkness. "I think I can manage. Besides, I have it on good authority that dancing is excellent exercise for the heart."

As they walked arm in arm through the lush Tiergarten, the concerns of the outside world seemed to fall away. The park was alive with the sound of birds settling in for the night and the distant laughter of other couples and families enjoying the evening.

"How are your studies going?" Erika asked. "Still buried in anatomy books?"

Stefan sighed dramatically. "I swear, I see bones and muscle groups when I close my eyes at night. But it's fascinating, truly. Today we started learning about the nervous system. Did you know that the human brain has about eighty-six billion neurons?"

Erika raised an eyebrow. "Is that so? Well, I hope you're using all of yours to remember our anniversary of our first kiss next month."

"As if I could forget," Stefan replied with a wink. "Speaking of which, any hints about what you might want as a gift?"

"Surprise me," Erika said, her eyes twinkling. "Although . . . a weekend trip to Dresden would be lovely. I hear the Semperoper is putting on a magnificent production of *The Magic Flute*."

Stefan nodded thoughtfully. "Dresden, hmm? I'll see what I can do. Maybe I can convince Professor Hartmann that I need to study the effects of opera on the human psyche."

They both laughed, the sound mingling with the rustle of leaves in the gentle evening breeze. As they neared the park's exit, Erika's expression grew more serious.

"Stefan," she began hesitantly, "have you given any more thought to what we talked about last week? About Hans?"

Over the previous two years, as war reshaped borders and blurred lines between right and wrong, a secret branch of British intelligence had taken root: the Special Operations Executive—the S.O.E. Its mission was sabotage, espionage, and resistance behind enemy lines. In occupied Poland, the Home Army—the Armia Krajowa—rose to prominence, with sources eventually providing nearly half the intelligence reaching the British. Somewhere within that underground network, Erika had found her place.

For some time now, Erika had moved between science and secrecy, walking a line sharpened by danger. Her contacts had links to S.O.E. communication channels, and recently she had made contact with the *Geschwistern Scholl*—the Scholl siblings Hans and Sophie, members of the White Rose resistance group in Germany. Like so many others, Erika was working in silent defiance, always with the hope that her quiet impact would ripple outward throughout wartime Europe.

Stefan's smile faded slightly. "Erika, please. Not tonight. I promise we'll talk about it, but can't we just enjoy this evening without—"

Erika squeezed his arm gently. "You're right. I'm sorry. Tonight is for us."

The tension eased as swiftly as it had arrived. Stefan stopped, turning to face Erika. "Have I told you how beautiful you look tonight?"

Erika pretended to consider. "Hmm, not in the last ten minutes, no."

"Well then, allow me to remedy that grievous oversight," Stefan continued, pulling her close. "You are the most beautiful woman in all of Berlin. No, in all of Germany."

"Only Germany?" Erika teased, her arms wrapping around his neck.

"The world, then," Stefan murmured, leaning in for a kiss.

As their lips met, everything around them seemed to fade away. In that moment, there was no war looming on the horizon, no vicious regime, no difficult decisions to be made. There was only Stefan and Erika, two young people in love, stealing a moment of happiness in a world growing darker by the day.

When they finally parted, both slightly breathless, Erika smiled up at Stefan. "Come on, Herr Romantiker. Let's go see this jazz band of yours before they throw us out of the park for public indecency."

Hand in hand, they made their way through the Tiergarten and into the vibrant Berlin night, determined to make the most of their evening together, come what may.

A few months later, late on the evening of May 27, Stefan sat hunched at his desk in a modest apartment on a narrow Berlin street, poring over a stack of documents. The room was sparsely furnished, with heavy curtains drawn against the fading evening light. A single lamp cast a warm glow over his work, illuminating the furrows of concentration on his brow.

Suddenly, the door burst open. Stefan's head snapped up, his hand instinctively moving to conceal the papers before him. But it was Erika who burst into the room, breathless, her eyes wide with a mixture of excitement and fear.

"Stefan!" she gasped, struggling to catch her breath. "You won't believe what I've just heard!"

Stefan rose from his chair, moving swiftly to Erika's side and taking her by the shoulders. "Calm down, Erika. What is it?" His voice was low and urgent. "What's happened?"

Erika took a deep breath, her words tumbling out in a rush. "There's been an assassination attempt on Reinhard Heydrich!"

Stefan's grip on her shoulders tightened. His voice dropped to a whisper. "The Butcher of Prague?"

Erika nodded vigorously, her hair falling across her flushed face. "Yes, yes! I overheard some SS officers talking about it on my way home. They were . . . they were rattled."

All that spring, Prague—like much of Eastern Europe—had been squeezed in the iron grip of German occupation. Czechoslovakia had been dismembered, with Bohemia and Moravia directly incorporated into the Reich as a "protectorate." The Nazis ruled with brutal efficiency, crushing any hint of resistance and implementing their racial policies with ruthless zeal.

SS-Obergruppenführer Reinhard Heydrich, mastermind of the ghoulish Wannsee Conference and one of the chief architects of the Holocaust, had been appointed Acting Reich Protector of Bohemia and Moravia eight months earlier in September 1941, beginning a regime marked by terror and oppression. Heydrich oversaw mass deportations of Jews to ghettos and concentration camps while simultaneously attempting to win over segments of the Czech population through a combination of modest concessions and relentless propaganda.

The Czech government-in-exile, based in London and led by President Edvard Beneš, worked tirelessly to maintain international recognition and rally support for the Resistance inside their homeland. They understood that a high-profile action against the Nazi occupation could galvanize both domestic and international support for the Czech cause.

And so Operation Anthropoid was born—a joint endeavor between the Czech Resistance and Britain's S.O.E. Czech and Slovak soldiers, specially trained by British operatives, parachuted into their occupied homeland under cover of night. Their mission: assassinate Heydrich, one of the most powerful and feared men in the Nazi hierarchy.

The tension in Prague was palpable. Citizens went about their daily lives under a cloud of constant surveillance and suspicion. Every knock at the door, every whispered conversation, every furtive glance could potentially lead to arrest, deportation, or worse. Yet beneath the surface, the flames of resistance continued to burn. Hidden in attics, in cellars, in coded letters passed in bread baskets and behind shop counters, Czech Resistance still lived, still breathed. And now it had struck.

Stefan's mind raced. If this news were true, it would be the most significant act of resistance since the occupation began. His heart pounded with a mixture of hope and dread. "Do you know if it was successful?" he asked, hardly daring to breathe.

Erika shook her head, her expression a mix of frustration and worry. "I'm not sure. The officers didn't say whether he was dead or alive. But Stefan . . ." Her voice trailed off, and she bit her lip.

"What is it?" Stefan prompted, though he could already guess what she was thinking.

"There will be reprisals," Erika said, voicing the dread they both shared. "Either way—success or failure—the Nazis will make someone pay for this."

Stefan nodded grimly. He released Erika's shoulders and began to pace the small room, his mind working furiously. "You're right," he said at last. "The Nazis won't let this go unanswered. They'll want to make an example, to crush any notion of resistance."

Erika sank into the chair Stefan had vacated, her excitement giving way to grim reality. "What do we do?" she asked, her voice small in the suddenly oppressive silence of the room.

Stefan stopped pacing and turned to face her. His expression was resolute, but Erika could see the flicker of fear in his eyes. "We need to be prepared for anything," he said. "If Heydrich survived, he'll be out for blood. If he didn't . . ." Stefan trailed off, the implications hanging heavy in the air between them.

"We have to warn the others," Erika said.

They would need to be careful. The Gestapo would be on high alert. Any unusual movement or gatherings could bring them down on Erika, Stefan, their small resistance network, and anyone else whom the Nazis chose to target.

The days that followed were a blur of tension, fear, and secrecy. News of the attack spread quickly, but facts were scarce. Stefan and Erika, along with their small network of conspirators and information sources, pieced together the events surrounding the attack. They learned that two of the commandos involved were close family friends of Stefan, and that Heydrich had initially survived the assassination attempt. For a brief, agonizing time, it seemed the mission might have failed entirely. But a week later, Heydrich succumbed to sepsis—the result of debris from the bomb blast becoming lodged in his body.

The irony—that Heydrich's death from his wounds might have been prevented had his doctor, Karl Gebhardt, administered sulfonamides to prevent sepsis—was not lost on Stefan, a medical student. But an underlying aversion to modern medicine among some in the Nazi regime, whose twisted ideologies were built on championing the "superior" health and strength of the so-called master race, had outweighed clinical judgment.

As Erika and Stefan discussed their next moves, the gravity of the situation settled over them like a heavy cloak. The assassination of Heydrich marked a clear turning point, igniting the full fury of Nazi vengeance. The reprisals were swift and merciless, targeting both the Resistance movement and innocent civilians alike. Stefan and Erika knew that even as far away as Berlin, the uneasy quiet of the occupation in Prague was about to be shattered.

And it was shattered, just as they'd predicted. But the aftermath was much worse than either of them could have imagined.

On a gloomy afternoon in late June, Stefan met with a contact on the outskirts of Berlin, exchanging information and sharing plans for upcoming acts of resistance. As Stefan turned to leave, his contact grabbed his arm. The man's weathered face was lined with grief.

"Stefan," he whispered hoarsely, "I have terrible news about Lidice."

Stefan felt his blood run cold. Lidice was a village near Prague, unremarkable in many ways but for one crucial detail: It was home to Stefan's cousins, his last remaining family in that region.

"What about Lidice?" Stefan asked, dreading the answer.

The man's grip on Stefan's arm tightened. "It's gone. The Nazis . . . they razed it to the ground. They killed all the men. Sent the women to concentration camps, and . . . and the children . . ." He couldn't finish the sentence.

Stefan staggered, his mind reeling. "My cousins?" he managed to choke out.

The man shook his head slowly, his eyes filled with sorrow. "I'm sorry, Stefan. There were no survivors among the men. The women and children . . . no one knows."

Stefan barely remembered the journey back to his apartment. The world around him seemed muffled and distant, as if he were moving through a thick fog. When he finally stumbled through his door, Erika was there, her face immediately registering alarm at his appearance.

"Stefan? What's happened?" She rushed to his side.

He looked at her, his eyes hollow with grief. "Lidice," he said, his voice cracking. "The Nazis destroyed it. My cousins . . . they're gone."

Erika's hand flew to her mouth, her eyes widening in horror. Without a word, she wrapped her arms around Stefan, holding him tightly as the full significance of his loss crashed over him.

Stefan's body shook with silent sobs as he clung to Erika. The reality of what had happened—not just to his family but to an entire village—was too much to bear. Lidice had been obliterated, its inhabitants murdered or scattered to the wind, all in the name of Nazi retribution.

As Erika held him, murmuring words of comfort that seemed woefully inadequate in the face of such tragedy, Stefan's mind raced. He thought of his cousins—of shared childhood memories, of family gatherings, of the lives they had built in Lidice. All of it gone, wiped away in an act of senseless brutality.

"How can they do this?" Stefan whispered, his voice raw with emotion. "How can they destroy an entire village, murder innocent people, for something they had no part in? How can they justify it?"

Erika stroked his hair gently, her own tears silently falling. "It's not about justice for them, Stefan. It's about cruelty and terror. They want to break our spirit, to make us too afraid to resist."

Stefan pulled back slightly, meeting Erika's gaze. In her eyes, he saw a reflection of his own pain but also a fierce determination. "We can't let them win," he said, his voice gaining strength. "We have to keep fighting. For Lidice, for my cousins, for everyone they've stolen from us."

Erika nodded, her hands cupping Stefan's face. "We will," she promised. "We'll make sure their sacrifice wasn't in vain."

As they stood there, holding each other in the fading light of day, Stefan and Erika felt the heft of their responsibility more keenly than ever. The annihilation of Lidice was not just a reminder of Nazi brutality—it was a reckoning. A call. A terrible proof of what was at stake.

The pain of loss would not fade quickly. It would linger, sharp and unrelenting. But in that pain, Erika and Stefan would find purpose. In the days and weeks to come, they would transform their grief into resistance, their sorrow into defiance. The memory of Lidice, now etched in blood and ash, would become their compass. Those who had perished would not be forgotten. Their legacy would live in every act of courage that followed.

Erika and Stefan would continue to fight, not only for their own futures but in honor of those whose futures had been stolen.

Erika and her beloved Stefan in Bromberg, circa 1943. Erika was under Gestapo watch beginning in 1943. She was part of the White Rose movement with the Geschwistern Scholl and a member of the Home Army, the Polish Resistance. Erika and Stefan both were spies.

CHAPTER TWENTY-ONE

A KIND OF SURVIVAL
(1942)

BLISTERING HEAT. BLINDING SUN. ENDLESS stretches of desert. The sun-scorched expanses of southern Italy and North Africa were as foreign and unforgiving as anything twenty-one-year-old Hellmuth had ever known—an assignment far removed from the comforts of home and family.

Yet here he was, navigating the treacherous skies as pilot of a Junkers-52, dodging anti-aircraft fire while delivering vital supplies to Field Marshal Erwin Rommel's embattled Afrika Korps. Though Hellmuth respected his commanding officer—the Desert Fox, revered by both allies and enemies for his mental acumen—each mission felt like a dance with death.

They called the Junkers the *Tante Ju*—the "Auntie Ju." It was a kind nickname for a slow, lightly armored aircraft in a war that had little room for sentiment. As the Luftwaffe's fighters were increasingly committed to supporting German ground forces and battling for air superiority over the desert, they were less available to protect the supply planes over the sea. That left the transports vulnerable: lumbering targets for the faster Kittyhawks and Beaufighters that prowled the skies at the behest of Britain's Royal Air Force. For Hellmuth, each trip meant dodging flak, navigating blinding light, and trying not to think too hard about what might be waiting on the other end.

The sky was a stage of violence: planes spiraling, gunners firing, engines screaming. Hellmuth would grip the yoke until his knuckles went white, forcing the aircraft into evasive dives and climbs it was never meant to handle. The roar of the trimotor engines drowned out the sound of his pounding heart but didn't erase it.

Three weeks into his assignment in North Africa, on the Southern Front, Hellmuth saw one of the unescorted formation Junkers take a direct hit. The troop transport plane spun once, then twice, and dropped into the sea with smoke trailing from its fuselage. Tiny black shapes tumbled from the falling plane. Some jumped. Others fell.

Men, Hellmuth realized in horror.

One of those airmen was his best friend Urs, who had shared his rations, his memories of home, his quiet fears beneath the bravado. Now Urs was dead. For Hellmuth, the glamour of flight died with him.

Between missions, Hellmuth clung like a drowning man to the letters from his family. Their words transported him back to a place of warmth and familiarity, to something human. He would trace his mother's sprawling handwriting, imagining the comfort of her embrace, or hear his father's steady, reassuring voice in his lines. These weren't just letters. They were proof that a different world still existed.

Yet even as he read their words of encouragement and love, a deep sense of guilt twisted in his chest. How could he reconcile what he saw from the cockpit—villages scorched, civilians staggering to safety, slave labor fueling the shrinking war machine—with the values his parents had raised him on? He had learned right from wrong. And yet here he was, delivering supplies in service of something he could not believe in.

In the oppressive environment of the barracks, where the air was always stifling, time seemed to crawl. The cramped quarters were pervaded by the stale scent of sweat and cigarette smoke, an inescapable reminder of hardship and the relentless march of duty. Hellmuth kept to himself, haunted but focused. Fear, duty, and the flicker of a life waiting back home—only these kept him going.

Easter Sunday, he sat at a battered table beneath the dim lantern light. His hands hovered above the paper for a long time before he began.

Liebe Eltern und Eka und Tita, I hope this letter finds you all well and in good spirits, despite the difficult times.

Hellmuth paused, the words catching in his throat as he thought of the celebrations they might be having at home.

Today is Easter, and I cannot help but feel so lonely. I am sure the house is filled with warm bread. I can almost smell it from here. I am missing you more than I can say.

His mind drifted to the memories of Easter mornings past, when they would awaken to the delicious aroma of Mama's freshly baked *kuchen* and the sound of Papa's violin filling the air. He could almost hear the laughter of his sisters as they searched for hidden eggs. That other life felt impossibly far away.

Carissima Mater, Beloved Mother, I miss you. I wish I could come home. It would take me fourteen days by auto, and that is much too long. We listened to the weekly Führer Rede today. Hitler says we are winning. He says this war will be over soon. I want to believe him. Meanwhile, I hope you are all safe and well and that the festivities brought you some joy amid the uncertainty that surrounds us. I think of you always. That helps me hold on.

Hellmuth signed his name with a flourish, folded the letter, and sealed it with a kiss.

As he slipped it into the envelope, he whispered a prayer for his family's safety and for the day when he could once again embrace them.

A few days later, from the cockpit of a Junkers retrofitted with floats, Hellmuth found a few quiet moments to write again. The pen scratched across the paper like an old habit. *Liebe Familie*, he began, his hand steady despite the weariness that had settled deep in his bones. *Ich sitze hier am Mittelmeer und habe keine Mittel mehr . . .*

It was a familiar play on the words *Mittelmeer* and *Mittel*: "I sit here on the Mediterranean with no money left . . ."

That is our motto! Hellmuth wrote, relishing the moment of humor.

His mind then drifted to the previous day, when he had indulged in a simple pleasure—a rare pause for a bath in the sea. The memory was a balm for his soul.

I swam yesterday. It felt so good, he scrawled, the sensation of the cool, salty water still vivid on his sun-kissed skin.

Yet even in that moment of tranquility, danger was ever-present. *We have to be careful*, he continued. *There are sharks.* The thought sent a shiver down his spine. Even the most serene settings, he knew, could harbor deadly threats.

Other perils also lurked in this unforgiving land. *I must watch for the snakes and scorpions,* he continued, a reminder of the constant vigilance required to survive.

Hellmuth signed off slowly. He held the letter a little longer before slipping it into the postbag. There wasn't much he could control out here—not the war, not his fate—but sending words home still felt like a kind of survival.

—

Ten days later, the sterile scent of a Sicilian field hospital filled Hellmuth's nostrils as he lay on a cot, his body wracked with fever and chills. He was a pale shadow of himself, his skin hanging loose against his bones. A coarse blanket itched at his chest but did nothing to warm him. The groans of fellow patients underscored the grim reality of their situation.

Hellmuth reached with a trembling hand for the paper and pen by his bedside. Each movement was an effort, but the need to write gave him a semblance of strength. The scratch of pen on paper was fainter now, the ink occasionally smudged by his weak grip.

Dear Family, he wrote, each word an exertion, *I am in a Lazarett in Sicily.* The looping letters were unsteady, written in a precarious hand. He paused, trying hard to collect his thoughts as he explained his presence in the military field hospital.

> *Malaria has caught me in its grip. The doctors say I will recover, but it is slow. I look gray. The fever is less right now, so I can write. I dream of home. Of you all and of peace.*

He hesitated before revealing more about his condition, but honesty compelled him. *I have hematuria,* he wrote simply, knowing they would understand. There was blood in his urine.

The room spun slightly. Hellmuth set down his pen and closed his eyes for a moment, breathing through the tightness in his chest. Then, with effort, he picked it up again and wrote. The words were raw and simple but absolute—a soldier's wish for respite from the turmoil that had become his entire world: *I long for this war to end.*

He folded the letter slowly, as if tucking away a part of himself within its creases. If it reached them, they'd know he was still here. Still fighting.

The door to the ward creaked open, and a nurse walked in, her face masked by cloth and concern. "Herr Hellmuth," she said gently, approaching his cot. "How are you feeling today?"

Hellmuth managed a weak smile. "Like I've been run over by a tank. But I'm still here."

The nurse nodded, kneeling beside his cot. "That's the spirit. We are doing everything we can. The chloroquine should shorten this episode. Is there anything you need?"

"Just this," he replied, holding up the letter. "Can you make sure it gets sent?"

She took it carefully. "Of course. Your family will be so glad to hear from you."

"Thank you," Hellmuth said, his voice barely a whisper. "And . . . thank you for taking care of all of us."

The nurse touched his shoulder. "We're all in this together. Rest now. You need your strength."

As she left, Hellmuth lay back, his mind drifting to thoughts of home once more. He closed his eyes, letting his memories of Bromberg wash over him and soothe his weary soul.

A sudden noise jolted him from his reverie—a fellow soldier, delirious with fever, crying out in the night. Hellmuth was not alone in the struggle; every man in this room was fighting his own battle, longing for home and the comfort of loved ones.

"Hellmuth," a voice rasped nearby. It was Dieter, a fellow pilot two cots over, who had also fallen victim to malaria. "What did you write to your family?"

Hellmuth sighed, turning to face him. "I told them about the malaria and that I am doing well. I didn't mention my shrapnel wound. They would worry about the safety of the Tante Ju." He still felt attached to the Junkers—such a great plane! It had won the Spanish Civil War for Franco. But look what it had done to Guernica—bringing death and destruction to so many civilians. "I cannot tell my family too much. I tried to keep it hopeful."

Dieter nodded, a sad smile playing on his lips. "It's all we can do, isn't it? Hold on to hope."

"Ja," Hellmuth replied, his words almost inaudible. "Hold on to hope."

The two men lapsed into silence, the import of their words hanging in the air. As Hellmuth drifted off to sleep, he cleaved to the hope that had sustained him thus far, praying it would be enough to carry him through the dark days ahead.

For Hellmuth, letters were sustenance. When weeks passed without one, the silence filled the space like static. Time stretched. Reading old pages was an act of survival.

On May 6, Hellmuth wrote again for Mother's Day:

> *Carissima Mater, I am thinking of you from far away. I have lost*
> *hope of seeing you anytime soon. Your son thinks of you so much.*
> *There will come a time when we can be together again. You are*
> *mine, and I, Hellmuth, am yours.*

Why do you write so infrequently? he scribbled later that month. The letter continued:

> *This heat is unbearable. Even with the tent flaps open, it feels*
> *like an oven, 65 degrees Celsius at least. We all had to shave our*
> *heads after a typhus outbreak. I look like a plucked chicken, but at*
> *least I am a bit cooler.*

He could almost hear his sisters' giggles and see his mother's worried frown.

> *The newest rumor is they may start offering officer training*
> *programs for us pilots. Can you imagine me barking orders?*

Hellmuth let out a hollow chuckle as he wrote, but it quickly turned into a bout of coughing.

Or maybe I'll simply request a decommissioning and return home, he continued after the coughing subsided. *Although I'm not sure what sort of "home" will be waiting by then . . .*

Hellmuth trailed off, his pen hovering over the page. So much weighed on his mind—the brutal heat, the interminable sickness, his uncertain future, the guilt over leaving his family to endure the war's hardships alone.

With a sigh, he continued:

> *It's been twenty days now since I've heard from Joachim. I hope*
> *Tommy hasn't seen him on the front lines yet. This silence is difficult.*

Hellmuth set down his pen as a fit of coughing overtook him. He doubled over, his body wracked with the deep, hacking barks that had plagued him for weeks. When the spasm finally subsided, he wiped his brow with a trembling hand. The tent offered little respite from the brutal rays of the sun. Sweat rolled down his forehead and stung his eyes.

"Here, drink this," a nurse said, holding a metal cup beaded with condensation. "You need to stay hydrated."

"Thank you," Hellmuth replied, his voice hoarse. He looked at the nurse, her face kind but weary. "Do you think they'll ever let us go home?"

The nurse sighed, her expression softening. "I hope so, Hellmuth. We all do. Just stay strong."

Hellmuth nodded, watching her leave before turning back to his letter.

Home. The word conjured up a flood of memories—cool evening breezes carrying the scent of the nearby river, the sound of Christa's melodies floating through open windows, laughter and stories shared around the dining table. A different kind of life, and one he hoped hadn't vanished completely.

With a weary sigh, he leaned back onto his cot, the thin mattress offering little cushion against the hard surface beneath. He closed his eyes for a moment, willing his mind to drift from this miserable place. But the incessant buzzing of mosquitoes and the coughs of the sick made such an escape impossible.

Forcing his eyes open once more, Hellmuth turned his attention back to the letter. He knew his family waited anxiously for any word, no matter how sparse. Perhaps some small anecdote or reassurance would help buoy their spirits, as their words did for him.

On June 29, Hellmuth wrote:

> *I know these letters bring you little comfort when they speak only of hardship. But I promise you, my dearest family, I'm doing all I can to stay strong. The doctors assure me this latest bout will pass soon, and I will be back on my feet before long. I am now in a Lazarett in Sorrento. Maybe we can all come here after the war.*

*I didn't take part in the siege at Tobruk like my squadron did. It's
a key port. Rommel took it quickly, they say. I still just hate war. I
want it to end.*

He paused, rolling the pen between his fingers as he carefully chose his
next words. A small smile tugged at the corner of his mouth as he recalled
the lively dynamics of their household.

*I miss our dinner table. The laughter. The arguments. Even the
noise. I miss it all.*

Hellmuth's smile faded.

*This wretched war cannot last forever. Sooner than we think, I
pray, the fighting will cease, and we will be together again.*

His energy waned, each word taking a toll. But he was determined to
impart some semblance of hope and reassurance to those he loved most.

*Until then, I find strength in thoughts of you. Please, take care
of one another and stay strong. I send all my love to each of you.
May you remain in good health, both in body and spirit.*

Hellmuth's hand trembled slightly as he signed his name with a flourish,
then tenderly folded the letter and slid it into an envelope. He set it aside
to be collected for delivery, repeating the prayers that always accompanied
such letters: for peace, for health, and for a way back home.

Hellmuth, always the daredevil, in Bromberg, 1940.

A pensive Hellmuth in North Africa, 1942.

CHAPTER TWENTY-TWO

THE WHITE ROSE
(1942-1943)

DESPAIR SATURATED THE ROOM. THE stench of antiseptic, bodily fluids, and gangrene hung thick in the air. Walls peeled in long curls of plaster, mingling with moans of delirium and the muted weeping of young men too wounded to hide their pain. The corridors of a crumbling Russian school building, once filled with schoolchildren's laughter, now rang with the clipped footsteps of exhausted medics, their arms full of bandages and tin bowls of weak broth.

Christmas was near, and the Battle of Stalingrad had been raging for four months—the deadliest conflict of the war. A nurse, her face etched with exhaustion, led Joachim down the corridor of the school hastily converted into a Lazarett, one of many makeshift hospitals dotting the Eastern Front. Where lessons once echoed through the halls, now only the shuffle of boots and the low groans of the wounded remained.

Pale faces—some staring vacantly, others contorted in agony—turned toward Joachim from crowded cots as he shuffled past. He kept his gaze low. There were too many wounds and too little strength left in him to bear them all.

An orderly gestured toward an empty cot beneath a frost-glazed window. Lowering himself, Joachim noticed a dark stain on the mattress—blood, dried but not old. He didn't speak. There was nothing to say.

The war had brought him here—not to a battlefield this time but to a place where the fight was for breath, for dignity, for life itself. He shuddered as nausea surged, regretting the thin gruel he had forced down earlier. His abdomen throbbed; sweat dotted his brow despite the chill. He tried to distract himself by studying the room, but so much suffering only deepened his dread.

A doctor pushed through the maze of cots with a worn medical bag. He looked young—hardly out of medical school—but his eyes were old, hollowed by what he had witnessed at the Front. Appropriate antibiotics were understood by those in his profession but still scarce in Europe, where wounds, infections, and countless illnesses were rampant in hospitals and battlefields.

"Where does it hurt?" he asked, kneeling. His tone was strained, urgent, fatigued.

"Everywhere," Joachim whispered, clutching his belly. "But mostly here."

The doctor nodded and began a brisk, practiced exam—impersonal but not unkind. "You've been through a lot," he murmured. "Severe dysentery, likely another bout of Askarid." He used the German word for a parasitic worm in the intestine. "And pneumonia on top of it. You're lucky we still have fluids left. Many have died from less."

Joachim barely registered the sting of an injection. As the fever pulled him under, he heard the doctor's voice from a distant place. "These fluids need to work fast."

Night fell and the ward sank into darkness. A few oil lamps flickered, casting long, eerie shadows. Orderlies moved among the wounded, dispensing water and changing soiled bedding when they could. Men moaned in German, Russian, and Polish.

Sometime after midnight, the low rumble of artillery shook the ward.

Joachim's eyes snapped open. The cot trembled beneath him.

Across the room, the nurse who had checked his fever stood frozen, knuckles white on her apron. "They're getting closer," she whispered, wide-eyed.

The doctor rushed in, his veneer of calm interrupted by necessity. "Prepare for incoming wounded! You two—clear this corner. We need triage space now!"

Chaos erupted: cots scraping, bandage rolls unfurling, elbows bumping plastered walls. The barrage swelled, each blast and concussion rattling windows and ribs alike. The whine of an air-raid siren cut through the low-pitched rumble.

"Take cover!" the doctor shouted over the klaxon. "They've called for strikes on this sector!"

Pandemonium followed. Patients tried to crawl beneath tables and doorframes; orderlies dragged those too injured to move. Plaster snowed from the ceiling.

Then—silence. Not peace. Just the sudden absence of sound.

When the ward's noises eased back to the typical hum—footsteps, low sobs, the hiss of a lamp—Joachim eased out from under his cot. The ward was wrecked: cots overturned, gauze spooling across the floor, a cabinet smoldering until someone stamped out the small flames.

Miraculously, there was no direct hit.

Dawn seeped through shattered panes. A few bodies lay still—too still. Others whimpered, bleeding from fresh shrapnel wounds. The doctor, face smeared with grime, kept moving—kneeling, stitching, checking pulses, barking soft orders.

Joachim pushed himself upright slowly, every muscle protesting. A soldier a few cots away—no older than nineteen—watched him through clenched teeth, his arm bandaged to the shoulder, his skin the color of ash.

"You're lucky," the young man muttered through clenched teeth. "At least your wounds are hidden."

Joachim glanced down. Blood was seeping through the gauze on the soldier's side, wrapped over a uniform torn and crusted. "How . . . ?"

"Shell outside Orel. Half my unit gone." His voice was flat. "Shrapnel in my arm and side. I bled a long time before they got me out."

Farther down the line, a man lay with his head swathed in bandages. A nurse gently changed his dressing, revealing a horrific wound.

"Sniper," she murmured in response to Joachim's stare. "Caught him just above the ear. He was one of the lucky ones . . . that day." She didn't look confident about his chances.

Ambushes. Snipers. Mines. Shelling. The faces changed; the stories were the same. There was no refuge, not even here, not even for the ill and wounded.

That night, as the ward quieted, Joachim remained awake. The air raid had shaken him, but something else stirred him now. Moments ago, from a dim corner of the room, he had heard hushed voices—eager and intense, unlike the groans and grief he had grown used to.

". . . and we can't just stand by while civilians are slaughtered," one was saying now. "There's still a way to resist."

"But how?" another whispered. "Speak out, and they kill you."

"Through writing," the first voice replied. "Pamphlets. Truth. Words that pierce."

Joachim thought of the words he had sent in a recent letter to his parents:

> *Liebe Eltern,*
> *I fear what we are doing here cannot be justified. The things I have witnessed, the orders we are given—they go against everything you have taught me about honor and humanity.*

Easing his sore body from the cot, hand pressed to his side, Joachim shuffled closer to four men clustered together. "Pardon me," he said softly. "I don't mean to intrude . . . I just overheard you speaking."

A lean young man studied him, guarded. "It's none of your concern. We'll keep it down."

Joachim didn't leave. "My family . . . we've spoken out against the regime too. My sister lives in Berlin . . ." He thought it wise to say no more for the moment. "I might understand more than you think."

The leader studied him for a long moment. Then he gave the slightest nod. "Very well. We're already half dead anyway. I'm Hans. Hans Scholl. We're the White Rose—nonviolent resistance."

"White Rose?" Joachim echoed, still cautious. Erika had been involved in the Resistance since they were all back in Bromberg, before he had shipped out.

"We began at the University of Munich," Hans said, voice low. "Students, philosophers, writers. We don't carry rifles—only words. Leaflets. Truth."

"Rhetoric over rifles," another murmured.

"How do you distribute them?" Joachim asked. "Surely it's dangerous."

The other men exchanged glances. "The first rule of revolution," one said with a faint smile, "is to get away with it."

"We're careful. Facts, analysis, language that cuts through the fog," Hans continued. "When people know about the war—the camps, the lies—some stop looking away. Stalingrad is a slaughter. For what? To support a regime that sends us to war while killing our families at home?" His voice dropped. "When enough people say no, even quietly, this regime won't stand."

"I'm Joachim," he said, offering his hand.

Hans clasped it. "When you're stronger, we'll talk more about what might still be possible."

The group melted back into the shadows. Joachim returned to his cot, body aching but eyes bright with thought. He pictured Adi, Tatjana, Hellmuth, Erika, Christa. None of them wanted this war. Did they know what the Reich was truly doing—all the senseless cruelty and destruction? Maybe, but he doubted that a full awareness of the depravity had reached Bromberg.

Either way, he understood more now: No one was safe. But no one was powerless, either. Small acts mattered—even here.

His fingers found the crumpled pamphlet Hans had slipped him. He smoothed it under the lantern's edge and read:

> *Nothing is so unworthy of a civilized nation as allowing itself to be "governed" by an irresponsible clique that has yielded to base instinct . . .*

The message was beautifully composed, mercilessly clear. Somewhere, across Germany—in dim kitchens, in crowded barracks—others were reading the same words, hands trembling, eyes opening.

Joachim glanced inside his rucksack, which contained little else but his necessities, paper and ink, a few buttons, scissors for making bandages. The scissors would have to do. Tonight, he decided, he would cut a small paper stencil: a white rose.

By dawn, he had finished the clandestine work. He folded the stencil inside a letter to Erika and sealed the envelope. Afraid of saying too much, he wrote only the following:

> *For your eyes only. Seek out enlightenment. I trust you to*
> *plant the seeds.*

Erika knew danger, and she wouldn't shy away. If anyone could breathe new life into the White Rose's ideals and continue the work of the Resistance in Bromberg and Berlin, she could.

And if he fell, perhaps a part of him would move forward through her.

The German army surrendered in Stalingrad in February 1943, a turning point on the Eastern Front that decisively shifted the balance of power to the Russians. Word reached Joachim—through Erika—that the core of the White Rose had been captured by the Gestapo: Hans Scholl and his sister Sophie had been executed by guillotine. The risks of resistance were higher than ever.

If Joachim and Erika were to communicate anything real past the censors, they needed a better method. Joachim had to change how he wrote home.

He asked Erika to send his favorite chemistry magazine, *Wissen und Fortschritt*—"Knowledge and Development." When it arrived at the military hospital near Orel, bundled with one of her usual letters from Berlin, he tore the envelope open, the thin paper crackling under his calloused fingers. Joachim read, hearing her voice.

> *Mein lieber Bruder,*
> *I pray this letter finds you safe, though I know the realities you face.*

It seems from your recent letters—and the news we hear here—that your situation grows more dire with each passing week.

I must warn you about something the soldiers call Panzer-schokolade, *tankers' chocolate. It is an amphetamine—Pervitin—that the army has been distributing to keep soldiers fighting for days on end without rest. There is talk now of its dangers—addiction, even psychosis.*

Joachim's hand stilled. Amphetamines, to wire men past sleep, past mercy. Another violence, this one from the inside out. He thought of his unit—boys already haunted. That such government overreach was acceptable, that the Nazis would stoop so low for performance enhancement, didn't surprise him. He swore to himself that the only sweets he'd accept would be those sent from home.

He turned then to the magazine. Within its scientific pages, he could hide a second text.

He penciled seemingly idle marks: underlines, marginalia, curious equations. To the untrained eye, he would be just a studious soldier. To Erika—trained to recognize his patterns—it would be data: troop movements, supply shortages, Panzer failures, weather. A cipher layered in chemical symbols and math, a map only she could read.

At the end, Joachim added a scrap of gallows humor: *Keine Läuse, keine Urlaub.* "No lice, no leave." He could picture her rolling her eyes already.

He folded the magazine and sealed it in an envelope. If intercepted, the message would be invisible to all but his brilliant sister.

When a chance came, he would entrust it to a fellow soldier who could get it safely to Erika. From her hands, it would pass into Stefan's—his comrade, his friend, and another voice in the Resistance. And the White Rose's mission would begin again.

That night, burdened with fatigue yet unable to sleep, Joachim felt something steadier than hope: purpose. In the shadows of a war without sense, he and Erika had found a way to speak. Separated by distance and danger, they were still part of the same resistance—threads of ink and code binding brother to sister, truth to courage, word to deed.

Letter from Joachim to Erika, December 1942. While in a field hospital near Orel, sick with Askarid, he met members of the White Rose movement and sent this white rose stencil to Erika.

CHAPTER TWENTY-THREE

HOHENLYCHEN (1943)

WHITEWASHED WALLS AND SHARP RED rooflines rose from the pastoral countryside. Despite her braced knee, Christa felt a thrill of hope upon seeing the hospital's stately, pristine facade.

After her difficult recovery from diphtheria myocarditis, Christa's return to figure skating had been a small miracle. Then, in early 1943, a fall on the ice nearly unraveled that fragile progress. Christa's doctor in Bromberg suggested a referral to Hohenlychen, nestled in a quiet rural area north of Berlin, for her injured knee. Given Christa's delicate cardiac condition, placing her under Dr. Gebhardt's direct supervision—so she could heal far away from the bombing raids and ration lines—sounded prudent, even ideal.

Still, leaving their seventeen-year-old daughter in a hospital outside Berlin felt unthinkable. In the doctor's office that day, Adi had exchanged a troubled glance with Tatjana.

"I understand your concerns," the doctor had told them. "But Hohenlychen is renowned for sports medicine expertise. The care is unmatched. Dr. Gebhardt himself will oversee Christa's treatment." Even among the general public, Dr. Gebhardt's name held prestige: *Gruppenführer* in the SS, *Generalleutnant* in the Waffen-SS, Himmler's personal physician, president of the German Red Cross.

Tatjana's fingers had tightened around Christa's hand. "With the war raging, how can we be sure it's safe?"

"Remaining in Bromberg amid the tumult may hinder her recovery," the doctor replied. "Hohenlychen's peace could be just what she needs."

"I want to get better, Mama," Christa whispered. "This might be my best chance."

Adi ran a hand through his hair, torn between Dr. Gebhardt's sterling reputation and the obvious risk.

"We're her parents," Tatjana said, voice strained. "We cannot simply leave her."

But in truth, Erika was still finishing her schooling at the Chemotechnikerschule in Berlin, where Stefan was deep into his medical studies. And Manja lived in Charlottenburg, on the city's outskirts. Christa would not be entirely alone.

"You wouldn't be leaving her," the doctor reassured them. "You'd be entrusting her to the most advanced orthopedic care available. And of course, you may visit."

Adi's eyes met Tatjana's. The decision was made in silence—etched not only in logic, but in love.

Once a tuberculosis sanatorium, Hohenlychen had long been an institution associated with recovery. In 1933, Hitler repurposed it as the Reich's first sports medicine hospital in preparation for the 1936 Olympics. Renowned orthopedic surgeon Dr. Karl Gebhardt—a protégé of Himmler and formerly a medical student under Himmler's father—was installed as medical director. His powerful connections would later carry him to the post of SS chief medical officer.

In 1942, Hohenlychen was repurposed yet again, when Germany was flooded with broken youth from the Eastern Front: countless young men returning from Russia, missing limbs, bearing burns and blast injuries, and suffering from trench diseases. Hohenlychen became the primary intake facility for the SS war wounded.

When Christa arrived at Hohenlychen with Tatjana in May 1943, the mood inside the hospital had shifted once more. Soldiers who once might have graced fields of sport now navigated hallways bearing the scars of battle. Bandaged limbs were everywhere. The tap of crutches resounded on polished floors. Hohenlychen's rhythm was no longer sport; it was recovery—or something that looked like recovery.

Tatjana moved through the halls with vigilant focus, instincts sharpened by the strangeness of it all: nurses clipped and precise, doctors brisk and distant. The cleanliness gave comfort. The silence did not.

At last, they reached Dr. Gebhardt's office. He rose from behind his desk with a rehearsed warmth. "Welcome, welcome! Please, have a seat," he said, clasping Tatjana's hand. "You must be Frau Dindinger. An absolute pleasure."

"Thank you for seeing us, Doctor," Tatjana replied, polite but tense.

"And this radiant young lady must be our patient—Christa, is it? We'll have you back on the skating team in no time."

His confidence eased Christa's nerves. "Thank you, Doctor. Truly."

"Think nothing of it," he said. "Now—your treatment plan . . ."

As he unfolded therapies and schedules, Tatjana's shoulders slowly loosened. Brushing aside the hospital's darker undertones, both women entrusted their hopes to Hohenlychen's polished care. Neither could have known how carefully the performance had been rehearsed.

By nightfall, Tatjana boarded a train back to Berlin. The hospital, washed in dusk, appeared peaceful, even noble. But part of her thought it seemed to be watching her—still and unblinking.

In the days that followed, Christa found unexpected comfort in familiar Bromberg accents among the wounded. Shared stories helped her forge a bond with other patients. Yet whispers threaded the corridors: strange procedures, wounds that did not heal, fear that did not lift.

But then—music.

In the hospital auditorium, Christa discovered a beautiful piano. It became her refuge. She played first for herself: Rachmaninoff's Prelude in C-sharp minor, rippling like raindrops. Then Chopin's nocturnes, followed by Beethoven's *Moonlight Sonata*. Each note carved out space for memory and escape.

Word of Christa's playing spread. Wounded men and nurses gathered at doorways, drawn by the grace and liveliness of her music. Requests followed; a crowd grew. For the length of a song, her magnificent, skillful fingers gave them all a place untouched by war.

Erika and Stefan often took the short train ride from Berlin to attend the evening concerts. Those visits also afforded them unremarked access to hallways and stairwells of a military hospital full of high-ranking Nazi officials. In listening to Christa's marvelous performances, they also heard bits of useful information from SS members and Wehrmacht soldiers, as well as haunting cries coming from the back corridors of the hospital. What little could be overheard, and what could not, was passed to the Home Army. Tatjana was aware of the risks they were taking, but they protected Adi from that knowledge.

The music Christa played, the reports they passed, the glances exchanged in hallways—each was an act of survival and quiet defiance.

One evening, as the final chord faded, a woman approached Christa—elegant, gloved, pale-eyed, with a practiced smile. "You play exquisitely," she said. "I haven't heard such a beautiful touch since my lessons in Vienna."

"You're too kind, gnädige Frau," Christa replied. "It's something to do while I recover."

"Modesty doesn't suit a gift like yours. Talent must be nurtured." The woman removed a glove. "I am the wife of the director of sanitation at Ravensbrück."

Christa's breath caught. Ravensbrück was a concentration camp just a few miles from Hohenlychen, where women from all over the occupied Reich were imprisoned and forced into slave labor. And "sanitation" meant the disposal of corpses and body parts.

The director's wife produced an envelope. "A letter of recommendation—and a pass from Dr. Gebhardt. You'll commute to Berlin twice a week for private lessons with a concert pianist. My friend."

Christa hesitated.

"He has agreed to take you on," the woman continued, voice crisp. "I expect you to make full use of the opportunity." It was not a suggestion.

Slowly, Christa reached out to accept the envelope—velvet and ashes all rolled into one. It was a dream, handed to her by someone complicit in the unthinkable.

"Tell your family," the woman added. "They'll be proud."

The family buzzed with the news of Christa's incredible opportunity—and of the complicated connection to higher-ups at the Ravensbrück labor camp. Adi wrote to Joachim at the Eastern Front. Tatjana spoke with her sisters, Manja and Fania. Erika quietly passed word to her Resistance contacts: She was now but a few degrees of separation from a leading official at Ravensbrück.

Amid the glimmer of Hohenlychen's respectability and renown, shadows lengthened. Walking the halls with their eyes and ears alert, Stefan and Erika noted a spike in deaths from sepsis—freshly wounded soldiers who were gone within days. They also noted, with surprise, some women prisoners from Ravensbrück in the back hallways who were there to undergo medical procedures.

Stefan recognized some of the women: distant cousins from Lidice.

They were survivors, sent to Ravensbrück after the Nazis razed the village in retaliation. For Stefan, the Resistance work suddenly became even more personal.

But he and Erika were not yet privy to the grim tableau within Hohenlychen's walls, where the vestiges of humanity were stripped away under the pretext of wartime exigency. As the war churned on, Hohenlychen's dual identity had hardened: hospital above, laboratory below—death masquerading as care.

Under the care of Dr. Karl Gebhardt—who had failed to save Reinhard Heydrich from assassination in Czechoslovakia—Ravensbrück prisoners were undergoing brutal, unethical medical procedures. The stated goal was advancing battlefield medicine. The result was suffering and death.

Hohenlychen and Ravensbrück were not separate worlds. They were partners in the same machinery.

CHAPTER TWENTY-FOUR

LOSS (1943)

THE RUINED STREETS OF KHARKOV stretched before them, cloaked in smoke and dust. Joachim's eyes burned from the acrid haze as he surveyed what remained, his heart leaden with the finality of their loss.

His unit had fought ferociously to hold the city in northeast Ukraine. But by the end of August, the war's momentum had turned decisively against Germany after the devastating losses at Kursk earlier that summer—the final strategic offensive the Wehrmacht would launch on the Eastern Front. In this grim panorama, Joachim's Panzeraufklärungsabteilung 3 found themselves entrenched along the blood-soaked banks of the Mius and Dnieper Rivers. Their tanks and antitank units, once believed invincible, now formed only a brittle shield against the implacable Soviet forces.

Above them, the skies belonged entirely to the Soviets. The Red Air Force, strengthened by reinforcements and the symbolism of the anniversary of its inception, showed no mercy. Fighters and bombers swarmed like hornets, their presence announced by a low, vibrating growl that swelled into a deafening roar before the payloads dropped—earth-shaking blows that shattered both ground and spirit.

On the ground, Joachim's unit had just received their first allotment of the vaunted new Panther tanks—Germany's long-promised answer to the formidable Russian T-34s. But even these feared behemoths proved a mere stopgap against the overwhelming numbers they faced. Joachim and his comrades soon realized their weapons could not penetrate T-34 armor. What's more, the Panthers' faulty fuel pumps and fragile transmissions betrayed them in the field, often immobilizing them in the heat of battle.

The Russians didn't just have the upper hand in technology; they vastly outnumbered the Germans, further tipping the scales. Even Enigma, the Reich's trusted intelligence tool, had become a poisoned gift. Just like at Kursk, unknown to the Germans, the British were feeding its decrypted contents to the Soviets, hastening the Wehrmacht's undoing.

Communications had devolved into brief, static-laced bursts over unreliable radios. Supply lines had collapsed. The situation grew increasingly dire, with each passing day bringing fresh losses—bodies, equipment, ground. Yet still they fought, until finally, the order came through the radio: *Rückzug!*

"Retreat."

The admission of defeat tasted bitter on Joachim's tongue. The Battle of Kharkov was over. Their strength had proved insufficient against the sheer force of the Soviet advance. The roads and railways leading forward had been rendered impassable by ceaseless bombardment. The enemy had come with numbers, with fury, and with resolve. In the end, the defensive line collapsed. The path to the Dnieper now stood open.

With each step of their weary retreat, Joachim saw it was not merely territory they lost but the last residue of hope. They were leaving behind a landscape haunted by the ghosts of their departed comrades. The decision to retreat was more than a military maneuver; it was an unspoken confession: Germany was no longer advancing. It was merely reacting.

As the reality set in, so too did understanding. This war, once expected to be a quick triumph, had become a long, consuming shadow with no clear end.

The Panthers, proud titans of German engineering, now retreated with the sullen grace of defeated gladiators, their steel hides scarred by the unyielding fury they had faced. The remnants of Joachim's unit, scattered and beleaguered, were a procession of war's weary children, clinging to the fragile lifeline of radio transmissions that crackled with the voice of command.

Among these soldiers, there was a commendable sense of duty and an admirable mental resilience. These were the *Landsers*, the native Germans, skeptical of Hitler's malevolent agenda but fiercely loyal to one another. They were the original Army Group Center, a unit whispered to harbor resistance sympathies—even assassination plots. But in the mud and fire of the front lines, there was no time for politics. They fought for one another—not because they believed in Hitler's war but because retreat meant leaving others to die.

In the weeks that followed their retreat from Kharkov, they found themselves embroiled in grueling, bloody conflicts against what had become a fearsome enemy. Outnumbered and outgunned, they fought the "subhuman Slavs," whether alone or in small clusters, often isolated from other friendly forces. Joachim and his unit knew they were the final line of defense against advancing Soviet forces.

With no contact from their infantry and surprise attacks coming from behind their lines, the situation was grim, yet he and his comrades held fast. They understood that yielding ground would imperil everyone they cared about. This wasn't grandiose heroism destined for the history books; it was a subtle, more intimate form of valor, born from a blend of emotional and physical tolls that surpassed any quantifiable measure, expressed in every bullet dodged and every moment they chose to stand their ground despite insurmountable odds.

During the first two weeks of September, the Ukrainian landscape disintegrated into a mosaic of battlegrounds, individual farmsteads becoming the focal points of brutal skirmishes. Elements of the Third Panzer Division, including Joachim's unit, pushed back against the relentless Russian advance with immediate counterattacks.

Tank crews were deployed around the clock. Sleep became a luxury. The regiment, desperate to conserve its thinning manpower, began rotating men between the front and the rear. Aboard battered trains now doubling as field shelters, soldiers caught brief fragments of rest, if not peace.

Joachim, exhausted and hollow-eyed, found himself on one such train. He stared out the window, the landscape a blur of destruction and despair. Sleep, even here, refused him. The war had followed him onto the train.

In his narrow berth, he wrote home.

> *Liebe Eltern und Eka und Tita,*
> *I hope this letter finds you well and in good spirits, despite the*
> *trying times we find ourselves in . . .*

As Joachim penned words to his family, threads of warmth were stitched over a fraying reality. He wrote of manageable discomforts, of jokes exchanged with comrades, of small victories—not of the dying or the fear that lived in his gut. He softened the edges of war with every line, sparing his family the details that clung to his skin like soot. These letters became his armor, a shield of ink and denial.

The train lurched to a halt, the sudden jolt snapping Joachim from his reverie. Around him, the compartment stirred. They were a motley crew now, a patchwork of veterans and green recruits, their uniforms stained with sweat and grime.

A voice crackled over the intercom, distorted and distant. "Fifteen minutes. Make it count."

The train's doors parted with a hiss, revealing desolation. Scorched earth stretched to the horizon. The air reeked of smoke and cordite. Somewhere beyond the hills, artillery thundered, a sound now so familiar that it registered less as fear than as fact.

Joachim pushed himself to his feet. His knees ached as he rose, the sudden movement jarring. He followed the others through the narrow passage, into the open air for fifteen precious minutes.

The soldiers dispersed, finding what refuge they could. Some sought camaraderie through shared smokes and hushed conversations. Others stood solitary against the expanse of ruin, their gazes empty, as if searching the horizon for answers they knew would never come.

Joachim, with a soldier's instinct, gravitated toward a lone tree at the train yard's edge. This stubborn sentinel, scarred yet enduring, stood in defiance of a war that had taken so much. Beside it, Joachim knelt, his hand gently tracing the bark's rugged surface, drawing a silent parallel between the tree's resilience and his own.

Here, in the shadow of this modest symbol of persistence, Joachim closed his eyes.

For a moment, the artillery fire faded to a low rumble in the distance. He allowed himself to feel the full force of exhaustion, of days and nights run together by the rhythm of war. There had been no time to grieve, no space to reflect, just the constant drag forward.

In this rare pause, he wasn't thinking of strategy—not here, not now. Instead, he sought the embrace of peace, ephemeral and precious. Around him, the world might be consumed by chaos, but within this small, sheltered space, Joachim found a whisper of the serenity he fought to preserve, for himself, for his family, for his nation, and for a future that seemed an ever-distant dream.

As he knelt there by the tree, time slowed, staying its march to grant the weary soldier a moment of reprieve. It was a moment to simply be, to breathe, to exist not as a combatant but as a man who longed for the simple grace of peace.

But the reprieve was short-lived. All too soon, the voice on the intercom pulled them back to the train. Joachim rose to his feet, his body heavy with the knowledge of what lay ahead. Making his way back, he allowed himself one final glance at the tree, its branches swaying gently in the breeze. He took a deep breath, the smells of war mingling with the faintest hint of something green and alive.

Back inside the train, he dropped into his seat. The wheels began to turn again, steady and mechanical, a familiar sound in an unfamiliar world. He fished out the stub of pencil and the battered notebook from his pack, the pages worn and creased from countless readings. Then, with a heavy sigh, Joachim opened to a fresh page, the blank expanse seeming to mock him with its emptiness.

For a moment, he simply stared at the page, his mind a whirl of thoughts and memories, each one vying for attention. He thought of his family back home, their faces etched into his consciousness with vivid clarity. He pictured his mother's gentle smile, his father's steadfast gaze, his sisters' infectious laughter. They were his tether, his reason for enduring in the face of the unrelenting horror that surrounded him. Slowly, almost reverently, he began to write again.

The words flowed from his pencil, each one a careful construction, a deliberate attempt to shield his loved ones from the harsh realities he faced. He spoke of camaraderie among his fellow soldiers, the small moments of levity that punctuated the bleakness of their existence. He wove tales of laughter, of friendly competitions and pranks played on one another. He described the breathtaking sunrises that somehow managed to break through the ever-present haze of smoke and ash, painting the world in vibrant hues that seemed almost too beautiful to be real.

He didn't lie, exactly. But he filtered the truth. What reached his family was what they would carry. Through it all, he strove to convey a sense of hope—that no matter how dire the consequences, there was still beauty to be found in the world, if one knew where to look. Woven through the letter was the quiet belief that even here, there were still things worth holding on to.

I am so proud of you, Eka, that you will soon move on to advanced studies in chemical engineering in the Sudetenland. And Tita! Soon it is your birthday. I will try to send you something from the Front. Please send me ice skating pictures. The dream of our reunion is what sustains me . . .

As he wrote, Joachim could almost see them gathered around the kitchen table: his mother blinking back tears as she read his words, Eka with that determined line to her jaw, Tita grinning and trying not to interrupt. He knew these letters to them mattered, creating a tangible connection to the son and brother they had sent off to war. And so, he poured his heart into every word, every sentence a carefully crafted message of love and resilience.

And though the road ahead may be long, I take comfort that you are there, waiting for me at the end of this journey. Your love and support are my guiding light, even in the darkest of times . . .

When the final sentence was done, Joachim lowered the pencil and exhaled. It wasn't much, not compared to what he owed them, but it was something—a bridge between where he was and where he hoped to return.

He folded the page, tucking it into his pack. The battle ahead was close. But for now, he let himself feel that bond with home, with peace—thin and battered now but unbroken.

CHAPTER TWENTY-FIVE

REVELATIONS FROM RAVENSBRÜCK (1943)

STEFAN'S HANDS TREMBLED AS HE made his way to Manja's flat in Charlottenburg, his bulky medical bag seeming heavier with each reluctant step. He had carried it through exams, through internships—but today it felt unbearable. The prospect of completing medical school had once filled him with purpose, but the lessons he'd learned over the past few days burdened him with knowledge too horrifying to bear alone.

The closer he got to the flat, the more certain he became: What he had seen could never be unseen.

He climbed the stairs and knocked, his heart pounding. When Tatjana opened the door, her warm smile flickered and died as she took in the pallor of his face and the haunted look in his eyes.

"Stefan, what's happened? Is Tita okay?" Her voice wavered as fear crept in.

"Tita's fine. It's about Ravensbrück," Stefan replied, swallowing hard. "Is Adi here yet?"

Tatjana shook her head slowly. "He won't arrive until tomorrow. Stefan, what is it?"

"I need to speak with you and Erika. It can't wait." He followed Tatjana into the living room, where heavy curtains softened the afternoon light into a muted glow. "The Nazis . . . There's more going on than we ever imagined."

The apartment—normally a space of warmth and conversation—went still. Tatjana and Erika sat down, exchanging tense glances.

Stefan remained standing. "I . . ." His voice cracked, and he cleared his throat, fighting to maintain composure. "I've seen things at Ravensbrück. Things that no one would believe."

The memories of Ravensbrück surged before he could stop them—vile, relentless, impossible to repress. His mind filled with the sickening clarity of what he had witnessed: skeletal bodies twisted in pain, vacant eyes that once held hope, and screams—so many screams—ripping through the night air, unanswered. He clenched his fists, trying to keep his voice steady—a battle he was losing.

He forced himself to continue. "Erika, the cries we heard in those back corridors at Hohenlychen—the cries we couldn't explain. We didn't understand then, but now I do."

Tatjana and Erika watched him silently, with growing alarm.

"They're . . . experimenting on the prisoners," he whispered, struggling to find the right words. "Innocent women, children . . . They're using them like test animals. It's not just a labor camp. It's a slaughterhouse."

Erika's arms shot out to grip his trembling hands. "You need to tell us everything, Stefan."

Tatjana closed her eyes for a long moment. When she opened them, her voice was steady yet tight with restraint. "Dear God. The Nazis."

Their gazes locked. In Stefan's eyes, they saw horror. In theirs, he saw something else: not panic but resolve. These women understood peril. They'd lived in the shadow of it for too long to be easily broken.

Stefan drew a breath, his voice steadier now. "The prisoners . . . many are Jewish women. Others are political prisoners—communists, Catholics, socialists. The screams . . ."

His voice broke again, and he shuddered.

"They're injecting gangrenous bacteria," he pressed on after a pause, hollow and drained. "They're watching people rot from the inside out so they can study the infections. Some patients get sulfonamides. Some don't. The suffering . . . it's monstrous."

Tatjana gasped, her face ashen.

Erika leaned forward. "This is worse than what we feared."

"Yes. These are brutal experiments," Stefan said, each word cutting like a blade.

For a moment, no one spoke. Stefan began pacing, as though trying to outrun the images that haunted every corner of his mind.

"And the doctors there . . . they're amputating limbs, removing bones, grafting flesh, extracting nerves—no anesthesia. Nothing," he continued, his voice rough. "And the severed limbs . . . they aren't discarded. They're . . . used again. The doctors graft them onto other prisoners. They're trying to test transplant viability. All without anesthesia."

Tatjana's breath caught. Her eyes darted to Erika, who gripped the armrests of her chair. Silence fell—heavy, suffocating.

Erika shook her head slowly, refusing to accept such a monstrous reality. "No . . . they cannot possibly believe that will work. It's barbaric."

"They do," Stefan answered grimly. "They think if they give men new arms or legs, they can send them back to the Front. After Stalingrad, they believe the cost is worth it—the cost of the lives of these Ravensbrück prisoners."

Erika's eyes narrowed, fury smoldering beneath her grief. How could such atrocities be happening just beyond their doorstep?

"These aren't nameless bodies in hospital beds," he added, the bitterness cutting through. "They're women: mothers, daughters, human beings—dismembered and discarded. But the Nazis don't see them as people, just disposable labor. Just parts to be used."

Erika's voice, when it came, was strained. "And what's happening to the wounded soldiers—the ones who receive the grafts?"

"The grafts fail, one after another," Stefan said, jaw tight. "Horrific infections, sepsis . . . Many die in agony. They're not receiving antibiotics."

The room held still, the weight of such cruelty pressing down on them all. The image of these experiments, conducted in the name of science, stained the very idea of humanity.

"And the man behind it all," Stefan continued, voice thick with disgust, "is Dr. Karl Gebhardt."

Tatjana's eyes widened. "Dr. Gebhardt? But he . . . he's Christa's doctor. He's been treating her for weeks at Hohenlychen."

"Yes," Stefan said grimly, exhaling hard. "Himmler's protégé. After Heydrich was wounded in Prague, Gebhardt refused to use the new sulfonamide antibiotics. Heydrich died a few days later. Hitler and Himmler never forgave him."

When the Nazis realized that sulfonamides might have saved the Butcher of Prague from sepsis, Dr. Gebhardt launched trials on Ravensbrück prisoners to ward off professional disgrace. He was claiming to study battlefield infections. In reality, he was trying to erase his failure, to rewrite his legacy. Desperate to save face, he needed data. Human data.

"Gebhardt is using these women to redeem himself—to prove sulfonamides don't work," Stefan continued, shaking his head. "He's using their pain as penance. It isn't science. It's revenge."

The final piece of a dreadful puzzle clicked into place.

Hohenlychen. Ravensbrück. Gebhardt. The Nazi concentration camps weren't just for imprisonment and slave labor; they were for experimentation and extermination. This savage, gruesome web had been around them all along. They just hadn't seen it—until now.

And somewhere inside it, tangled and unaware, was Christa.

Late the next night, long after the rest of the family had drifted into uneasy sleep, Tatjana sat at Manja's kitchen table with Adi, newly returned from Bromberg. A single bulb cast dim light over the room, stretching shadows across the walls—shadows that mirrored the weight still hanging from the previous night's revelations.

Tatjana reached out, her hand trembling slightly as it found Adi's. "Stefan brought news yesterday about Ravensbrück . . . and Hohenlychen," she began, her voice barely above a whisper.

The words tumbled out, ragged and raw, each one a knife twisting in her chest: the unbearable conditions; the women dying of starvation, disease, and brutality; the descent into medical depravity. Under roofs marked with red crosses, the line between treatment and torture had vanished. Hohenlychen had become a site of systematic human experimentation, where Dr. Gebhardt presided over a range of inhumane procedures and unnecessary deaths.

Authorized at the highest echelons of the Nazi regime, these operations—from forced sterilizations to tendon and bone harvesting to amputations—were justified with a chilling calculus: The suffering of a few, especially when those few were "inferior" people, was rationalized as a chance to save many German soldiers. Gebhardt viewed his methods as contributions to battlefield medicine. In truth, he had transformed operating theaters into laboratories of suffering.

The cries from Ravensbrück prisoners echoed through Hohenlychen's back halls—cries not only of pain but also of souls being extinguished. And sometimes the silence that followed was worse. Had Christa heard the terrible screams, the ghastly silence?

Tatjana's mind flashed back to her own experiences on the Bromberg Death March when the war began. The memories surged, replete with the haunting images she had fought so hard to bury. She shuddered, pushing the thoughts away, refusing to let them surface now, when she needed all her strength. Then her eyes found Adi's once more.

His face drained of color, Adi tightened his grip on Tatjana's hand, as if trying to ground himself in the reality of her presence. His eyes searched her face. The fear, the rage—it was all there, simmering just below the surface.

"Mein Gott," he whispered, his words breaking under the strain. "Christa . . . she must leave that place as soon as possible."

The silence that followed was encumbered by the horrors they now shared. The air in the room seemed harder to breathe, as if it had absorbed unspeakable darkness.

When Adi spoke again, his voice was a low rumble, heavy with sorrow but edged with fury. "We have to do something, Tatjana. We cannot let this madness continue."

Tatjana looked at him, her heart breaking for the man who had always tried to shield their family from the worst. She had no plan, only this: They could no longer pretend not to know. "We'll find a way," she replied simply. "We must. For them . . . and for us."

Her thoughts spiraled. The truth of her heritage—her hidden Jewish identity—rose like a warning flare. Only Adi and Joachim knew. If it came to light, it wouldn't just be her own life at risk.

"I've heard news from Lithuania at last," she said quietly. "Where my Uncle Reines founded his yeshiva." The word felt foreign on her tongue—*yeshiva*—like an echo from a life she was no longer allowed to claim. "The Lithuanians didn't wait. The pogroms began as soon as the Wehrmacht arrived, the very first week of Operation Barbarossa."

Her hands tightened around Adi's.

"Most of the killing wasn't even done by soldiers. It was the SS units behind the lines. Our Joachim wouldn't have seen this firsthand. But he must know something. The exterminations . . ." Her voice faltered, almost too much to bear. "Entire Jewish communities wiped out. Men, women, children . . . no one spared."

Adi squeezed her hand tighter, his breath catching. It was as if the world itself was turning against them, and there was nowhere left to hide.

"We knew about the work camps," she continued softly. "My work as a translator has made me aware of so much evil. But this?" She shook her head. "Ravensbrück . . . it's beyond anything we could have imagined."

Adi pressed a tender kiss to her forehead, though she could feel the tremor in his lips. "We'll get through this," he whispered, his voice thin with hope. "We have to believe that."

Tatjana nodded, drawing strength from his words, from his unwavering belief that they might all somehow survive this war. "Adi, there's something else," she began, voice low and thoughtful. "Joachim, Erika, Stefan . . . they're working with the Resistance. Erika has shared this with me."

Adi's eyes widened, his expression flickering in a way Tatjana recognized instantly. It was the same churn of emotions she herself carried: the fierce pride of knowing their children were standing up for what was right, and the terrible dread of knowing what it might cost them.

"We've raised them well," Adi said, his voice rough with emotion. "Now we must trust them, as we surely believe in them."

Tatjana nodded, a bittersweet smile forming through her tears. "But we keep Christa out of this. She is too young and too innocent. And she is already caught in the middle of it at Hohenlychen."

"Agreed," Adi said firmly. "We'll protect her as best we can."

They sat in silence, the enormity of their situation—of the dark tides of mankind that defied comprehension, of how far cruelty could reach—filling the small kitchen. Yet in that silence, something held. Not hope, exactly, but something close to it. A resolve to cling to what was still theirs: their family, their purpose, their humanity. And to fight quietly, steadily, in whatever ways remained.

After Christa returned to Bromberg, letters from the hospital haunted her. Men she had known were dying. The dead were piling up. One patient, a man named Erwin Wodtke, described the death of a fellow soldier.

NOVEMBER 17, 1943

Christa,

I write because your music lifted our spirits and we miss you. Yet another life is gone from the blood infection, sepsis, after surgery by Dr. Gebhardt. There have been many. There is something very wrong here.

Erwin's letter was not just a warning but proof. The deaths were not random.

Stefan and Erika relayed firsthand accounts like Erwin's to the Polish Home Army and the British S.O.E., unmasking these atrocities for the

Allies and for the sake of history. But inside Hohenlychen's sealed corridors, and in Berlin's dim apartments, their resistance didn't feel like history. It felt like fear, like rage—like grief they could not show.

None of them could see the full shape of what was coming, but they understood enough to know the price of silence was too high. In a regime built on forgetting, they chose instead to remember.

And to bear witness.

Hohenlychen
am 17. November 1943

Liebe Christa!

Nachdem ich vor einigen Tagen aufgrund eines
so traurigen Anlasses Euch schreiben musste, muss
ich Ihnen heute wieder aus ähnlichem Anlass
schreiben.

Sie erinnern sich wohl noch jenes schönen Som-
mertages, an dem Sie uns das lustige Gedicht vor-
lasen, das Ihnen der Obersturmführer Schwein-
berger widmete, auch, dass ich ihm von Ihnen
Grüsse bei meiner Ankunft bestellen sollte. — Nun
ist er nach beinah' 2 jährigem Leiden nach einer
von Prof. Gebhardt vorgenommenen sigsten Operation infolge zu grossen Blutverlustes in der Nacht
vom 12. zum 13. November verstorben. — Gestern wurden seine sterblichen Ueberreste in seine Heimat
überführt. —

Es ist doch wirklich schade, wieviel junges, tap-
feres Blut in diesem Krieg vergehen muss, und
wer weiss, welche Opfer er noch fordern mag.

Letter to Christa from fellow Hohenlychen patient Erwin R. Wodtke, dated November 17, 1943. He describes the death from sepsis of yet another young man operated on by Dr. Karl Gebhardt. There had been many such deaths. Dr. Gebhardt often worked in conjunction with Dr. Josef Mengele from Auschwitz. Dr. Gebhardt was later tried and convicted at the Nuremberg Doctors Trial. He was Christa's doctor.

Wie ich von Edeltraud hörte, sind Sie nun
wieder in Braunsberg, und werden Sie meine
Zeilen dort wohl auffinden.

Im Moment möchte ich Ihnen nicht viel von mir
bzw. meinem Zustand erzählen, das mag neben
dem Vorstehenden sich nicht recht ausnehmen.
Genug, ich habe einen Gehgips seit gestern und
werde früher als vermutet wieder zuhause sein
können.

Es wird mich dann freuen, Ihnen so manches
von hier erzählen zu können, und bleibe ich
bis dahin
        Ihr Ernst R. Wödtke.

P.S.: Grüße an Eltern bitte auszurichten!

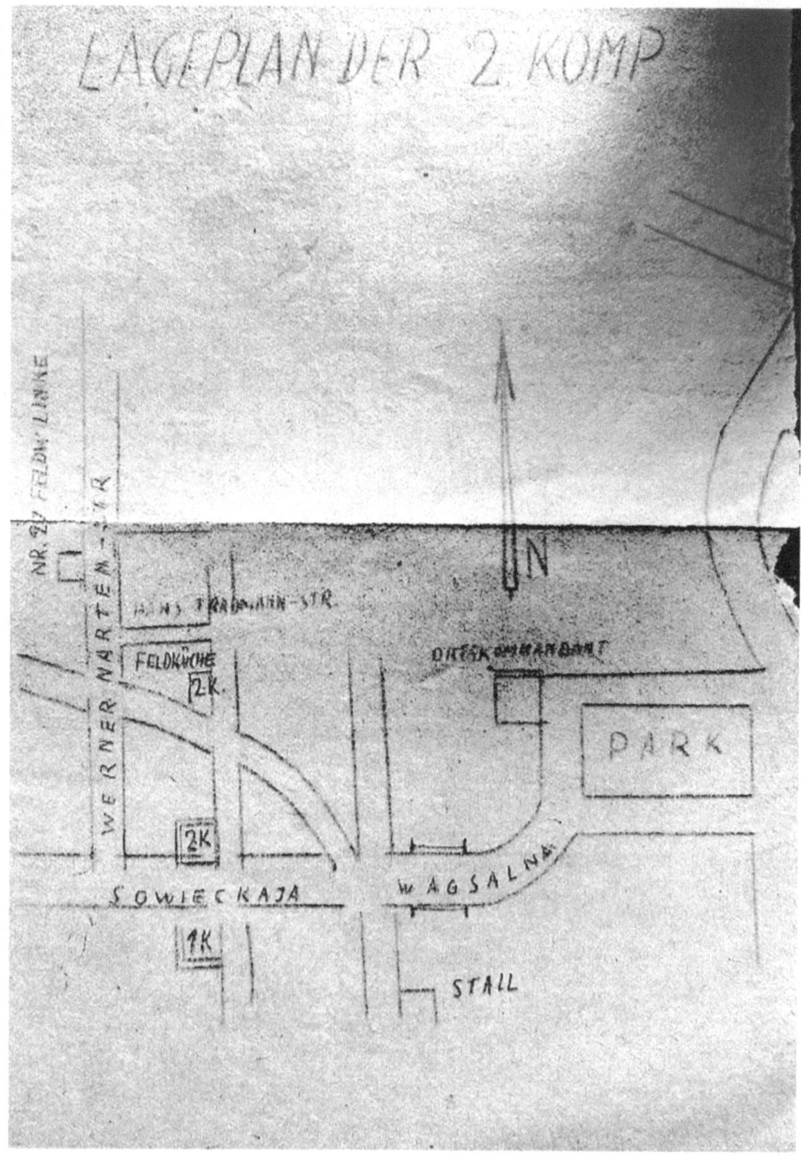

Site plan of the second camp, early 1943. Joachim sent this to Erika to provide more information regarding troop locations and movements to the Resistance. He sent it late in the war when the censors were more lax; they let it go through.

CHAPTER TWENTY-SIX

PEKARI (1943)

JOACHIM STOOD QUIETLY AT THE edge of the chaos, taking in the faces of the soldiers around him. Their eyes were dulled by fatigue, but beneath the surface lay something more enduring—fear laced with unspoken determination. No one said it aloud, but they all knew what was coming. The worst always found them again.

The harsh realities of war had already taken a staggering toll. Medical teams were stretched to their limits, tending to the 315 wounded men who had piled up in just the first few weeks of September. There was no time for ceremony, no space for grief. There was only the relentless task of keeping men alive long enough to return to battle.

With this sobering reality in mind, Joachim's division launched a crash training program for replacements, a desperate attempt to harden green recruits before they were fed to the Eastern Front. For every soldier who lay silent on the field, another stood ready to fill the empty space, his fate a coin toss in the chaos of conflict.

As Joachim oversaw the training of these recruits, he couldn't help noticing another group among them: correspondents, still photographers, and filmmakers dispatched to Ukraine by the Army High Command. At first he naturally assumed they were there to document the truth. But that illusion didn't last. The cameras didn't follow the pain; they followed a script.

Lights were ever present, as soldiers were directed and choreographed in their movements and actions.

Slowly, it dawned on Joachim: They weren't there to record what was real. They were fabricating what should be believed—a Hollywoodesque portrayal of a far less picturesque conflict. The tragedy of war was being reframed through a lens of propaganda.

Disgust welled up in Joachim as he saw polished fiction masquerading as truth, belittling the sacrifices they had made. Hitler was orchestrating psychological warfare, a manipulation of public perception. This was not lost on troops already disillusioned with the Reich and its machine.

The staccato crack of rifle fire tore through the haze, sharp and sudden, snapping Joachim from his thoughts. Bullets ripped through smoke-filled air, slamming into mortar and brick with sickening finality. Joachim pressed flat against the meager cover of a low wall, heart pounding. The Soviet assault had begun in full.

"Dindinger! We're pulling back!" his commanding officer shouted over the gunfire. "Fall back to the rally point!"

Joachim risked a glance over the wall, eyes stinging from the acrid smoke. Through the haze, figures darted from one precarious bit of cover to the next in a hasty retreat. With a low groan, he slung his rifle and ran.

Boots pounded over broken stone. The air howled with artillery. Buildings burned to his left. A shell landed behind him, dust and heat sweeping his back. This wasn't the war the cameras captured. This was the part they cropped out—the running, the panic, the desperate calculus of staying alive.

Somehow, Joachim made it to the rally point and joined the remnants of his unit—ragged, soot-streaked, eyes haunted. There was no time to catch his breath. The rumble of approaching tanks grew, the vibration climbing through his boots. The enemy was close.

"Panzerfaust teams, make ready!" came the order up the line.

Joachim scanned the rubble and spotted the antitank teams huddled behind a shattered storefront, bazookas cradled in their arms, protected like a flicker of hope. In skilled hands, the weapon could punch through turret rings or gun mantlets. It wasn't much, but it was something.

A Soviet T-34 tank rounded the corner, casting a long shadow across the battered street. Its main gun thundered, the blast staggering Joachim. A shell smashed into the upper floors of a nearby building; masonry and glass rained down.

Then came the response. The Panzerfaust teams sprang into action. The first rocket streaked forth, smoke and flame carving a line that found its mark, punching through the turret ring. The machine shuddered to a halt, belching oily smoke as its crew scrambled to escape the fire inside. No time to cheer—more tanks poured into the street, guns barking in a thunderous chorus.

To the left, the Third Panzer held firm. To the right, the Twenty-Fourth was collapsing.

Sleek T-34s and hulking KV-1s emerged from the smoke, turrets swinging toward the gap like predators scenting blood. The German line splintered into isolated pockets. They were being overrun, outflanked, and exposed.

Then a new threat flared: Russian partisans, emboldened by the shifting tide against their occupiers, materialized from ruins and tree lines. Bullets sliced past in tight bursts. Joachim hit the ground as rifle cracks braided with tank thunder. It wasn't a Front. It was a crossfire.

Somehow, Joachim and most of his unit survived the onslaught as they fell back toward the Dnieper. Then came the rain—steady, unrelenting, pattering against Joachim's helmet as he crouched in his forward reconnaissance position.

The soil turned to sludge, cold and dragging at every step. They were ordered to secure vital Dnieper crossings ahead of the SS-Panzergrenadier Division Wiking. The order was clear: *Hold at all costs.*

Even as Joachim watched the terrain, unease pressed in. The SS were infamous for merciless violence. He knew the whispered stories: exterminations, mass graves. The contrast with his own unit could not have been starker: They fought to survive; the SS fought to dominate. But the alliance was tactical, not ideological. Pragmatism had to replace principle. The Red Army was gaining. If survival meant temporary alignment, he would endure it—for his comrades, for his family, for the faint hope that something might still be salvaged from this disastrous war.

The Dnieper crossings were quiet on the night of September 25. Too quiet. Boats slid silently through moonlight. On the far bank, the illusion shattered. Hitler's hubris had once again overruled sound strategy: There were no defenses—no bunkers, no trenches—only open ground. They were standing in exposed terrain with no prepared fortifications. It was an oversight so catastrophic it felt intentional.

Engineers were ordered to carve positions from the unforgiving earth. Joachim labored alongside his comrades, muscles burning as they hacked shallow dugouts while distant tanks growled nearer. Mud crippled the soldiers' mobility, and sightlines were poor. Still, they worked, praying something might hold. They were sculpting their own fortress from the land they had sought to conquer, seeking sanctuary in the bosom of a motherland that was not their own. In the irony of their endeavor, there was a bitter lesson about the nature of war: The conqueror could be reduced to seeking solace in the trenches of the conquered.

The dawn of September 28 brought new orders: *Move northwest—immediately.* They traveled one hundred kilometers along the Dnieper's western bank, every step a risk. The region crawled with partisans and Soviet airborne troops. The sand along the riverbank offered no protection, only danger.

On October 1, rain-soaked ground trapped the division's tanks and assault guns in treacherous *balkas*—ravine-like gullies. Joachim's armored reconnaissance battalion, reassigned to an infantry division, was ordered to seal off and eliminate a Russian bridgehead near Pekari. Visibility was poor; coordination frayed. The silence warned more than soothed.

Then, without mercy, it snapped. A blistering crossfire tore open the quiet, bullets furrowing mud at Joachim's feet. Amid the churn and smoke, he spotted a transport, hopelessly bogged, with two wounded soldiers trapped inside. He went without hesitation. To him, their safety outweighed his own.

The bullets, too, did not hesitate. There, as Joachim strained against the sucking mire to free the vehicle—as rounds stitched the air—a single bullet found him.

It did not hesitate.

It did not miss.

Joachim fell beside the vehicle he had tried to save. The flame that had driven him—duty, courage, love—burned on in the choice he made.

The *Wehrpass* issued to Joachim and released to his family upon his death as a keepsake. The fifty-four pages include battles fought, units served with, injuries, and miscellaneous notes. The open-wing eagle cover was used mid and late war, as opposed to the Wehrmacht-style eagle used early on.

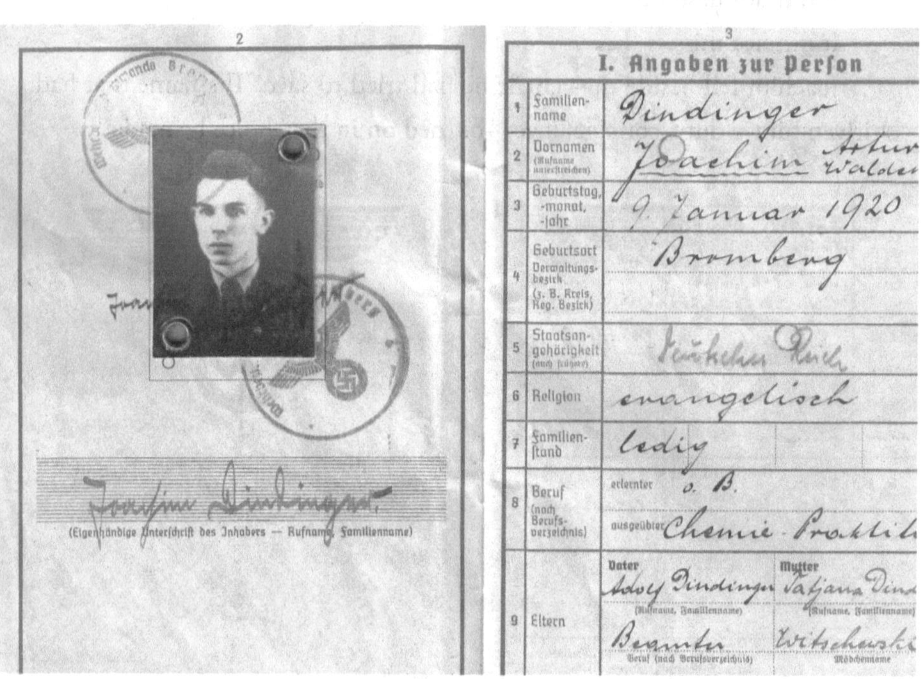

Wehrpass, first page.

22. 6.—9. 7. 41	Doppelschlacht von Bialystok u. Minsk
	Im einzelnen:
22. 6. 41	Durchbruch durch die Grenzstellung (Bug-Übergang)
23. 6.—28. 6. 41	Kämpfe im Pripjet-Gebiet ostw. Brest (Verfolgungskämpfe bis zur Beresina
29. 6.—9. 7. 41	Vorstoss gegen und über Swislotsch und Beresina
	29. 6.—1. 7. Beresina-Übergang bei Bobruisk
	2. 7.—9. 7. Kämpfe bei Rogatschew und Shlobin
10. 7.—31. 7. 41	Schlacht bei Smolensk
	Im einzelnen:
10. 7.—14. 7. 41	Durchbruch durch die Dnjepr-Stellung (Dnjepr-Übergang bei Stary Bychow und Durchbruch durch die Stalin-Linie)
15. 7.—31. 7. 41	Abwehrkämpfe am Ssosh (Kämpfe bei Propoisk)
1. 8.—8. 8. 41	Schlacht bei Roslawl
9. 8.—20. 8. 41	Schlacht bei Kritschew und bei Gomel (Vernichtungsschlacht bei Klimowitschi-Miloslawitschi)
21. 8.—26. 9. 41	Schlacht bei Kiew
	Im einzelnen:
21. 8.—5. 9. 41	Verfolgungskämpfe bis zur Dessna (Einbruch in die Dessna-Stellung. Umfassung der Feindkräfte im Raum um Gomel)
6. 9.—26. 9. 41	Verfolgungskämpfe in der Schlacht bei Kiew
	6. 9.—15. 9. Schlacht bei Konotop; Romny und Lochwiza; Schliessung des Kessels von Kiew
	16. 9.—26. 9. Abwehrschlacht bei Romny
27. 9.—3. 10. 41	Doppelschlacht bei Wjasma und Brjansk
	Im einzelnen:
27. 9.—3. 10. 41	Schlacht bei Brjansk (Durchbruch auf Orel)
4. 10.—5. 12. 41	Vorstoss gegen Moskau und Woronesh
	Im einzelnen:
4. 10.—31. 10. 41	Vorstoss auf Tula
1. 11.—17. 11. 41	Kämpfe um Jefremow und Tula
18. 11.—5. 12. 41	Schlacht um Tula und Vorstoss auf Rjasan und Kaschira
5. 12.—4. 2. 42	Abwehrschlachten vor Moskau
	Im einzelnen:
6. 12.—20. 12. 41	Abwehrschlacht im Raum um Jefremow und Tula
21. 12.—25. 12. 41	Abwehrkämpfe an der Oka
26. 12.—2. 1. 42	Abwehrkämpfe nordwestl. Liwny
6. 1.—4. 2. 42	Abwehrschlacht bei Kursk
	6. 1.—25. 1. Abwehrkämpfe im Raum um Wypolsowa
	26. 1.—4. 2. Abwehrkämpfe nördl. Schtschigry

| 12. 1.— 17. 9. 43 | Feldzug gegen Russ... | 5. / Pz. |
| 18. 9.— 1. 10. 43 | Einsatz Ost | 2. / Pz. |

The partial list of battles in which Joachim participated until he was killed in Pekari on October 1, 1943. The Wehrpass and his personal toiletries were returned to his father as souvenirs two months later.

Joachim Dindinger
(Rufname, Familienname)

Nummer der Kennkarte

Nummer des Arbeitsbuches	Nummer der Erkennungsmarke (im Kriege)
447/01213	L/Kf. Ers. Abt. 3, Rathenow 5765

Bromberg, den 10. April 1940
(Dienststelle des Wehrbezirkskommandos) (Tag, Monat, Jahr)

I.V.

Hauptmann
(Unterschrift und Dienstgrad, Dienststellung)

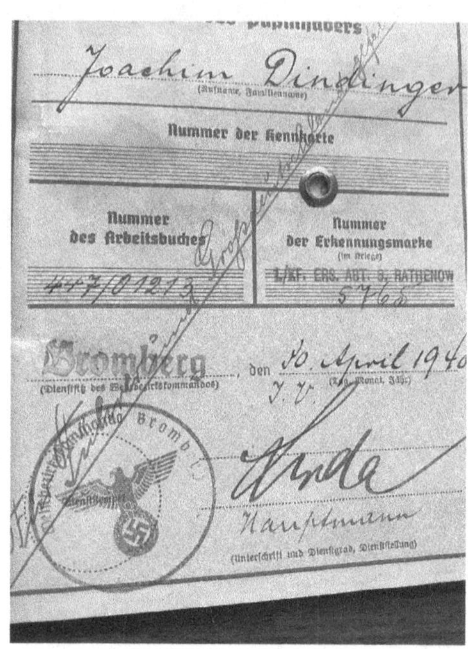

Wehrpass for Joachim with the red line and words saying he had fallen and died for the Führer and Greater Germany.

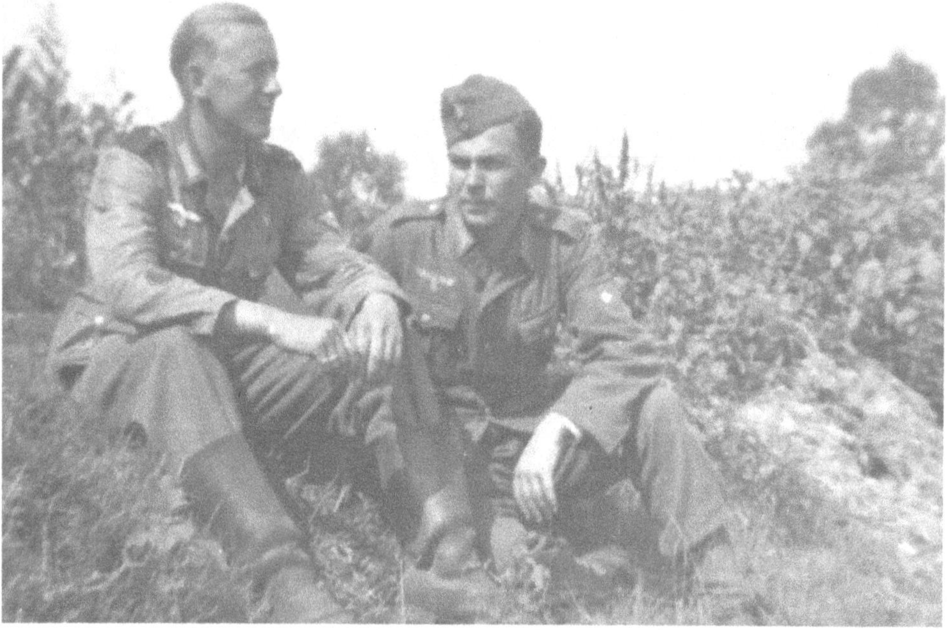

Joachim, right, and a Wehrmacht officer on a rare warm April day on the Eastern Front, 1942.

PART V

Heartbreak

CHAPTER TWENTY-SEVEN

HARDENED RESOLVE
(1944)

EUROPE WAS BLEEDING, AND THE wounds showed no signs of healing. Czechoslovakia remained a paradox within the Reich's tightening grip. The Czech Resistance grew bolder, forging stronger bonds with the British, even as the German occupation exposed its own contradictions: The Reich despised the Slavic population, yet permitted just enough leniency in its treatment of the occupied inhabitants to keep Czech factories running. Those plants had become a crucial artery in the German war machine, churning out aircraft, tanks, artillery, and myriad other armaments to feed the Reich's insatiable appetite for destruction.

Erika entered into this tense, shifting terrain when she arrived in Reichenberg, deep in the occupied Sudetenland, to continue her studies in chemical engineering. The timing was cruel: one door opening as another slammed shut.

The news about Joachim had reached Bromberg three weeks after his death, severing the family's last threads of hope when they hadn't heard from him. There were no ringing doorbells, no minister at the door—only silence, followed by letters returned to his family, stamped *gefallen*: killed in action.

Tatjana's world collapsed. The tears came like a flood. She had known, and yet the knowing did not soften the fall. Adi was carved hollow, the echo of his son's laughter replaced by unanswerable questions. Hellmuth's reply from Nordhausen—he had been transferred back there after Rommel's North Africa campaign officially ended in Axis defeat in May 1943—was stained with tears. Christa went quiet as her eighteenth birthday arrived without Joachim. The house that once held music and chatter became a sanctuary of grief.

Erika just burned with rage.

Joachim, her beloved brother—the confidant of childhood, the steady lodestar of her youth—was gone. The letters she so eagerly awaited, each a lifeline, would never arrive. No more requests for essential supplies. No more teasing questions about her exam results. His familiar sign-off, *Viele Grüße und Küsse*, had shifted from a promise into a farewell. She had read his last letter so many times, it seemed part of her. Now it lay folded in the bottom of a drawer she could not bring herself to open.

Weeks later, the commander's letter arrived in Bromberg. It offered no answers, only a portrait of Joachim's final moments: chosen, not suffered. *Joachim died a hero*—the commander wrote—*a Heldentod*.

The Panzer commanders called men like him *stille Helden*, "quiet heroes." US President Dwight Eisenhower would later say the grunts were the real heroes, for their unwavering endurance in all conditions. There were right and wrong sides of this war, but there were heroes on both sides.

But to Adi, Joachim had always been more than a hero. He was a light. Even as a boy, Joachim's moral compass had steadied the family, guiding them as protector, arbiter of fairness, defender in small skirmishes, and ally in innocent dreams. The soldier he became was still that son: compassionate, resolute, uncorrupted at his core.

Joachim had dreamed of peace beyond Hitler's cruel dominion. Now those dreams were buried in the blood-soaked soil of eastern Ukraine, along with a man who was more than a soldier: a son, a brother, a reminder of what remained pure. No stone would bear his name; no row of crosses would mark his place or that of his comrades. The field where he fell would remain unknown to his family—a void that could not be filled, a story without the solace of a grave.

As Erika began to experience the tumult of 1944, the shock of her brother's death hardened into something colder, more determined. Her sorrow became fury. Her grief became resolve. Joachim's legacy—his unyielding spirit, his protective love—would not fade. It would galvanize her.

Already deeply involved in the Resistance, long before the White Rose began distributing pamphlets in Munich, she now vowed to be an instrument of retribution, a quiet harbinger of justice. Amid the clamor of factories repurposed for conquest, Erika's intelligence and discipline became weapons against the oppressor. Every move was aimed at undermining the machine that had claimed her brother's life. She would fight on for him, because of him. Her work, she decided, would honor him not only in memory but in deed. She would honor Joachim not with tears but with action.

In Erika's makeshift lab in Reichenberg, beakers and glassware cast long shadows across a dimly lit bench. Fumes stung her nose as she added a final reagent; the solution bloomed a deep crimson that seemed to mock the blood spilled for the Führer's delusions. Her hands were steady—not from calm but from necessity.

Erika's scientific work carried bitter irony. Her expertise in propellants—knowledge she had hoped would serve humanity—was being fed into the maw of war. So, she fought a quiet duel with that perversion of science: When she could, she subverted yields, delayed results, misreported data. Notes that looked like progress for Berlin were, in truth, seeds for sabotage and intelligence for the Resistance. Each small sabotage was a silent refusal.

Hitler's regime—the force that had stolen Joachim—had lit a fire in Erika that could not be extinguished. She pored over schematics and formulae, mind whirring with calculations and possibilities. Each equation, each meticulously "successful" compound, was a step closer to striking at the Reich's heart.

Across the table, Stefan recorded their findings, brow furrowed. Joachim's best friend had become Erika's partner in this dangerous dance of defiance. Their eyes met, renewing the unspoken covenant that bound them. This was more than the usual Home Army or S.O.E. task. It was a vow born of love and loss.

Rumors darkened by the day. The rocket program—SS Werner von Braun's domain—haunted Erika. Reports filtered in of V-1s and V-2s: ballistic missiles lashing at the British across the English Channel. To Erika, von Braun's name, whispered with reverence and fear, was a reminder of science bent to cruelty. And beneath it all came the chill of nuclear talk—a horizon she prayed mankind would never cross.

From the Harz Mountains, Hellmuth's letters arrived in careful phrases and between-the-lines reports. After he had been reassigned near Nordhausen, he learned that underground tunnels had been carved into the Kohnstein in response to the August 1943 bombing of the secret rocket development center at Peenemünde. Hellmuth confirmed what Erika feared: The Reich's worst ambitions had not been slowed, only buried out of sight.

Few outside knew what lay beneath the forested slopes: Mittelbau-Dora, a subterranean hell where enslaved prisoners built rockets. On intermittent security detail, Hellmuth encountered skeletal men, the reek of unwashed bodies and chemical dust, the metallic cough echoing off stone: death made industrial. Each shift left him with less room to rationalize, less distance between duty and conscience.

He found ways to speak. During brief visits and in letters couched in family news, he passed along what information he could. Erika's Resistance cell was able to map logistics with new precision: rail routes, fuel blends, failure rates, launch rhythms. The information mattered for sabotage—and for bearing witness.

Hellmuth's disillusionment became quiet rebellion. He could not abandon his post, but he could refuse to stay silent. Erika listened carefully while reading between the lines of his letters and worked even later into each night, turning data into resistance. She did not know how history would bend. But for people like Erika, who risked everything to dismantle the Reich's machinery, the path was still clear. She would fight the looming darkness from within so that Joachim's sacrifice—and the sacrifice of so many—would not be in vain.

It was not science that betrayed humanity.

It was silence.

Tears stain the page of the letter Hellmuth sent from Nordhausen after learning of Joachim's death on October 1, 1943. News traveled slowly in those days. This letter, full of grief, is dated October 30, 1943.

CHAPTER TWENTY-EIGHT

ARREST (1944)

THE LOSS OF JOACHIM HAD cast a pall over the Dindinger family, an aching silence that hung in the air like a thick fog. Their routines became subdued, each day haunted by what horrors might come next. Tatjana, once the steady center of the family, now moved with a tension that never eased. Her face, formerly a canvas of warmth, was traced with lines of sorrow.

Yet even under the weight of grief, Tatjana pressed on. Her work with the Resistance deepened as she tried to help Fania escape Germany. Christa's piano lessons in Berlin had provided a convenient cover for her movements. Now, with Christa back in Bromberg, Tatjana met with others in back rooms and train compartments, where every glance might mean betrayal—especially in late 1944, when even the smallest freedoms had withered.

The Gestapo's reach felt closer every week. Letters had to be smuggled out of the country with extraordinary care, each one a fragile thread of hope for her sister's escape—and a potential death threat for herself.

Tatjana's mind never quieted. She rehearsed lies in case she was questioned, tracked safe drop points obsessively, reread coded letters by candlelight, and sought signs that plans might go awry. Göppingen—just thirty miles outside Stuttgart in the Württemberg region where Fania lived—had become a place of shadows. With each trip into town, each pause at a café, she scanned for watchers, informers. Familiar alleys now felt like traps; the friendly nod of a passerby might conceal a report to the authorities.

But the ever-present fear of discovery did not dictate her steps. The mission was too urgent, too personal.

One morning, she walked briskly through the early Göppingen mists, a letter tucked into the lining of her coat. It was more than mere paper and ink; it was Fania's last chance at freedom in Palestine.

Tatjana's visits to her sister had been cloaked in secrecy. She knew the Nazis' stranglehold was tightening. Arrests were happening closer to home. But still, she moved forward—not with naïveté but with the grim courage of someone who had already lost too much to stop now.

As Tatjana rounded the corner, her heart leaped into her throat. Two men in crisp uniforms stood outside the bakery, their eyes scanning the street with hawkish intensity. Her steps faltered for half a second, but she forced herself to maintain a casual stride, her mind racing for a plausible excuse should they question her.

But the men paid her no heed. She passed them without so much as a glance, slipped the letter into the hollowed-out space beneath the bakery's windowsill, and kept walking. A wave of relief washed over her, followed quickly by the thrum of strategy. What now, and how soon?

She didn't see the black sedan.

Just a few blocks later, it pulled up fast and close. Before Tatjana could react, the door flew open and she was yanked inside. The world narrowed to the slamming shut of the car door.

The ride was a blur, a whirlwind of shouted questions and accusations, punctuated by the sting of sharp blows to her head. In the face of such terror, Tatjana drew upon an inner well of strength—her love for her family, her commitment to the Resistance—to bolster her through the ordeal. Tatjana remained silent, her bloodied lips pressed into a thin line, her eyes defiant even as her flesh bruised and swelled. Silence was all she had left to give.

It wasn't until she was dragged into the stark interrogation room that the reality of her situation settled in. The Gestapo officer loomed over her, his face twisted into a sneer as he brandished her letter.

"So, Frau Dindinger," he hissed, his voice dripping with contempt. "You really thought you could get away with this? Aiding and abetting the escape of a traitorous Jew from Württemberg?"

Tatjana said nothing, her gaze unwavering.

"We'll see how long the silent act lasts," he snarled, motioning for the guards to take her.

As they dragged her away, her body slumped slightly from pain and fatigue. But her resolve did not falter. She thought of Christa. Of Fania. Of Erika. Of Adi and Hellmuth. Of the tiny hope stitched inside every secret message she'd risked delivering. She didn't know if it would be enough to help change the path of this war. But if her suffering brought them one more day of freedom, it would have to be.

When Tatjana did not return from Württemberg as expected, the Dindinger home became a crucible of anxiety. Adi, haunted by foreboding, moved like a specter through the rooms where her absence was felt most acutely. He kept running his fingers through his hair in a gesture of deep unease. Each glance out the window was a search for the familiar silhouette of his wife, each moment without sight of her a further descent into catastrophe. The home that once resonated with the warmth of family now echoed with the silence of waiting—and the cold dread of the unknown.

"She should be back by now," Adi murmured, more to himself than to Christa, who was curled up on the couch, the worn threads of an old blanket slipping through her anxious fingers.

Christa swallowed hard, her throat constricting with the fear she tried so desperately to push down. She was trying to write music, but the melodies fell apart mid-phrase, collapsing into silence. "Maybe she got held up," she offered, her voice small and unconvincing.

Adi shook his head slowly, his jaw clenched. "No, something's wrong. I can feel it," he declared, cursing the intuition that came with nearly three decades of love and marriage.

When the clock struck the hour, its chime rang too loudly in the stillness, jarring them both. Adi resumed his pacing, each step a somber cadence in the growing symphony of dread.

Christa abandoned her composition, her hands trembling as she clutched the blanket tighter around her shoulders. She watched her father trace the same path over and over again—first the window, then the far wall, then back again. The room had shrunk to the radius of his worry.

As they waited, one hour became two and then three. Outside, the night stretched on, endless and unforgiving. Inside, the air thickened with fear, with all the terrible shapes their imaginations could make from her absence.

The deafening silence was shattered by a pounding at the door, the sound reverberating through the home like a gunshot. Adi froze. Christa turned to him, her face already drained of color.

Adi moved toward the door with leaden steps, his body refusing to believe what his mind had already guessed. He pressed on until his trembling hand closed around the doorknob as he drew a shuddering breath.

The door swung open to reveal two Gestapo officers, their expressions grim and uncompromising. Without preamble, they brushed past Adi, their boots thudding heavily on the hardwood floor.

"Adolf Dindinger?" one of them barked, his eyes sweeping over the room with a scrutinizing gaze. The question was less a query than a declaration.

Adi nodded mutely, his mouth dry with dread.

The officer fixed him with a cold stare. "Your wife, Tatjana Dindinger, has been arrested for associating with the Israelite community and facilitating unauthorized departure from the Reich."

The words hit Adi like a physical blow, stealing the breath from his lungs. He reeled, groping blindly for something to steady himself as the room spun around him.

Christa let out a strangled cry, her hands flying to her mouth in horror.

Tears sprang to her eyes, spilling down her cheeks in torrents as she shook her head in disbelief.

The officer's expression remained impassive as he continued, his voice devoid of emotion. "She has been charged with treason against the Reich and will be deported to KZ-Lager Bergen-Belsen for further processing. You and your daughter are advised to remain in your home. Do not interfere."

Then they left, their boots retreating down the hallway in a staccato rhythm, leaving behind a silence that was all at once a void and a scream.

The door clicked shut behind them, and Adi leaned against it, the wood cool under his palms. Unable to breathe, he turned to Christa. She was crying harder now, tears sliding down her cheeks. She didn't speak. Adi felt the world tilting on its axis as the officer's words crashed over him again and again: *deported to Bergen-Belsen.*

Tatjana. His Tatjana. Deported to a concentration camp. The mere thought was inconceivable, a nightmare from which he longed to awaken, but the grim reality stared him in the face. His world, already reeling from the loss of Joachim, now seemed to crumble into dust.

Adi's knees buckled, and he sank to the floor, the carpet scratching against his hands. The home they'd built, once brimming with music and laughter, was filled with heartbreak now.

Christa knelt beside him, her arms wrapping around him in a futile attempt to ward off their new reality. He barely felt her touch. They stayed like that—father and daughter—frozen in the space left behind.

Tatjana was gone. Not just gone—taken. Again. And there was nothing Adi could do.

His mind reeled, grasping for the shape of what should come next. He tried to imagine the future and found nothing—just gray, as far as he could see. Their lives, once tethered to the warmth of music, meals, and shared days, had been severed in a single knock.

Finally, his daughter's grief, small and sharp, broke through his own. He felt Christa trembling and pulled her closer. He couldn't reach Tatjana, but he would not lose his daughter too. He would not let the cruelty that had stolen his wife take the rest of them.

Not without resistance.

Adi stayed kneeling on the floor, one hand still pressed to the rug, breathing through the pain. And when he finally stood, it was not because the grief had passed. It was because it hadn't—and he'd decided to carry it forward as resolve.

CHAPTER TWENTY-NINE

CAPTURE (1945)

IT WAS GRADUATION DAY—APRIL 18, 1945—and the auditorium was a galaxy of academic stars. Erika, dressed in the ceremonial garb that symbolized the passage from student to scholar, could almost hear the rustling of her mother's dress, the gentle clearing of her brother's throat—as if they were there beside her, witnessing the fruition of her odyssey.

The gown felt heavy on her shoulders, as though it carried more than fabric, more than academic achievement. It bore the memory of those who could not be there—her mother, her brother—and the quiet vow she'd made not to let their absences become erasure. She would carry what they had taught her: knowledge, compassion, precision, purpose.

The world outside teetered precariously, as if at any moment it might plunge into the abyss of its own violent creation. Adding to the grim shadow cast by war, Franklin D. Roosevelt had died not a week earlier. The steady voice of the American president had gone silent just as the final acts of war were accelerating across Europe.

But even as chaos and grief pressed inward, something inside Erika had solidified. Her mother was gone and her brother lost, their lives ripped away by the machinery of cruelty. Yet there could be no surrender to despair. Erika would not allow their sacrifices to be consumed by silence.

At Reichenberg, she had thrown herself into her studies with a fervor that bordered on obsession. The lab became her refuge, a space where the cold logic of chemistry offered structure—even sanity. Day bled into night as she pored over data, her notebooks dense with scribbled formulae and half-formed insights. The rhythmic click of glassware, the hum of fume hoods, the smell of acetone and iron filings—these were constants she could hold when nothing else made sense.

Her research was meticulous. Each solved equation, each successful trial, felt like clawing back a fragment of meaning. There were setbacks—compounds that degraded, measurements that refused to align—but Erika met them with a stubborn, almost desperate persistence. If she could not change the war, she would outwit it, molecule by molecule.

She still heard her mother's voice in her mind, clipped and steady: *To yield is to wither.* It was a rallying cry, a quiet rhythm, a beat that kept Erika moving forward. She'd whispered it while cleaning beakers, mouthed it over and over while solving an equation. Those words weren't lofty. They were practical. They reminded her that movement was life.

There were moments when her brother returned to her. Not in ghostly visions but in memory—the way he held his breath when reading something complicated, the way his brow furrowed when he was trying not to laugh. She saw him in the swirls of a reaction turning clear and in the soft blue flame of a Bunsen burner catching just right. Those moments hurt, but they anchored her in purpose.

And where would she be without her other anchor—her beloved Stefan? Erika scanned the crowd for him, her gaze piercing the sea of faces until she found him standing near the back—smiling, steady, proud. Stefan, her fiancé, her confidant, who had been by her side through every late night, every collapse into doubt, every improbable breakthrough.

This graduation day wasn't an ending. It was the moment between what had been and what might be. Her heart lifted, but there was a catch in her throat too. The hardest trials were still ahead.

As the ceremony began, Erika's mind drifted back to the lab—to the crackling hush of candlelight over a scrawled notebook, the acrid tang of solvents on her hands. She could still feel the sleepless nights in her bones . . . still remember the thrill when a line of numbers resolved into something elegant . . . still hear Stefan's voice coaxing her away from her desk when she'd forgotten to eat.

It had taken so many hours, so many weeks, so many private reckonings with fear and failure. And now, it was here: this singular moment.

One by one, the names resounded across the vast auditorium, each met with applause. Erika sat still, her palms damp, her heart thudding in her chest.

"Erika Dindinger."

She rose, her legs trembling ever so slightly, and made her way toward the stage. As she ascended, the applause was not merely for her but for the indomitable will of all who had walked the razor's edge of peril to emerge into the realm of possibilities. The doctoral hood was draped across her shoulders, cloaking her in a profound sense of accomplishment—not merely a personal triumph but a victory for all those who dared to dream.

Approaching the podium, Erika let her eyes travel across the room. So many faces: some strangers, some friends. She wouldn't see her mother or Joachim, but she imagined them anyway. She would speak to the role she now held but also to the path she had taken to get there and what it had cost.

"Ladies and gentlemen, distinguished guests, and fellow graduates," Erika began, her words cutting through the stillness, resonant and clear. "This isn't the kind of journey measured by semesters or syllabi. It's shaped by the things we carry and by the things we've lost."

She paused, letting the silence settle. There was no need for grand metaphors or calls to arms. The weight of the moment was enough.

"We stand here today not only as scholars but also as survivors of a world still unraveling," she continued. "We are not untouched by war. We are shaped by it. And still, we choose to learn. To build. To believe there is something worth building."

Nearing the end, she allowed herself to push forward the truth, in a mosaic of memory and hope.

"I carry with me the memory of those who could not be here," she announced. "Their absence lives in everything that I do. I hope I've honored them today."

A standing ovation greeted her closing words, a chorus of hands that spoke of recognition and respect.

"We stand at the confluence of past and future, at a point where our actions define us not just as graduates but also as custodians of the world we inherit," she finished. "We are the architects of tomorrow, and within our minds lies the potential to build a future illuminated by the light of knowledge and human decency."

The very next day—April 19, 1945—they were waiting for her.

Gestapo.

Erika saw their dark silhouettes first, under the streetlamp near the old tram depot: two men with broad shoulders and dark coats, standing too still. Even before her mind caught up, her body knew.

The documents under her coat suddenly felt enormous, heavy against her ribs. She couldn't breathe, couldn't think. She'd been so careful. Every meeting was planned, every exit mapped, every lie rehearsed. Still, they had found her.

Stefan was in the apartment, waiting for her. She had to warn him. But how?

In the half second before they noticed her, she turned and ran.

The deserted alleys whispered threats—every shadow concealing the enemy, every sound signaling treachery. The secrets she clutched beneath her coat could become damning evidence.

She sprinted back the way she had come, feet pounding the cobblestones. She had come close to exposure during her involvement in the White Rose a few years earlier. Now she was far more deeply embedded in the Resistance. The thought of betraying the cause, of allowing the sacrifices of so many to be in vain, was unthinkable.

The night erupted with shouts. Erika's lungs burned, and her muscles screamed, but still she pushed forward. A narrow gap between two build-ings—just wide enough—offered a sliver of hope. She slipped through it, into a dim courtyard where shadows granted a brief reprieve. Her chest heaved; her heart hammered.

The commotion closed in. A gunshot cracked behind her. She stumbled but kept moving, driven by fear and the raw refusal to give in. To be caught now wasn't just *her* end—it was the end of everything.

She thought of Stefan, alone in the apartment—of the coded messages, the quiet handoffs, and the lies stacked so high, they felt like a second lan-guage. There would be no way to explain.

So she kept running.

The shadows shifted, and suddenly they were upon her like a pack of wolves, jackboots crunching the cobbles. Her resolve dipped for a breath as the full weight of the moment crashed down. The documents—her shield and sword—lay trampled in the courtyard mud.

She struggled. It was useless.

Cold metal snapped around her wrists. Orders were barked. The court-yard spun as they dragged her up. Her shoulder ached. She stayed upright.

One officer yanked her close. "You think you're clever?" he hissed. "We'll see how long that lasts."

She met his eyes and said nothing, thinking, *Don't give them anything.*

A shove. She stumbled, caught herself. Faces flickered in windows above—some afraid, some fascinated.

With another violent push, Erika was thrown into the back of the truck. Thoughts careened: *Papa . . . Christa . . .* Would her arrest tell them anything of Tatjana's fate—or only repeat it? She thought of Hellmuth, of Joachim— not his voice, but the steadiness in his eyes when she was afraid.

Then, as the truck rumbled to life, Erika sat up straighter. She would face whatever lay ahead with the same unwavering resolve that had defined her brother.

CHAPTER THIRTY

KEEPING HOPE ALIVE (1945)

THE MOURNFUL STRAINS OF TCHAIKOVSKY'S Violin Concerto drifted through the quiet halls of the Dindinger home, a haunting melody giving voice to the depths of human sorrow. Christa paused in the entryway, her breath catching in her throat as the familiar notes washed over her, each one a poignant reminder of the anguish that had engulfed their family.

Adi sat hunched over his violin, body tense, eyes closed. His fingers moved with practiced precision, but his face betrayed the effort it took to contain his sorrow. The loss of his beloved Joachim had devastated him. The arrest of Tatjana threatened to consume him entirely.

The news of Erika's capture had yet to reach them in Bromberg. But already, in the months since Tatjana's arrest, Adi had retreated into a shell of silent grief, his once-vibrant spirit dimmed by these crushing losses. No words could soothe the ache in his soul. But in the plaintive notes of the Andante, he found a language that transcended speech, a way to give voice to the depths of his sorrow.

As Christa watched her father pour his heart into the music, her own pain threatened to overwhelm her. Tears streamed down her cheeks, and her body trembled with a force of emotions she could no longer contain. The melody spoke to her very core, resonating with a truth that was both achingly beautiful and utterly devastating. The violin's voice was crying the tears Papa could not shed.

The final strains of the Andante faded into silence. Adi slowly lowered his violin, his shoulders slumped as if the weight of the world had finally become too much to bear. Christa stepped forward and wrapped her arms around him.

"Play with me, Christa," Adi said softly, his voice steady though his eyes were rimmed with tears. "They loved to hear us play together."

And so they played. Not a performance, not a rehearsal—just a conversation in music, a father and daughter stitching something back together, however temporarily, through shared sound. The voices of the violin and the piano wound through the house like breath, overlapping and parting.

When they finished, their eyes locked. Christa saw the raw anguish reflected in her father's eyes, a pain so deep that it threatened to swallow them both whole. But there was something else there, too, something quieter: the steadiness that had kept him upright through each unimaginable loss.

"Do you remember," Adi began, struggling with emotion, "your first recital at the conservatory?"

Christa's smile was faint. Adi's recollection conjured a time when their world was whole, when music was a celebration rather than a lament. "How could I forget?" she replied. "I was so nervous. But the moment my fingers touched the keys, it was like I became someone else entirely."

Adi nodded, his gaze distant as he recalled the scene. "The entire audience was spellbound. Your mother and I were bursting with pride, watching you share that precious gift."

"That was before everything changed," she said sadly.

His voice gentled. "Yet you're still that same girl, Tita. The one who could stop a room cold with a few bars of Brahms. You haven't lost her."

Christa's mind drifted back to the night of that first recital—to the feeling of pure joy as she played, lost in the magic she was creating. "Will we ever be that happy again, Papa?"

Adi didn't answer right away. His hands, warm and seasoned from the strings of labor and love, enveloped her colder ones. "Happiness, Tita, is like the music you played—it's not a place to arrive at but a melody to be played, a series of notes to be strung together across the days."

He drew a breath as if to pull strength from the air around them. His next words carried the weight of a promise.

"We will find our way back to joy, piece by piece, note by note."

Christa's eyes teared as she thought of their beloved Joachim. "He was the purest melody of us all, wasn't he?" she said, with a ghost of a smile.

Adi closed his eyes briefly. "He taught us how to live. That was his gift."

Christa nodded, a tear escaping. "And Mama . . . I pray that she'll come back to us, that they haven't . . ." Her words were cut off by a quiet sob. They didn't talk about what might have happened to Tatjana. It hurt too much, gave too much shape to the fear.

"Your mother is the strongest woman I have ever known," Adi murmured. "She faces adversity with a courage and grace that humble even the bravest of souls. If anyone can make it through whatever hell she's had to face, she can."

He pulled Christa close, his embrace a shelter from the storm of dread that threatened to overwhelm them both. He could feel the tension in her slender frame, the silent anguish that had become an all too familiar companion in the wake of Tatjana's arrest.

"So we must keep hope alive—for her, for all of us," he said with conviction. "Your mother's spirit, like ours, isn't easily dimmed. We must trust in her strength and love. That has always been the core of our family."

"She's always been the glue that holds us together," Christa whispered, her voice trembling. "Without her, we're . . . scattered."

Adi's hand smoothed her hair. "Then we must remember how she did it. And we hold the line until she comes home."

Christa allowed her mind to drift back to the countless moments they had shared as a family, the laughter and warmth that had once filled their home. "Do you remember how she used to sing to us when we were little? At night. Always the same songs," Christa said, her voice saturated with nostalgia. "Those lullabies were like magic, bringing light to the shadows."

Adi closed his eyes and smiled. "Ah, yes. And that one refrain, which made no sense, but you all loved it anyway . . ."

"It chased the dark away," Christa whispered. "Every time."

She looked up, and in her eyes was something deeper than grief—a flicker of the strength Tatjana had planted in all of them. It was a strength that, somehow, endured.

"We have to believe she is still out there, Papa," Christa whispered, "fighting to find her way back to us."

Adi nodded. "And we'll do everything in our power to bring her home. No matter how long it takes."

In that moment, neither of them doubted it. Hope wasn't just a feeling—it was a tether, thin but unbroken. In that dim room, their belief in Tatjana's return made the dawn seem possible again.

In late April 1945, however, news of Erika's arrest threatened to shatter what little remained intact. Joachim was gone. Hellmuth was still battling malaria, making his whereabouts difficult to track. And now, in the war's final stretch, Erika had been ripped from them too. The storm of war had swept away another one of Adi's children.

Day after day, he and Christa sat in silence, the house too quiet. Even the walls seemed to absorb their grief. Adi bore the weight of a father's powerlessness, of losing the future they had all fought for.

One day, a sharp rap at the door made them both start. Adi stood quickly, his heart pounding in his chest. Were they coming for Christa next? But it wasn't the Gestapo.

It was Stefan.

He looked pale, drawn. The collar of his coat was damp with sweat and rain. "I heard . . . I heard something about Erika," he said quietly.

Christa held her breath.

"She didn't go easily," Stefan continued, his voice catching. "I was told it took four of them. She fought until the cuffs were on, even as they beat her."

Adi shuddered, then rested a hand on Stefan's shoulder. "You didn't see it happen?"

"No. And I don't know what information they may have found on her. But I haven't heard of anyone else being taken. Not yet," Stefan insisted. "Erika won't break. She's stronger than they are."

"How could they . . ." Adi's voice was cracked and raw. He raked a trembling hand through his hair, a gesture of helpless frustration. "She's just a girl. What threat could she have been?"

Christa's voice was barely audible. "She thought too much. She challenged. And she hated Hitler. She wouldn't stay silent." The tears on her face marked the map of their family's dissolution. Their family would never be whole again—not without Joachim, without Eka, without Tatjana.

Adi looked at her, then away. His hands curled at his sides. "But she has the fire of our family in her. They can't extinguish it."

Christa fell into her father's embrace, drawing strength from his unwavering optimism. "I miss her so much, Papa. I miss them all."

Adi pressed a kiss on the top of her head. "But we have to believe we will see them again. It's all we can do." His grip on her tightened with both gratitude and grief. "She has the heart of a lion. We have to believe it's enough."

Christa nodded. "She's out there fighting," she finally said. "We have to fight too. And survive."

Stefan's jaw clenched. "Survive . . . that's what we must do. Eka won't give up. Neither did Joachim. And neither will Tatjana. We must keep going, however we can."

The room was still, the silence weighted with the effort of holding hope aloft.

"And Hellmuth?" Adi murmured then.

Stefan shook his head. "Still no word. But he's resourceful. He's been through worse than most. We must not lose hope."

For a long moment, none of them moved. They stood in the hush of a fractured home, stitched together by what remained—loyalty, love, memory. And a hope that they wouldn't let go.

Because the war would end. The Allies were approaching, bringing with them a path to liberation. And the ones who survived would need someone waiting on the other side.

CHAPTER THIRTY-ONE

REMEMBERING HOW TO HEAL (1945)

TATJANA LAY HALF-CONSCIOUS ON A bed in the Bergen-Belsen infirmary. She didn't remember the name of the girl who'd cleaned her face with warm water or the boy who'd brought her broth in a chipped tin cup. But she remembered the way they'd looked at her—not with pity but with something close to recognition. For the first time in years, she felt hope. It was even stronger than medicine.

Drifting between fever dreams and memory, she saw Adi—his face, his hands—and remembered the shape of his embrace. She imagined Hellmuth as she'd last seen him: eyes bright, talking too fast. Erika and Christa came next—smiling, running, chasing one another around the kitchen table—and finally Joachim. These weren't visions of the future. They were pieces of a past she needed to touch again. Clutching them in her mind helped her hold on.

It was not strength, exactly. More like refusal.

In the first five days after the camp was liberated, medical help had arrived too slowly. There were too few doctors, too little medicine, and no real infrastructure. The surviving prisoners were given army rations—canned meat, chocolate, condensed milk—that their weakened bodies couldn't handle. Malnourished for so long, thousands collapsed from digestive failure—from the well-meant food and the lack of immediate care.

It was Heinrich Himmler who had unlocked the gates of Bergen-Belsen on April 15, 1945—not out of conscience but with calculation. British forces had pushed through the Western Front, crossing the Rhine and pressing toward a concentration camp that few outside Germany had ever heard of: Bergen-Belsen. As the Red Army advanced on Berlin from the east, Himmler offered the camp to the British under the guise of humanitarian concern. He claimed that typhus, a disease that had claimed millions of German lives in Russia during the First World War, was rampant within the camp. But the truth was far colder: Himmler hoped to leverage the gesture in peace negotiations, even as Germany collapsed around him.

After a German truce party crossed enemy lines and requested a limited ceasefire, the British took control of the camp—a pragmatic solution that overrode the complete and unconditional surrender demanded by the Allies. When the British 11th Armoured Division entered Bergen-Belsen, what they found defied comprehension.

When the soldiers came, Tatjana was clinging to the cold metal bars of the entrance gate, her fingers thin and stiff from hunger and cold. She was unrecognizable from the woman she had been. Her hair, once golden and full, hung in damp clumps around her face. Her skin had gone waxen, stretched thin over sharp bones. Her clothes were little more than shredded cloth.

Her eyes—those bright, curious eyes Adi had always loved—were now hollow, as if sight itself had become too much to bear. Squinting into the distance, Tatjana was just barely able to make out the line of British soldiers, their uniforms incongruously clean against the mud and filth of Bergen-Belsen.

Around her, the prisoners—sick, skeletal, barely upright—began to stir. They swayed as if caught in a silent rhythm, their eyes fixed ahead, afraid to believe. A ripple moved through the crowd—first a murmur, then a rustle of breath, as if the camp itself had exhaled. Could it be true?

Tatjana pressed her face closer to the gate, her chest heaving. Her heart pounded beneath her ribs, sharp and painful in its urgency. She didn't trust her own eyes. The rumors had come and gone before. Was this another cruel illusion?

Then someone whispered, voice rising from the depths of a collective purgatory, cracking from disuse: "Sie sind gekommen."

"They have come."

Tatjana's throat closed around the words she couldn't speak. Tears welled, stinging her dry eyes.

As the soldiers drew closer, their faces came into focus. Some looked straight ahead with grim determination, but most wore unmistakable expressions of disbelief and dawning horror. Tatjana searched their eyes for something she couldn't name. Maybe it was humanity. Maybe it was mercy.

As the gates of Bergen-Belsen creaked open, the soldiers stepped into a nightmare that no one had prepared them for. The air hit them first— thick with rot and something worse, a sourness that clung to the back of the throat and refused to let go. Then the gate gave way with a groan, and for a moment, no one moved. Then the current surged, like the parting of the Red Sea.

The survivors, if they could be called that, began to move toward the soldiers—staggering shadows of humanity, their limbs barely holding them upright, their ribs visible through tattered clothes. A low, guttural moan rose through the crowd. It wasn't language—it was pain, grief, something primal.

Corpses lay in the open, twisted and skeletal, their eyes frozen wide in silent testimony. One soldier turned away and vomited, his body rejecting what his mind could not yet process. Another dropped to his knees, sobbing and shaking, his helmet slipping from his head into the mud. Behind him, others stood stunned, silent, covering their faces with a sleeve, unable to speak or move.

Even as the soldiers faltered, the prisoners pressed forward, reaching out with trembling hands, touching their sleeves, gripping their jackets. They had no strength for asking questions. They just needed contact—proof that help had come, that the soldiers understood the magnitude of what they were seeing, that the world beyond the barbed wire still existed.

The soldiers held steady for a moment—frozen, stupefied. Then they wiped their faces, straightened their shoulders, and forced themselves forward. Through the stench and the shock and the rising panic, they walked deeper into the camp as witnesses, as lifelines.

The prisoners poured forward, stumbling through the opening like floodwater breaching a broken dam. Tatjana stumbled with them.

All around her, prisoners surged ahead, not with strength but with instinct. Starved bodies brushed against one another, skeletal hands reaching for water, a hand, a face—anything that might mean help had come. Each step Tatjana took seemed pulled from some reserve of strength far beyond what her frail body should have allowed. And yet she moved.

Then her legs gave out and the world tilted, but strong arms caught her before she hit the ground. A soldier held her upright. His face swam into view, pale and stricken.

"You're safe now," he said softly.

The words didn't register at first. When they did, Tatjana's body began to shake. She clutched at his sleeve and wept uncontrollably, her body wracked with waves of catharsis and ineffable gratitude.

Around her, others did the same. Some collapsed to their knees. Some shouted. Some simply stood still, unable to move at all. All sought comfort in the embrace of their saviors, their cries ebbing between chords of joyous relief and the somber dirges of remembrance.

In the soldier's arms, Tatjana felt herself begin to return—to her body, to the earth, to the fragile possibility of life beyond this. She didn't know what would come next. But for the first time in years, she believed something might. Her spirits lifted in concert with the surge of humanity around her.

The British troops, though prepared for hardship, found themselves entirely unready for what Bergen-Belsen had become. Corpses were everywhere. Some had been dead for days, others weeks. A few were so withered, it was hard to believe they had ever been alive. Others were bloated, their skin stretched by decay. The soldiers stepped around them in silence—unable to look, unable to look away.

They had come ready to fight. But there was no enemy here—only the aftermath of one.

They had read the briefings. They had seen what the Nazis had done in France, in Belgium, in Poland. But for these battle-hardened liberators, knowledge and understanding were two very different things. No prior confrontation with death had prepared them for the scale of this extinction of life. They had come face to face with the enemy on open fields, but here lay evidence of a concealed war—a massacre executed on noncombatants with chilling precision. Here there was no gunfire, no uniforms. Just silence, broken by the shuffling feet and the quiet cries of people too weak to scream.

Yet somehow, in the middle of it all, people clung to life. Men, women, and children who had survived months, even years, of starvation and disease still tried to stand when help arrived. Their survival wasn't symbolic—it was something simpler and harder: breath after breath.

Though tens of thousands still lived, there were nearly as many corpses. The camp reeked of sickness and rot, and each day brought hundreds more deaths, even after liberation. Tatjana, lying curled on a straw mat inside one of the huts, barely conscious and too weak to move, was almost one of them.

Her face was sunken, her eyes dulled by fever. She didn't speak. She hardly stirred. Typhus and dysentery had reduced her to rubble. But she still held on. When a soldier passed by and knelt beside her, she turned her head. That flicker of life still burned within her, a defiant spark that refused to be snuffed out by all the misery. Even in this state, Tatjana still held something deep within: the faint echo of a will that hadn't been broken.

Then the medical students came, ninety-five of them, young, tired, and fresh out of London—some had never treated a patient before. But they rolled up their sleeves and moved with urgency, not panic. They took vitals. They cleaned wounds. They lifted bodies gently from soiled bedding and laid down fresh straw. They spoke softly, and they stayed.

The air began to clear, not only of the stench of death but of the intangible miasma of despair. The introduction of DDT and industrial disinfectants was swift and thorough, a revelation to both the survivors and their caretakers. Bathing stalls were erected among the ruined barracks, and the daily routine of delousing began. The clouds of DDT clung to skin, clothing, bedding—everything—and the visible drop in typhus cases made the dust feel like a small miracle. Few understood the chemical's risks. What mattered was survival.

Tatjana was moved to the infirmary. Each day, she grew a little stronger. Her limbs trembled, but they moved. The cramps in her stomach began to ease. She no longer gagged at the smell of warm broth or backed away from food she didn't recognize. Meals that once left her doubled over now passed through her organs with less violence. Her body, battered as it was, began to remember how to heal.

As her strength returned, so too did her sense of the world around her: the changing rhythms of the infirmary ward, the quiet pulse of something like order reasserting itself, the occasional echo of laughter.

The death toll, once a steady and numbing count, began to slow. Fewer cots were stripped bare in the mornings. The lines at the infirmary shortened. The students—still exhausted, still underequipped—began to look more assured. Their hands steadied. Their voices calmed. With each recovered patient, something shifted in the air: not joy, exactly, but less fear.

Amid this fragile rhythm of survival, something unexpected arrived. It was just a box—plain, wooden, unmarked. Not bandages or gauze. Not food or medicine. The soldiers eyed it with suspicion, muttering that someone in London must be out of touch with reality. What use was luxury here?

But when the box was opened, it silenced the yard. Inside were dozens of tubes of lipstick: bright reds, coral pinks, deep wines. Cheap brands, mostly. But new. Unused. Clean.

The soldiers shook their heads. The medics exchanged glances, bewildered. What could possibly matter less than cosmetics in a place where teeth were falling out and fevers burned through the night? But the women understood.

No one said a word. One by one, those who could stand stepped forward. Those who couldn't propped themselves up. Some hands shook so badly, they could barely twist the caps open. But still they tried.

A woman with missing teeth applied a crooked swipe of crimson to her mouth and smiled for the first time in weeks. Another passed a tube to the woman next to her, nodding silently. There was laughter, but it came softly, as if they were afraid of breaking the spell. It wasn't just makeup. It was memory. It was defiance. It was a thread connecting past and future, reminding them that there had been beauty once—and might be again.

Tatjana watched from her cot, still too weak to rise. But someone passed her a tube—a dull red—and she held it in her hand like a relic, turning it over, watching the light hit the smooth casing.

Applying the lipstick became a stroke of rebellion, a touch of normalcy, a whisper of days gone by and a promise of the days to come. It wasn't vanity or even comfort. It was a reminder that her body was hers. That she could still choose to mark it. And that, somehow, was enough.

In her mind's eye, she imagined Adi's grin. Joachim's unwavering affection. Hellmuth's pride. Erika and Christa laughing as they passed a mirror, experimenting with colors. She held on to those faces like lifelines. That small gesture—applying lipstick—felt like a message to them all: *I haven't disappeared.*

After weeks of intensive medical care, Tatjana was deemed strong enough to travel. The Red Cross was working to reunite her with her family, to inform them that Tatjana was alive. And finally one morning, the hospital doors opened and Tatjana stepped into sunlight.

She was thinner than she'd ever been. Her body still throbbed with pain, and her hair had become brittle. But she stood upright. She was leaving Bergen-Belsen. She had survived.

Each breath that Tatjana took felt like a miracle. But she wasn't walking away from the camp empty-handed. She was holding the knowledge of what had happened, and the memory of lives that hadn't made it out.

As she climbed into the Red Cross transport, she didn't look back. She closed her eyes and carried her family forward with her, a prayer she held in her chest like a second heartbeat.

Adi—her constant, her pillar of strength. Where was he now? Had he and Christa made it through? Had he found a way to protect their children from the storm that had swept across everything they once called home?

She pictured Hellmuth, always moving too fast for the world around him. Was he still chasing his ambitions? Or had the war and malaria taken that future away?

And Erika—brave, indomitable Erika, who refused to bend even when it would have been safer to do so. Had her defiance saved her, or had the Nazis destroyed her?

Were they alive? Tatjana didn't know. The road unspooled before her, uncertain and long. She was thin. She was aching. She was alone and uncertain.

But she was alive.

PART VI

New Beginnings

CHAPTER THIRTY-TWO

THE WILL TO GO ON (1945)

WEEKS HAD PASSED, AND STILL there was no news of Erika. Adi, Christa, and Stefan chased every lead they could find—through the Home Army, the British, even the Czech Resistance—but each attempt came up empty.

The timing of Erika's capture was a bitter irony. On the very day she was taken in Reichenberg—April 19, 1945—General George Patton of the US Army crossed into Czechoslovakia, his sights set on liberating Prague. Orders from the US High Command turned him around. Had the war's course shifted, Erika might have met liberators—and a nation might have sidestepped decades of communist rule.

On May 5, a national uprising ignited in Prague. On May 8, Nazi Germany surrendered unconditionally. Soviet troops arrived on May 9.

Still there was no news about Erika.

Stefan tried to keep moving, as if action might stave off the rising dread in his chest. But it didn't. Erika's absence gnawed at him. Sleep brought no rest, only images of her face—the way she furrowed her brow when deep in thought, the stubborn set of her jaw. If he sat still long enough, he could still hear her laugh.

As the war lurched to its bitter end, the Sudetenland morphed into a cauldron of vengeance. Overnight, the Czech Revolutionary Guards transformed from resistance heroes to oppressors. Within weeks, they began sweeping through towns and villages, rounding up ethnic Germans with blunt, indiscriminate force. It didn't matter what they had done during the occupation. Bloodline was enough to condemn them.

In Brno, Stefan witnessed a scene he couldn't forget: A woman stood screaming in front of her home while a mob beat her husband to death on their doorstep. Their teenage son lunged to protect him, only to be knocked unconscious. No one intervened—no one dared.

The guards weren't alone in their violence. Ordinary Czechs, fueled by years of anger and the rhetoric of opportunistic politicians, joined in. Some seemed to revel in it. It was chaos posing as justice.

Stefan avoided eye contact in the streets and kept his papers close at hand. He found himself wondering what counted as guilt now. Survival? Silence? Speaking the wrong language at the wrong moment?

The air smelled of ash and boiled potatoes, of sweat and tension—the kind that settles over a place when everyone is watching everyone else and no one feels safe.

And still no sign of Erika.

Stefan realized he could not stay in Czechoslovakia. His German surname—despite his years in the Resistance—marked him as a target. Brno no longer felt like a city; it was a gauntlet. Each day brought new disappearances, brutal beatings, and executions carried out in public squares, all under the guise of justice.

The liberation he had once prayed for became a different kind of nightmare. Every unexpected knock at the door made his pulse spike. Sleep was scarce, and when it came, it brought visions of Erika: imprisoned, beaten, or worse. Was she suffering? Had she already died, nameless and unseen? The questions chased each other through his mind, unanswered and unbearable.

Staying meant risk, but leaving was just as perilous. Checkpoints now choked every major road, staffed by Czech guards with their own grievances and their own lists. If you didn't have the right papers, you didn't pass—and some didn't even survive.

That night, under the dim light of a single bulb, Stefan sat at his desk in Reichenberg and began to write. His hand shook, the pencil's tip scratching against the page like a whisper he could not voice aloud.

MAY 23, 1945

Adi,

I hope this letter finds you in better spirits than mine, although I suspect that's unlikely. The silence around Erika has settled over all of us like a second war. Time blurs, each day more torturous than the last with no news of her . . .

Believe me when I say I have left no stone unturned in my search. I have combed through each neighborhood, speaking to anyone who might offer a scrap of information. But every question is met with silence. No sightings. Just silence. It's a cruel echo of the reunion we once imagined at war's end.

The Czechs, I am sorry to tell you, have become what they once despised. I've seen it—revenge without restraint. Families torn from homes, children watching helplessly as their fathers are dragged away . . . And now we have the Russians.

Recounting the horrors he had witnessed, Stefan's hand shook, a teardrop falling and blotting the paper. He took a deep breath, steadying himself before continuing to write.

I cannot stay here much longer. The risk is growing, and I have drawn too much attention already. I must resume my medical studies—it's the only way to explain my presence without questions. It will also give me more freedom to travel, to search.

But Adi—please know this: I haven't given up. Not on Erika. Not on us. Wherever she is, she's still with me. Every day.

As Stefan pondered the conclusion of his letter, his writing faltered as he choked with emotion.

> *And if the worst has happened, I promise you her name will not disappear into the mist. She will never be forgotten. Her vibrant spirit, her fervor, her resilience—all that made her remarkable—will endure through our memories. In the quiet courage she passed on to us. In the fight still left in me.*
>
> *Yours always,*
> *Stefan*

A single tear rolled down Stefan's cheek as he signed his name with a determined stroke. Then he folded the letter, placed it in an envelope, and sealed it with a sense of finality.

———

Holding Stefan's letter, Adi felt his own tears blur the script as he read the painful details from Czechoslovakia. The mystery of Erika's disappearance tormented him incessantly. Each day was more unbearable than the last as he pondered her fate, his mind haunted by the distressing possibilities. He had written to embassies, followed whispers through refugee networks, even bribed former soldiers who claimed to know someone who knew something. But the trail always ended in the same way: a shrug, a refusal, a lie. Adi hadn't stopped searching, but it felt more like flailing than resolve.

His daughter's absence had hollowed him, left him walking through rooms as if some essential dimension had vanished from the world. He rarely slept without dreaming of her. Sometimes she was running toward him, sometimes away. Most nights, she said nothing at all.

Christa was a small light in the darkness gathering around them. Amid the repercussions of violence and loss, she remained animated by her music, her presence a kind of defiance. Adi, increasingly consumed by his search for his older daughter, found himself anchoring to his younger one—protecting what little innocence remained in their family.

Over breakfast, he would ask about twenty-year-old Christa's latest composition, forcing warmth into his voice.

"It's a waltz, Papa," she'd reply, eyes alight with pride. "Herr Meissner says I have captured the rhythm beautifully."

Moments like these pierced the fog of despair, if only briefly. Christa's playing was a ritual, an escape, an offering.

Enrolling her at the conservatory had been one of Adi's clear choices since the war ended. The school gave her a rhythm to follow, teachers who challenged her, and a world not consumed by grief. Watching her disappear into the discipline of her practice, he felt a bittersweet comfort. She was still able to dream. Each piano lesson marked a quiet victory.

But when the house fell silent, so did Adi's quiet performances of hope. Each night, he returned to the search: scanning casualty reports, tracing Red Cross archives, interrogating bureaucrats with worn photographs in hand. He was methodical, obsessive. Sleep only arrived when his body gave out.

On his nightstand, a photograph of Erika and Stefan—their smiling faces, their arms entwined—offered tender motivation. It captured a moment of youthful love and joy—an image Adi clung to, preferring to remember them in that carefree, blissful state.

Each day began with a silent vow: *one more attempt.* One more day of examining ledgers, of combing through police records, of visiting refugee shelters, hoping something had changed overnight.

On the morning of May 27, the light filtering through Adi's bedroom curtains felt no different. The air held the faint, warm smell of Christa's fresh bread, a smell that once brought comfort but now was just a reminder of all they had lost.

He came to the table and ate anyway, the crust dry in his throat. And when the knock came at the door, he stood slowly, expecting another rumor, another disappointment.

Still, he opened it.

For a moment, everything stilled. The sight of the Red Cross worker was like a freeze-frame in the otherwise continuous motion of Adi's life. He steadied himself against the doorframe. The sound of Christa's laughter echoed in from the kitchen, dissonant against the tight, unfamiliar swell in his chest.

"Herr Dindinger," the woman began, her voice solemn. "We received word . . ."

Her words trailed off, but it was enough.

Adi's knees wobbled, and he barely kept himself upright as the wave of relief and gratitude flooded through him. Tatjana, his beloved wife, was alive. Somehow, through everything, she had survived.

Relief hit first. Then anguish. Then guilt—for the nights he'd doubted her endurance, for the ache of having imagined a future without her. He pressed a shaking hand to his mouth, unable to speak. Tears came hard and fast.

Christa was at his side in an instant, her arms wrapping around him. He tried to put words together: Tatjana was in a hospital, she was safe, and they would soon be together again.

There would be details to manage, choices to make, and devastating news to share. Adi would have to tell his wife about Eka. But for now, he let himself feel it—the fragile lift of something close to hope.

A few weeks later, on a quiet June morning with hints of jasmine on the breeze, Adi opened the door for her.

Tatjana moved with careful, halting steps, leaning into him for support. She was thinner than he had imagined, her body hollowed by months of deprivation. Her eyes—once bright and lively—now bore the shadows of profound trauma.

Adi helped her across the threshold, steadying her with both hands. Her fragility made him feel helpless. Her hands trembled in his. This was his wife—the same woman who had once stood so firmly at the center of their family, whose quiet strength had always held them together.

Seeing her this way broke something open in him. It wasn't just the physical toll of her suffering. It was what had been taken from her, and from all of them.

Still, she was here. That was enough, for now. She had come home.

Tatjana's gaze moved slowly across the room, pausing on the curtains, the couch cushions, each familiar shape. A flicker of recognition crossed her face, though it seemed distant—like she was seeing it all through a fog. She took a shaky step forward, struggling to reconcile the safety of home with the horrors from which she had just returned.

Her eyes caught on the family portrait in the foyer. A tear slipped down her hollowed cheek. She drew in a dry breath, then let it out in a soft gasp.

"My darlings," she whispered, her voice thin and wobbly. "I dreamed of this . . . but seeing you here—it almost hurts. I'm back, but I don't feel like the person I was. Hellmuth is ill. Joachim . . ." Her voice cracked. "And Erika . . . Eka is gone. Our fighter."

Adi felt the depth of her grief in his own chest. The way she said Erika's name—so final—carved into him. Rage flared briefly at the captors who had reduced his wife, this strong, luminous woman, to someone haunted by shadows. But he forced it down. There had been enough anger.

He stepped forward and wrapped his arms around Tatjana carefully, mindful of her delicate frame. She collapsed into him with a quiet sob. He stroked her brittle hair, rocking her gently, and the memories of decades returned in waves: the sound of her laughter, the warmth of her hands, the way she used to sing in the kitchen without realizing it.

So much had been taken. But so much was still here.

"You're safe now, meine Liebe," he whispered, kissing her cheek tenderly. The words felt small against the weight of what she'd survived, but they were all he had to give. "We're together again. And we'll find Eka. I promise."

As Adi held Tatjana close, he felt the rush of her breath against his collarbone—shallow, uneven, but undeniable. The soft beat of her heart was real. She was home. The certainty of it settled in slowly. He let himself believe it: He was alive. She was here.

When her crying slowed, Tatjana leaned back slightly, searching his face. Her eyes, rimmed red and sunken, held questions she was reluctant to voice. "Is it really over? Am I really home . . . and safe? Did Fania make it out?"

"Yes, you're safe," Adi replied. "And because of you, Fania was able to escape through the Caucasus to Palestine." He cupped her face gently, his thumbs brushing the lines worn deep by fear and hunger. "We are all here. It's not the same, but it's a beginning. And I'm not letting go."

For a moment, Tatjana just looked at him, her gaze inscrutable.

But somewhere behind the exhaustion in her eyes, Adi saw it: the faintest trace of the woman he'd so devotedly loved. Not untouched, not whole, but still there. Still his.

It would take time to confront the full horrors of what Tatjana had endured—longer than any of them could yet grasp. But that was for later. For now, even in her silence, Adi felt that boundless will within her—flickering, faint, but alive.

CHAPTER THIRTY-THREE

RESCUE (1945-1946)

BY LATE SUMMER, THE NEED for Germans to flee Poland was no longer in question. The Russian advance was relentless, and every rumor carried the same refrain: looting, rape, murder. At the Potsdam Conference on August 1, 1945, Truman, Churchill, and Stalin agreed that German nationals in occupied territories would be "transferred" to Germany. It was a diplomatic word for something far messier.

For those on the ground, navigating the violence and terror at the end of German occupation and then the chaotic dawn of liberation meant days lived on the edge of panic. For some, despair ran so deep that walking into the nearest river became the only escape. The psyche of ethnic Germans like the Dindingers was under immense, destructive pressure.

Adi had to get his family out of Poland.

By November, the remnants of the family were prepared to join the largest westward migration in European history. Adi was burdened with responsibility not only for his young daughter at home but also for a wife still struggling with the traumatic aftermath of her incarceration. And somewhere out there was Erika, if she was still alive.

Then, days before their planned November departure, a letter arrived from the Red Cross. Adi stood at the kitchen table, staring at his name written in unfamiliar script. He broke the seal slowly, as if rushing it might change the words inside.

Tatjana came up beside him, her fingers brushing his sleeve. "What is it?"

Scanning and rescanning the letter, Adi didn't answer right away. Then, unable to breathe, he handed the letter to Tatjana. "They think they've found her."

Tatjana's eyes moved over the page, her lips parting. Six long months had passed since Erika's disappearance—five since Germany's surrender. "A girl matching Erika's description . . . holding center for political prisoners . . . near death from typhus . . . unable to give her name."

The location written on the page was in Austria, a holding center in North Tyrol.

Tatjana looked up. "Near death."

Adi nodded once, the motion tight and almost imperceptible. "But alive."

They clung to each other, tears spilling freely, caught between disbelief and relief.

"She's alive," Tatjana whispered, her voice shaking. "Our Erika . . . she's fighting. Adi, you have done the impossible in finding her. We must tell Stefan."

For a moment, neither spoke. The sounds of the street outside—the clip of boots on the cobblestones, a wagon wheel rattling over a rut—suddenly seemed too loud. Then Tatjana folded the letter carefully, her hands trembling despite her effort to be steady.

"You go," she said simply, gripping the letter as if it might vanish. "You go now. I will watch Tita."

Adi swallowed hard, forcing back the rush of emotion. The thought of Erika imprisoned, ill, yet still breathing brought both fury and a flicker of hope. He had never stopped looking for her.

Within the hour, his bag was packed and arrangements had been made for travel to North Tyrol.

On the train, the countryside slid past Adi's window unnoticed. In his mind, he saw Erika as she'd been: head thrown back in laughter while skating on the ice, daring and unafraid. Eyes bright as she bent over a chemistry experiment. Each memory sharpened the ache of lost months and unknown suffering yet also fed the stubborn belief that she could recover.

Adi rehearsed what he might say when he saw her, knowing no words could undo what had been done. More than anything, he longed to take his daughter in his arms as proof that she had made it through, to let her feel the unbroken thread of her family's love.

When the train slowed for its final stop, Adi's pulse quickened. He gathered his few belongings and his thoughts, refusing to be overwhelmed by the moment. Then, following the directions he was given, he walked through unfamiliar streets until the holding center came into view: squat, gray, guarded.

A stone-faced sentry looked him over before stepping aside and waving him in where the air was cold and stale. When the moment finally came, Adi braced himself. But the figure before him stopped him short.

Erika's beautiful hair had been roughly, raggedly shaved. Her scalp bore the unmistakable marks of brutality: angry, red indentations that looked like drill holes. Her teeth, those perfect pearls that once flashed such brilliant smiles, were gone, leaving her mouth a sunken cavity. The pale skin of her arms was a lattice of scars and wounds telling a vicious, unwanted history.

Then Adi's eyes dropped to her feet, which had once skimmed over the ice with easy confidence but were now swollen and blackened from frostbite. But what haunted him most were her eyes. Once bright with curiosity, they now stared past him, dull and unfocused. Her lips moved as if to speak, but only broken sounds emerged, the voice unfamiliar.

Adi's stomach lurched at the implications of such savagery inflicted upon his child. He stood rooted, the sound of the room fading. A single thought cut through the shock: *I was not there to keep her safe.*

Up close, he saw Erika's arms hanging limp, her body slack, as though each muscle had forgotten its purpose. Whatever had been done to her had gouged away her spirit as much as her frame. The question raced into his brain before he could stop it: *Who could do this to someone so young?*

A hard, hot anger rose in his chest. His fists curled, his jaw locked, and for a moment he wanted to strike something—anything—that might bear the weight of his fury. But beneath it ran a deeper ache, knowing that no act of revenge could restore what had been taken from her.

The sight of Erika, the shell of the girl he had raised, pulled his thoughts to Tatjana. Gratitude came first: Both she and Erika had survived. But would survival be enough?

Adi could not yet imagine what life might look like for them now, with these vile, inhuman memories carved so deeply into body and mind. His heart ached with the knowledge that even in their reunion with family, the shadows of their past would linger.

The doctor's words were clinical, each one landing like a blow: "Catatonic schizophrenia." Erika had nearly died of typhus after arriving at the Austrian holding center five months earlier, the doctor explained, and had been unresponsive since her arrival. The frostbite to her lower legs from prolonged exposure was severe.

Adi's gaze dropped to her feet, and he straightened. "No amputations," he said, his voice firm. "We'll find another way."

The doctor closed his notes. "The vascular damage is significant, but we can start with conservative treatments and monitor closely."

Erika's feet, once so quick on the ice, lay still.

Adi looked into her vacant eyes. "Eka . . . It's Papa. We'll get through this. I promise."

Her eyes moved, just slightly, toward his voice.

It was barely a sign, but Adi held on to it, willing it to mean that somewhere inside her mind, Erika was still there.

He listened as the doctors outlined the neuropsychiatric treatments ahead. Each faint squeeze of her hand, each flicker of her eyes, would be a victory for which they would have to fight.

"Tell me what she needs." Adi spoke without hesitation. "I'll fight for her with everything I have."

The doctor, seeing his resolve, laid out a rigorous treatment plan, including therapies that ranged from the conventional to the experimental. Adi took it all in. Whatever it required, he would do.

"We'll get through this," he murmured, taking Erika's hand in his. "Stefan has been looking for you."

Her eyes flickered once more, and again he held on to that faint sign of awareness. The path ahead would be long, but he was ready to walk it—for Erika, for Tatjana, for all they had survived.

In the days and weeks that followed, Adi allowed himself to imagine Erika's laughter filling their home again, her spirit shining as it once had. That vision became his compass.

On January 25, 1946, Erika was loaded onto a transport bound for the Provinzial-Heil- und Pflegeanstalt Galkhausen—a nursing home in Cologne. Adi could only guess at the pain she endured on the journey; although it was rough, the jolts left her unmoving, her gaze fixed far away.

When the vehicle stopped before the asylum and orderlies eased the stretcher from the truck, he felt both relief and dread. This cold, institutional building would now be Erika's refuge and her challenge.

Adi walked beside her, taking her hand and giving it a gentle squeeze. "We're here, Eka," he said softly. "This is where you'll start to heal."

Her eyelids shifted just enough for him to notice.

Inside, the hallways were hushed except for Adi's own footsteps. A man in a white coat approached, his face set in professional reserve. "Dr. Felix Weissenfeld," he said. "You must be the father?"

"Adolf Dindinger. My daughter Erika."

The doctor thumbed through a thin file. "No records came with her from North Tyrol. She was the only patient without documentation."

Adi nodded. "The Red Cross told me she was near death from typhus when they found her." His voice caught. "She's been through . . . more than I can put into words."

The doctor studied the scars all over Erika's body, his gaze pausing on the deep marks along her scalp. "An extreme case of political persecution," Dr. Weissenfeld said quietly. "One of the most severe I've seen. She was a spy, yes?"

Adi's chest tightened as he nodded. The words confirmed what he had feared as he forced himself to meet the doctor's eyes. "What are her chances? Will the catatonia last?"

Dr. Weissenfeld exhaled. "In cases like these, there are no guarantees. The body will recover slowly but steadily. The mind . . ." he hesitated, "we cannot predict. We'll use every treatment at our disposal: psychotherapy, electroshock, sedatives if necessary. But the road ahead will be long."

The doctor's bluntness struck harder than Adi had expected, stripping reality of any comfort. Images of Erika as she once was—laughing with her siblings, talking animatedly over supper—sent him reeling. The thought of that light dimmed beyond reach was almost too much to bear. Still, he felt a spark push back against the despair in the doctor's warning. Dr. Weissenfeld did not know Erika—her resolve, her sharp mind, the strength that carried her through other trials—as he did.

He met the doctor's gaze. "Then I walk that road with her. Whatever it takes."

Dr. Weissenfeld studied him for a moment before nodding. "We'll do all we can. But you should prepare yourself, Herr Dindinger. The recovery will be slow, and the Erika you remember . . . she may not fully return."

The words landed heavily, but the spark remained. Adi knew the months ahead would hold anguish and setbacks, yet he would not abandon Erika to the shadows.

Failure was not an option.

Letter from Dr. Felix Weissenfeld describing the arrival of Erika in January 1946, on a group transport from Austrian Tyrol without documents or medical history. Erika was catatonic when she was found, unresponsive and covered with wounds and scars. He relates that it was one of the worst cases of political torture that he had seen. Her head had been shaved and her skull wounded. Her teeth had been knocked out. Dr. Weissenfeld diagnosed her as a catatonic schizophrenic with an unknown future.

CHAPTER THIRTY-FOUR

SEEKING REFUGE (1946)

AMID THE CONFUSION AND DEVASTATION of the war's aftermath, Adi faced the grim logistics of resettling Tatjana and Christa in a displaced persons' holding center in Munich while still trying to care for Erika in Cologne. Bromberg, now called Bydgoszcz again, was no longer safe for them. They took only what they could carry, knowing that every possession left behind would be lost forever.

Adi cradled his violin under one arm—the instrument that had sustained him through so many of life's trials—and gripped two small suitcases. How quickly a life could be packed up, reduced to fragments that fit into a few square feet of worn leather and wood. One of these suitcases had carried Tatjana and Adi out of Russia during their flight from the Bolshevik Revolution. On the inside of its lid, the inscription Adi had etched in 1916 was still clear: *Ich bleib Dir treu*—"I remain true to you." The words, as steady now as when he wrote them, had carried them through years of upheaval.

Inside were the memories of their former life: Joachim's letters from the Eastern Front, written in the sweeping hand of a man who tried to keep hope alive. Adi's Great War dog tag from his service with the 8ten Kompanie Garde-Füsilier-Regiments and the Kaisergarde. Photographs from years when their faces were unlined by grief. Birth certificates, the proof of their existence. And forged identity papers for Tatjana, created in quieter, more dangerous days when her safety depended on being someone else.

The other suitcase held the things one takes when beginning again, the distilled remnants of a life built with effort. Nestled among those items were twelve slender silver spoons, each engraved with a daughter's initials. For Tatjana, they were more than utensils; they were a quiet link to her children, a tangible thread to hold fast to while the world shifted around her.

Tucked carefully into the second suitcase, Christa's belongings reflected her world at the piano: sheet music worn soft at the edges, her own scored compositions, and a few simple dresses for the stage alongside everyday clothes. Among these items was her newest piece, the pages crowded with pencil marks and scratched-out notes. This was the music she turned to when the outside world became too loud.

By then, the Dindingers were part of the endless tide of displaced persons, or DPs. The Allied Forces defined DPs as civilians pushed by war outside the boundaries of their country, now unable to return home without assistance. More than eleven million people bore that designation after the war, their lives shattered and their futures uncertain. Entire lives were reduced to a bureaucratic number: Christa was 226934. Tatjana was 226937.

Adi clung to the idea—fragile but persistent—that somewhere ahead lay a place of safety. Whatever came, they would face it together.

When they reached their assigned housing in Munich, on Cimbernstraße 97/0, each carried what little they had with quiet determination. The building's gray facade offered no welcome, only the blunt reality of where their journey had brought them.

Adi's grip tightened on the worn suitcases until the seams pressed into his calloused palms. Tatjana's arm slipped through his, her grip wordless but steady. Christa kept her eyes low, as if bracing for what lay inside.

The apartment building's door opened to a foyer dim with dust and the smell of damp plaster. A stern-faced woman sat behind a desk, her gaze scrutinizing them as they approached.

"Names and papers," she barked, her tone leaving no room for pleasantries.

Adi passed the documents across, his jaw tightening as she slowly read each line. At last, she gave a clipped nod and pointed toward the stairs.

"Third floor. Room twelve."

The hallway upstairs was lined with identical doors. Room twelve held nothing but bare walls, worn floorboards, and a few threadbare pieces of furniture. It was a place stripped of history. Adi stood in the center of the room for a moment, reading the space like a problem to solve. Even here, in the blankness, there was a flicker in his eyes: the stubborn thought that they could make it theirs.

"We'll have to use every bit of this room wisely," he murmured, already measuring possibilities, his mind ticking over like the engineer he was. "We've faced worse than this. We'll make it a home—even if it's only for a little while."

Tatjana gave a small nod, a faint smile playing at her lips. She began unpacking with a mix of efficiency and care, as if each treasured object carried its own heartbeat. From Adi's inscribed suitcase she lifted a framed photograph: Joachim, Hellmuth, Erika, and Christa, all caught in a moment of unguarded joy. She set it on the nightstand, the image a quiet anchor in an unfamiliar room.

At a small desk, Christa ran her fingers over the worn surface before opening her bag. Out came her composition notebook and a few pencils, arranged with the neatness of a ritual. Within minutes, she had carved out a corner for her music—a refuge amid the unsettled world.

Adi watched them both as pride and grief wove through his mind. They had lost so much yet retained the rare gift of finding comfort in small acts, of shaping order and meaning from whatever lay at hand.

Christa looked up from her notebook, her expression brightening. "Papa, we could turn the desk chair and a plank into a music stand. Then I can keep working on my compositions."

Adi's smile came easily. "An excellent idea, my goldenes Tita. Let's do it."

By evening, they had begun to claim the space as their own. Tatjana strung the twelve silver spoons from a length of twine, their soft chime drifting in through an open window. Adi fashioned the music stand just as Christa imagined, and soon her pencil was moving again, shaping melodies that wove through the air, gentle but sure.

When night fell, they gathered on the narrow bed, Tatjana leaning against Adi's shoulder, Christa curled beside them. "Tatjana," he said quietly, "I'll need to travel to see Eka in a day or two. Dr. Weissenfeld will need our new address."

Tatjana's eyes met his. "We'll manage until you return."

In the flicker of a candle stub, they spoke of better days, their laughter carrying just enough defiance to soften the silence. For now, bleak or not, this would be home.

It lasted only a few days.

A sudden knock at noon cracked through the stillness. Christa froze, then moved to the door, her pulse thudding in her ears. Through the peephole she caught the rigid stare of an American officer. She opened the door a fraction.

"Miss Dindinger? No parents home?" His voice was flat, stripped of warmth.

Christa nodded, dread tightening her throat.

"You and your parents are to gather your belongings immediately. This residence is being reassigned." The words came like a verdict, clipped and final. The family would later learn that Frau Zeune, the wife of a former SS officer, had falsely accused Adolf Dindinger of stealing furniture.

A chaplain stepped forward from behind the American officer, his presence lending a ceremonial gravity to the eviction. "You are to report to Cimbernstraße 15 without delay. Any attempt to take furnishings or other property will be treated as theft."

Christa's thoughts spun into a panic. Papa was in Cologne visiting Eka. Mama was at the Deutsche Bank, fighting to get Eka's medical care upgraded to a higher category. Neither of them could help her now. Christa was alone, staring down the hard truth of their vulnerability.

"You have until December 5 to vacate these premises," the officer said, his voice edged with threat. "Fail to comply, and your father will be arrested immediately."

The words knocked the air from Christa's lungs. She managed only a mute nod. The chaplain cast a brief, sympathetic glance before following the officer out, leaving the silence heavier than before.

Christa sank onto the worn sofa, her hands over her face. Boxes lay half-unpacked around her, their contents—a family portrait, Tatjana's battered Bible—small claims of permanence now stripped of meaning. This place had been meant as a pause, a breath between upheavals. Now, it was over before it had even begun.

Christa did not know that Polish authorities had refuted the accusations, telling American Corps Intelligence Control that they were false. The claim had been investigated by the criminal police and dismissed. The letter from the Polish authorities stated:

> *We cannot believe that a Polish DP family should be robbed of their rights for the benefit of an SS family, who participated in harm to so many people.*
>
> *We cannot believe that such intrigues should find the support of an American officer.*
>
> *The Dindinger family has helped the Polish people and had no connection with the Nazis . . .*
>
> *We believe in justice and we beg you to protect the innocent DP family Dindinger.*

Polish intelligence knew Erika's wartime role and what it had cost her. A *Fragebogen*—a "purification" questionnaire used by the Allies—noted that Erika had been under Gestapo watch since 1943 for association with foreigners, the *Ausländerin*: the Brits and the Poles. And her covert work passing intelligence to the S.O.E. had been unearthed. But there were no reparations for those accused of spying against Hitler—only punishment.

Polish intelligence also knew that Tatjana had survived Bergen-Belsen.

Yet bureaucracy moved forward. Adi, Tatjana, and Christa were uprooted yet again. There would be no true refuge for them.

FERNSPRECHER NR............................

BANKKONTO: DEUTSCHE BANK STUTTGART NR. 40515, GYMNASIUMSTRASSE 3

Frau   ⑭ STUTTGART S, den 17.5.46
D i n d i n g e r   BÜRO MÖRIKESTRASSE 24
                                                 L/Kn.
K o r n w e s t h e i m
Weimarstrasse 11

.Sehr geehrte Frau Dindinger!

Wie Sie uns gestern mitteilten, übernimmt das Versorgungsamt
Stuttgart die Kosten der Behandlung für Ihr Frl. Tochter, Erika
Dindinger im Bürgerhospital Stuttgart. Wie Sie uns sagten, übernimmt das Versorgungsamt jedoch nur die Kosten, die für eine Behandlung in der 3.Klasse entstehen.

In Stuttgart ist die Sache nun folgendermassen geregelt. Kommt
ein politisch Verfolgter in Krankenhausbehandlung, so übernimmt
das Versorgungsamt bzw. die Ortskrankenkasse die Behandlungs-
kosten der 3.Klasse.Die Differenz von der 2. zur 3.Klasse wird
vom Wohlfahrtsamt übernommen. Da Sie nun in Kornwestheim wohnen
bitten wir Sie, sich mit dem für Ihren Wohnsitz zuständigen
Wohlfahrtsamt in Verbindung zu setzen, damit dieses die weitere
Kosten übernimmt.

Sollten Sie auf Schwierigkeiten stossen, so bitten wir Sie, sic
nochmals mit uns in Verbindung zu setzen.

                              Hochachtungsvoll

A letter from the Repatriation Center for Former Political Prisoners on May 17, 1946, to Tatjana. Tatjana tried to negotiate a higher class of medical care for Erika with the Deutsche Bank. The cost of medical care, clothing, and toiletries remained issues long after the war ended. There were no reparations for *Halbjudin*, "half-Jews," or spies.

CHAPTER THIRTY-FIVE

STUTTGART (1946)

BY MARCH 1946, ADI, TATJANA, and Christa arrived in Stuttgart, the city of Adi's childhood. Hellmuth had recovered enough from his most recent episode of malaria to join them. For the first time in years, four members of the Dindinger family were under one roof. The ache of separation eased, if only a little, replaced by the tentative comfort of familiarity.

Their new flat was modest and worn, but it was theirs. Christa traced her fingers along the windowsill, pausing at a flake of paint. The silence felt different here—less ominous, less temporary. It was not a shelter, not a hiding place, but a home.

Tatjana unpacked their few salvaged belongings with quiet reverence. Each object—folded linens, a chipped teacup, the faded family portrait— was placed not as decoration but as a declaration: *We are still here.*

"It feels strange, doesn't it?" Adi's voice was a hushed whisper, his gaze moving over the small rooms. "To have a place to call our own again."

A melancholic smile tugged at the corners of Tatjana's mouth as she nodded slowly. "Strange but not unwelcome."

Adi wrapped an arm tentatively around her shoulders.

The city outside bustled with postwar urgency. Markets were reopening. Tram bells were clanging. Children were darting between rubble and rebuilding. The world had cracked open and was somehow beginning again.

Still, grief remained a silent tenant in the new flat. Erika's absence filled every room. Her name was spoken less often now—not because she was forgotten but because her story was one of sorrow. And Hellmuth's health was unpredictable. His malaria, brought back from North Africa, reminded them daily that healing rarely followed a straight path.

That evening, as the sky shifted from gold to rose to dusk, Christa began to hum a tune at the edge of memory. It was uncertain at first, as if testing whether joy still had a place here. But she kept humming.

Adi's gaze drifted from the window to the family portrait. His eyes paused on Joachim's smile—still, frozen in time. Grief flared in his chest, but he pushed it down, refusing to let it take over. They had fought too hard to make it here.

"Do you remember the day this was taken?" he asked, voice low, as if not to disturb the silence. "Joachim had just gotten that little chemistry set. He couldn't wait to show it off."

Tatjana moved beside him, her fingers tracing the outline of Joachim's face. "He was always so curious," she murmured. "Endlessly full of questions. That day, he explained every vial like it held a secret."

Christa leaned against the windowsill, her eyes never leaving the portrait. "He never lost patience with me," she added softly. "Even when I asked the same thing ten times. He could make anything sound simple."

Hellmuth's voice came from across the room, barely audible. "He wanted me to be a doctor." He gave a small, pained laugh. "Said we'd all work together after the war. That we would support Christa's musical education in Vienna. He had it all mapped out."

Silence settled between them, suspending all else as each of them sifted through memories, sorting through the pain of Joachim's loss.

Adi swallowed hard. "He was meant for more than this war. He had a mind that lit up every room and a heart that welcomed all."

The light continued to dim outside, and the flat grew still. Tatjana was the first to move again. Her voice, when it came, was quieter than before.

"He's gone, but he saw a future for us," she said. "We can't forget that." She reached for Adi's hand. "Not to chase it blindly, but maybe just to step into it. One step at a time."

Adi gave her hand a gentle squeeze. "You're right, Liebling. We'll always carry Joachim with us," he insisted. "But we still have each other. And we still have time."

Later, Tatjana's fingers paused at the edge of a frayed tablecloth, the fabric thin and sun softened. With each object she unpacked, the life they had built in Bydgoszcz flickered back—faint but stubborn.

"Mama, look!" Christa's voice rang out from the corner of the room. She held up a silver frame, the glass slightly fogged. "It was our last Christmas together, remember?"

Tatjana crossed the room quickly. Her hand went to her mouth, holding back unspoken words.

Hellmuth stepped closer, his eyes scanning the photo. "That was 1940. Before Joachim and I went to war." He hesitated. "Before the world changed."

Tatjana reached over and picked up the frame. Six of them, gathered tight around the Christmas tree, smiling, leaning into each other, unaware of what was coming. Her thumb brushed over Joachim's face.

"We'll find a special place for this," she whispered.

Adi appeared in the doorway, a small stack of books balanced in his arms. The spines were scuffed, some barely holding together. "These made it," he said, and set them down carefully on the wobbly table. He ran a hand over the top one, a volume of Goethe, its pages slightly warped from dampness. "It's something. Not much, but something."

Tatjana joined him, her eyes moving over the titles. Her fingers brushed the spines lightly. "Joachim loved these," she murmured. "He'd spend hours with them."

Together they stood in silence, their hearts united by the enduring legacy of the son and brother they had loved so deeply.

She paused at the corner of a worn score. "And here—your beloved Beethoven and Mozart," she said to Christa, managing a small smile.

Christa sank to the floor beside the pile, flipping gently through the pages. Hellmuth crouched next to her, one hand resting on a volume's cover. Tatjana watched them, her hand still on the table.

"These books have been with us so long," Adi said, almost to himself.

"Long before any of you were even born." He wrapped an arm around Tatjana's waist, pulling her in as they gazed around the small room.

Though still sparse, it seemed warmer now. The books on the table, the picture propped against the wall, the scent of old paper in the air . . . The past still hovered at the edges of daily life, but for the first time in a long while, it wasn't the loudest presence.

"It's a start," Adi said, his words brushing Tatjana's ear.

Tatjana rested her head against his shoulder and peered out the window, where twilight streaked the sky. "It's more than we've had in a long time," she murmured, her fingers closing gently around his. "And for now, it's enough."

The September air was sharp, tinged with woodsmoke and something harder to name: expectation. Adi, Tatjana, Hellmuth, and Christa made their way through Stuttgart's crowded streets, joining the quiet press of bodies headed toward the square.

Many people were gathered there, sitting shoulder to shoulder, their faces lined by war and want but now turned cautiously toward something new.

Christa tapped the side of her seat with restless fingers. Her eyes flicked across the crowd, then up to Adi. "Papa," she whispered, "what do you think he'll say? Do you really think things can change?"

Adi didn't answer right away. His gaze moved over the gathering. There were so many faces—some still hollow with hunger, others marked by cautious hope. "I don't know, Tita," he said finally. "But we've made it this far. We can't afford to stop hoping now."

Tatjana reached across to still Christa's hand, offering a small smile as the crowd shifted anxiously. The noise settled when James F. Byrnes, the US Secretary of State, stepped to the podium. His presence pulled the square into silence. His voice, when it came, was steady and precise.

"I have come to Germany to learn firsthand the problems involved in reconstruction—and to share the views of the United States government on these matters," he announced. "We believe their resolution will determine not only Germany's future, but that of Europe as well."

A hush settled over the crowd as his words rang out, unwavering.

"Freedom from militarism will give the German people the chance—if they will seize it—to apply their energies to the work of peace. It will give them the opportunity to earn the respect of peace-loving nations and, eventually, to take an honorable place among the members of the United Nations.

"It is not in Germany's interest—or the world's—for this country to become a pawn in a new military struggle between East and West. We advocate for economic unification. And if that cannot be fully achieved, then we will strive for the highest level possible."

Tatjana's fingers tightened around Adi's. For so long, their lives had been held in place: borders redrawn, orders issued, futures suspended. But now Byrnes was speaking of choice, of governance and reconstruction, of Germany no longer being managed like a problem to solve.

Hellmuth leaned forward, eyes wide. "Papa," he whispered, "does this mean I could still go to medical school?"

Christa glanced between her parents. "He's saying it might be up to us now. Isn't he?"

Adi gave a small nod, not trusting himself to speak yet.

Tatjana kissed Christa's temple, then reached for Hellmuth's hand. "It's a beginning," she said. "And for the first time in years, it feels like ours. Our chance to shape our own destinies. Carpe diem."

As Byrnes stepped back from the podium, the crowd erupted, louder than Adi had expected. Not just applause, but something beneath it: release and relief. Adi rose, pulled to his feet by the force of it. He looked over at his family, eyes shining.

"This feels real," he said, his voice low. "Like something might finally change."

As they left the square, the streets were still humming with movement and conversation. Byrnes's words echoed in the way the Dindingers walked, a little straighter now. His "Speech of Hope," delivered that September 6, signaled a major shift in US policy toward postwar Germany—moving away from economic dismantlement and toward reconstruction.

For the Dindingers, it wasn't certainty. But it was something close—the first real, public glimpse of a different future.

CHAPTER THIRTY-SIX

NEWFOUND PURPOSE
(1946)

CHRISTA'S FINGERS DANCED ACROSS THE ivory keys, the rich tones resonating through the practice room. Her brow furrowed in concentration as she navigated the intricate passages, losing herself in the music's ebb and flow.

Adi watched from the corner, his chest swelling with pride at the sight of his daughter's unwavering dedication. A mere two weeks since their arrival in Stuttgart, and already Christa had immersed herself in the city's vibrant musical scene. The Staatliche Hochschule für Musik had welcomed her with open arms, offering her a place in their prestigious master classes. Adi had wasted no time in securing her enrollment, determined to provide Christa with every opportunity to reclaim the passion that had once consumed her.

The final notes faded into a poignant silence, and Christa's shoulders slumped, a sigh escaping her lips. She turned to face her father, her expression a mixture of frustration and determination.

"It's still not quite right," she murmured, her fingers trailing over the keys in contemplation. "I can't seem to capture the nuances—the life of the music."

Adi crossed the room, settling onto the bench beside her. "Give it time, Tita," he said gently, draping an arm around her shoulders. "You've been through so much, and yet here you are, pouring your heart into your music once more."

Christa leaned into his embrace, drawing strength from his unwavering support. "I know, Papa," she replied, her voice thick with emotion. "It's just . . . the piano has always been my escape. And now, after everything, I feel like I'm grasping for something that once came so naturally."

Adi pressed a kiss to the top of her head, his heart aching for the pain she had endured. "Then we'll keep fighting for it, my love," he vowed. "We'll fight for every note, every crescendo, until the music flows through you like it did."

Her fingers poised above the keys once more. "Play with me, Papa?" she asked, her voice hopeful.

Without hesitation, Adi positioned himself beside her, his hands ready above the keyboard. Together, they began to play a duet, their melodies intertwining in a beautiful, haunting dance. The music swelled around them, filling every corner of the room.

Christa felt something shift within her. The weight of the past—the pain and uncertainty that had threatened to consume her—began to dissipate, replaced by a newfound sense of clarity and purpose. Perhaps this was her path, her journey back to the life she had once known and loved. With her father by her side guiding her every step, she felt a strength she had almost forgotten existed.

Christa turned to Adi, her eyes shining with unshed tears. "Thank you, Papa," she whispered. "You never gave up on me. You believed in me when I couldn't believe in myself."

"Always, my darling," he murmured, pulling her into a warm embrace. "Always."

The practice rooms at the Staatliche Hochschule für Musik hummed with a constant flow of melodies, each one a testament to the dedication and passion of the students who called this revered institution home. The walls seemed to absorb and then release the music, creating an atmosphere of perpetual inspiration. Yet even amid the multitude of sounds, Christa's melodies rose above the rest, their purity and emotion capturing the hearts of all who heard them.

Within weeks, Christa was back in top form. Her fingers danced across the keys with a newfound vigor and precision that left even the most seasoned instructors smiling in admiration. Word of her extraordinary talent spread quickly through the halls. Soon, a steady stream of admirers gathered outside her practice room door, eager to catch a glimpse of the prodigious young pianist at work.

Christa remained blissfully unaware of the whispers and glances. She was lost in the intoxicating world of music that had once again become her refuge. Each note, each crescendo was like a brushstroke on a canvas painting a masterpiece that spoke of resilience, hope, and the indomitable spirit that had carried her through the darkest of times. Her music was not just a performance; it was a narrative of her journey, a tribute to her strength and passion.

One afternoon, during a particularly intense practice session, the familiar strains of *Moonlight Sonata* filled the room. Professor Albrecht, the esteemed head of the piano department, was drawn to the haunting melody. Over the years, he had heard countless renditions of the iconic piece. But this was different.

He stepped into the practice room, and his breath caught. Christa's fingers glided across the keys with a fluidity and grace that defied belief, each movement imbued with a depth of emotion that eclipsed mere technique. Her playing wasn't just skilled; it was transcendent, carrying the weight of her experiences and the light of her hopes.

The final notes hung in the air, and Professor Albrecht found himself overwhelmed. Without a word, he turned and left, his mind racing with plans to showcase this remarkable young talent to the world.

Later that evening, Christa bounded up the stairs to the flat two steps at a time, breath quick with exhilaration and cheeks flushed from the chill night air. She flung open the door—a burst of cold wind and pure joy sweeping into the warm glow of the dining room. Adi and Tatjana looked up, their quiet conversation stilled at her radiant expression.

"Professor Albrecht just offered me the opportunity of a lifetime," Christa breathed, words tumbling out in a rush. "He wants me to be the featured soloist at the upcoming concert! Papa, Mama—it's really happening!"

For a heartbeat, Adi simply stared, letting the weight of her announcement sink in. Then his face broke into a grin that lit up his whole countenance. "Goldenes Tita, that's incredible!" he exclaimed, drawing both wife and daughter into his arms. "We always knew your gift would carry you to greatness."

Tatjana cupped Christa's face, her hands warm and steady against the cool flush of her daughter's cheeks. "Oh, my darling, we're so proud of you," she murmured. "This is just the beginning. I can feel the rest of your story unfolding."

They gathered at the table. Adi reached for the wine with a flourish that belied the mist in his eyes. He filled each glass and then stood, raising his own glass high.

"A toast," he declared, warm and resolute. "To our Christa—whose music moves souls, inspires hearts, and will, from this night forward, chart a path of triumphs too numerous to count."

Their glasses met with a crystalline chime—the overture to a new chapter in all their lives.

The night brimmed with laughter and easy joy as they lingered at the table, trading stories and weaving dreams for the future. The heaviness of the past seemed lighter now, replaced by a hopeful anticipation of what was to come.

Christa let her gaze travel from her father to her mother, her heart swelling with a quiet, abiding love. They had been her anchor through every storm. Now they would stand beside her in the sunlight of her triumphs.

Adi, Tatjana, and Christa stepped out from their modest flat, the night air greeting them with a crisp chill. Their breath curled in pale clouds, each exhalation mingling with the electric hum of the streets. The current of energy in the air was almost tangible, hinting at promises waiting just beyond the horizon.

Just outside the door, Adi paused to behold his wife and daughter, his eyes lingering with unmistakable pride. Tatjana had worked wonders with the few garments they'd managed to salvage; in her hands, threadbare fabric had been coaxed back to life, the stitches carrying not only skill but devotion. Christa's simple blue skirt, mended and pressed, flowed gently as she walked, its color a serene contrast to the creamy blouse her mother had pieced together from scraps of cloth. A delicate lace collar framed Christa's face, adding a touch of elegance to the garment's humble beginnings.

Tatjana herself moved with quiet grace in a modest black dress. A string of pearls—one of the few luxuries she had carried through the upheaval—gleamed softly at her throat.

Adi, too, had made an effort: crisp shirt, trousers marked with razor-sharp creases. He might have lacked the finery of other gentlemen who would fill the grand hall that evening, but the quiet pride in his bearing lent him a distinction no tailor could craft.

They set off toward the concert hall, the sound of their footsteps echoing pleasantly along the lamplit street. Adi's hand found Tatjana's, their fingers intertwining in the familiar comfort of decades shared. With his other hand, he gave Christa's shoulder a gentle, grounding squeeze.

"My darling Tita," he murmured, "words will never be enough to say how proud we are of you. Tonight, you'll let the world hear not just your music but your heart—your strength, your resilience, your truth."

Tatjana nodded, eyes glistening. "You've overcome so much, my love. Through everything, your music has carried us. Let it carry you now."

The concert hall rose before them, its grand facade bathed in warm lantern light. Christa took in the sight, drew a steadying breath, and squared her shoulders. Her chin lifted—not with arrogance but with the quiet certainty of someone stepping fully into her calling. Tonight she would play for herself, for her family, and for every soul who had dared to dream in the face of adversity.

Adi and Tatjana remained outside the performers' entrance, hands still linked, watching their daughter disappear backstage. Then Adi, wearing a small smile, guided his wife toward their seats, weaving through the crowded aisles without once taking his eyes from her face. This night belonged to all three of them.

The lights dimmed, casting the grand hall in a soft, expectant hush as the orchestra tuned. Adi leaned toward Tatjana, his forehead gently meeting hers, their breath mingling in the quiet before the first note.

The conductor stepped to the podium, baton poised like a painter's brush before a silent canvas. Christa sat at the piano, her hands resting delicately on the keys. She closed her eyes for an instant, shutting out the crowd, the gilded balconies, the rustle of anticipation. She thought of the long path to get here: the hours and years of practice, the nights when grief threatened to silence her music, the unwavering hands of her parents guiding her forward.

The baton fell, and the music began.

Christa's fingers moved with a grace born of both discipline and destiny, coaxing from the piano a sound so pure, it seemed to rise beyond the hall itself. Notes shimmered like water in sunlight, carried sorrow into the depths, and rose again with bright resilience.

The audience leaned forward, caught in the thread she wove.

From their seats, Adi and Tatjana watched, hearts caught between pride and awe. Christa surrendered to the music entirely—no longer a child striving to prove herself but a woman claiming her place in the world.

The final notes lingered, then gave way to silence. Then came the applause—an eruption that rose like a wave, carrying admiration, gratitude, wonder.

Christa rose, cheeks flushed. She bowed deeply, eyes glistening with the knowledge that she had given everything she had to give. Then she glanced toward her parents for a heartbeat—a single look filled with love and triumph—and smiled.

Adi and Tatjana joined in the standing ovation, their hands stinging from the force of their applause. Somewhere in that thunder, they knew this was not just the end of a performance. It was the beginning of a life fully claimed—a dream no longer deferred.

CHAPTER THIRTY-SEVEN

REJOINING THE WORLD (1946)

THE WINDOW IN ERIKA'S HOSPITAL room was cracked for air, but the room still felt oppressive to Christa. Quiet pressed into the corners; machines murmured in place of words. It was the first time she had seen her sister since the Gestapo took her.

The whole family had been relieved when news came that Erika was being transferred from Cologne to the Bürgerhospital in Stuttgart. But as Christa stood at the foot of the bed now, that word—*relieved*—felt too neat, too sterile for what churned inside her.

Papa had tried to prepare her. "Your sister has been through things we can't imagine," he'd explained. "Try not to expect . . . the Erika you remember."

At the time, Christa had nodded, thinking she understood. Now, she realized she hadn't.

Hellmuth stood beside her, silent, still holding his bag full of schoolbooks. His shoulders were stiff and his face ashen. He had survived the war, survived the loss of Joachim—and yet even he looked unmoored as he took in the figure on the hospital bed.

Eyes still closed, Erika stirred ever so slightly, her brow furrowing as if reacting to something only she could hear. Her skin was nearly translucent, with bruises old and new surfacing.

Christa's breath caught as she watched her sister's eyelids flutter, the faintest hint of movement sending a pulse of hope through her chest. Without thinking, she reached for Erika's hand. It was weightless, cool.

"Eka?" The nickname, once so easy on Christa's tongue, stumbled out. "It's me, Tita. Can you hear me?"

There was no answer—only the rhythmic beep of the heart monitor and the faint hum of the machines that kept Erika tethered to the world. Then, slowly, Erika's eyelids parted, just a crack. A glimmer of glazed blue met Christa's eyes but didn't seem to register anything.

Christa blinked back tears. "You're safe now," she whispered, her voice hoarse. "We're all here."

From the corner of her eye, Christa saw movement—her mother stepping closer. Tatjana's expression was unreadable, carved from the same stillness she had learned to wear through her own years of hiding and loss.

What must it be like, Christa wondered, *to see your child returned like this—body beaten, spirit unreachable?*

Tatjana said nothing. She simply lowered herself into the chair beside Erika's bed, her hand settling gently atop Christa's. The two women sat without speaking, holding on to the daughter, the sister, the silence.

Time lengthened. The monitor kept rhythm. Erika's eyes drifted open and closed, her gaze never quite landing. Christa leaned forward, her own eyelids heavy with exhaustion, just as Erika's lips parted.

"Nazis . . ."

The utterance was little more than a whisper, but it carried the weight of a thousand horrors. Christa's stomach turned; her breath caught. Across the bed, Tatjana froze, a sharp inhale escaping her lips.

Erika's eyes shot open—wild now—darting to the corners of the room as if searching for an exit. Her chest rose and fell in quick, frantic bursts.

"Nazis . . ." she gasped again, her voice rising in a keening wail of pure, primal fear. "Nein, nein, bitte . . ."

In an instant, Adi was at her side, his strong hands coming to rest on her shoulders. "Easy now, Eka," he soothed, his voice a low, gentle rumble. "You're safe, I promise. The Nazis cannot hurt you anymore. They're gone."

Indeed, the Nuremberg Doctors Trial would soon be underway, where Erika and Stefan's reports would be read into the record. Nazis like Dr. Karl Gebhardt, whom they had reported to the S.O.E. for his crimes at Ravensbrück, would be convicted of war crimes and crimes against humanity, and then executed for their crimes. The Nazis couldn't hurt Erika anymore.

But they still lived on in her mind, and Erika didn't seem to hear Adi's words. Her eyes stared through them all, trapped in a waking nightmare from which there seemed no escape. Her mouth hung slightly open, her face slack with terror.

"What's going on here?" a new voice demanded, the tone clipped with authority. A nurse, watching from the doorway, had stepped into the room.

Tatjana was on her feet in an instant, her hands wringing together. "Please," she implored, her voice trembling, "my daughter needs help . . ."

The nurse's expression softened just a fraction as she turned to look at Erika. "We're doing everything we can for her," she said, gentler now. "But she's been through an incredible ordeal. It will take time."

"Time?" Tatjana's voice sharpened with disbelief. "She has already suffered so much, for so long. Surely there is more that can be done?"

The nurse met Tatjana's gaze levelly. "Such as?"

Tatjana straightened. "We informed the Americans on the Fragebogen. She has no clothes. Nothing warm. They want to help her. So, please—a pair of socks. Her feet remain so cold! A winter dress. And a winter coat."

She paused, struggling to keep her voice level.

"My daughter has lived through unspeakable horrors," she continued, lowering her voice to an urgent murmur. "I beg you—help me give her back even the smallest shred of dignity. Help us make her feel human again."

For a long moment, the nurse simply stared at Tatjana with an unreadable expression. Then, giving a slow, solemn nod, she turned on her heel and walked out. The door clicked shut behind her, leaving only the soft, broken sounds coming from Erika.

Tatjana crossed to the bed once more, sinking into the chair at Erika's side and reaching out to tenderly stroke her daughter's sweat-dampened brow. "It's okay, Eka," she murmured. "Mama's here."

She said nothing more—just kept her hand there, gentle and steady, her thumb brushing lightly over her daughter's temple whenever a tremor came. The hours stretched on, yet Tatjana did not move. Anchored to that bedside, her presence quiet and unwavering, she barely blinked.

Christa sat nearby, watching her mother, and felt something rise in her chest—grief, yes, but also awe. Her mother had withstood more than any human should have to bear. And somehow, even now, she kept showing up, not with speeches or force or complaint, but with hands that didn't pull away, with words that stayed soft. Her love was resilience, and her resilience was love.

Her simple, insistent, loving presence was the most powerful thing Christa had ever seen.

The days and weeks that followed blurred together, with Erika mired in a haze of medication and therapy. She drifted in and out of relative lucidity, her body present but her mind still caught in the aftermath of torment and suffering. Nightmares persisted, each one leaving her shaken, confused, clutching at the sound of her mother's voice or the touch of Christa's hand.

Despite the doctors' best efforts, Erika's afflicted mental state showed little improvement within the confines of the Bürgerhospital. She rarely spoke, and when she did, her words were just disjointed fragments, echoes of memories no one could place. The nights were the worst.

Amid a tangle of consultations and anxious waiting for some change in Erika's status, Tatjana stayed close. When Erika slept, Tatjana read to her— old poems from Heinrich Heine's *Buch der Lieder*, stories from childhood, anything she could remember that had once brought comfort. She sometimes sang softly songs Erika had known as a little girl. But still, there was no sign of return.

Finally, after several agonizing months, Erika's physicians explained to Adi and Tatjana, with grave expressions, that more intensive psychiatric treatment would be required. They recommended another transfer, this time to a prolonged inpatient stay at a facility in nearby Göppingen that was better equipped to handle the depths of Erika's trauma.

It was not what Tatjana had hoped to hear, but she did not argue. She only nodded, steady and composed, as if she had been preparing all along for this next step. It was from Göppingen, a few years earlier, that she had helped her sister Fania escape to Palestine. Now she prayed she could help Erika escape her imprisonment too.

But the place looked nothing like healing. Adi hesitated as the gates to the facility groaned shut behind them. The sound echoed—metal on metal, final and heavy. Ahead, the stone building loomed, gray and institutional. Tatjana, beside him, shivered.

Dr. Blessing, Erika's new physician, met them in a dim office just off the ward. His expression was grave, his brow furrowing as he chose his words with care. "In cases such as this," he began, "where the mind has become profoundly disconnected from reality, we sometimes consider more . . . intensive interventions."

Tatjana exchanged a glance with Adi but said nothing.

"I'm recommending a course of electroconvulsive therapy," Dr. Blessing continued, calmly and cautiously. "Administered in brief, controlled sessions, under sedation, with close monitoring. The goal is to interrupt persistent cycles of delusion and depression, and thus to allow space for new neural pathways to form."

The silence that followed was absolute.

Tatjana felt her chest tighten. Shock treatment, seizures, electrodes attached to Erika's scalp . . . after the Nazis had tried to drill holes in her skull? How could they allow it, after everything, after the violence Erika had already survived?

Adi spoke first, his voice low. "You want to electrocute her?"

The doctor didn't flinch. "It's not what it once was," he replied. "This is not punishment. It is not torture. It is a medical procedure—regulated, precise, and in some cases, lifesaving. Your daughter's current condition is grave. She is trapped in a cycle of fear and trauma. Without intervention, she may not return."

Tatjana stood frozen, her hands clenched at her sides. The air felt suffocating. Her daughter was barely recognizable—silent, unreachable. But to subject her to this? Surely it wasn't the only answer.

Dr. Blessing softened his tone. "The decision is yours. As parents, you have the right to decline. But my clinical advice remains unchanged."

Tatjana's hands trembled as she stepped into the hallway. Adi reached for her, but his grip felt uncertain and full of the same dread.

"It doesn't feel like a choice," Tatjana whispered. "To agree to that kind of violence, even if it's cloaked in medicine . . . It feels like handing her over yet again."

Adi didn't answer right away. "What other choice do we have? Dr. Blessing said she won't come back on her own."

Tatjana gave a strained nod. "I know. But it still feels wrong. More like a surrender than an agreement."

They stopped outside Erika's room and looked in through the glass. She was curled tight on the bed, her knees drawn in, her face turned toward the wall. Her arms were wrapped around herself, as if to hold something in—or keep something out.

"We can't leave her like this," Adi murmured. "Not if there's a chance. Any chance."

Tatjana pressed a hand to the window, her fingers splayed against the cool surface, before turning to Adi. "Then we tell them yes," she said quietly. Her eyes were red but clear with purpose. "We tell them we'll try."

The hallway felt colder on the way back to Dr. Blessing's office. Neither Adi nor Tatjana spoke. When they entered the office, the doctor stood. His expression didn't change, but something in his posture softened.

"We'll go forward with the treatment," Tatjana said, steady now. "We want to give Erika every chance."

Dr. Blessing nodded solemnly. "And we'll take every precaution. I'll oversee her treatment plan personally to ensure her safety and comfort."

Tatjana and Adi exchanged a glance—nothing more than a breath in length, but it was enough. They had made their decision.

"Thank you," Adi said quietly. "We just want her to come back to us."

"I understand," Dr. Blessing replied. "This is not a promise, but it's a chance."

When the day of the first treatment arrived, Erika was wheeled into the treatment room, her parents following closely behind. The room was stark and clinical, the equipment intimidating. Tatjana's heart ached as she watched the preparations.

Dr. Blessing met them at the door, serious but reassuring. "She will be closely monitored throughout. We'll begin with a low dose and adjust as necessary."

Tatjana nodded, her eyes never leaving Erika's face. "Please . . . take care of her."

"We will," Dr. Blessing promised. "You can wait just outside. I'll update you as soon as we're finished."

Tatjana and Adi took seats in the waiting area, their hands clasped tightly together. They didn't speak. The clock made a noise that felt too loud for a hospital.

At last, Dr. Blessing returned, his expression carefully neutral. "The procedure went smoothly. We'll monitor her closely, but this is a good beginning."

In the recovery room, Erika lay still. Her expression looked calmer now, her breathing steady. The sight brought tears to Tatjana's eyes. For the first time in days, she felt something close to hope.

"We're here, Eka. Papa and I are here," she whispered, taking her daughter's hand.

The next afternoon, Tatjana kept vigil as usual in Erika's room. Sometimes she sang. Sometimes she just sat, her hand resting lightly over Erika's. Then she turned back to Heine's *Buch der Lieder*, or *Book of Songs*, choosing her words carefully now. "Du bist wie eine Blume," she read softly. "You are like a flower."

The very next afternoon, as Tatjana read again from Heine's *Buch der Lieder*, Erika's fingers twitched slightly against the blanket.

It was the smallest of movements but enough to make Tatjana catch her breath. She leaned in. "Eka, can you hear me? If you can . . . squeeze my hand."

Nothing at first. Tatjana's heart started to sink. And then—pressure. The faintest squeeze against her fingers.

Tears blurred her vision as she looked at Erika's face, hoping for another sign. Erika's expression hadn't changed. But her hand was still holding on.

Then Erika's eyes fluttered open.

"That's it, Eka," Tatjana whispered, her voice trembling. "We're here. Hold on."

At the foot of the bed, Adi stepped forward. "Did she . . . ?"

Tatjana nodded, her voice caught in her throat. "She squeezed my hand, Adi. She's with us again."

The breakthrough reinvigorated their resolve. They doubled down, working closely with the medical staff to tailor Erika's plan. Electroconvulsive therapy continued. Dr. Blessing, seeing the family's dedication, arranged for additional therapies, including art and music, hoping to reach Erika through different pathways.

Adi began bringing his violin, playing softly at her bedside. The familiar melodies seemed to soothe her. Christa would sing or sometimes just hum.

One evening, as Christa sang an old lullaby, Erika's eyes opened and held steady. She looked at her sister—not past her but *at* her.

"Christa . . ." she murmured, her voice weak but recognizable.

Christa choked on a sob as she rushed forward. "Eka, you're back," she whispered, kissing her sister's forehead. "You're really back."

Erika's eyes filled with tears as she looked around the room: Mama, Papa, Tita. Her family. "I—I'm so scared," she admitted, her voice shaking. "Everything is so dark."

Tatjana took her hand again. "We'll walk through it with you."

Adi laid his hand on Erika's forehead. "One step at a time. And together."

Little by little, in the weeks that followed, Erika began to return—to herself and to them. Her progress was slow, uneven, sometimes difficult. The nightmares still haunted her, and she saw Nazis everywhere. Some days were harder than others.

But within the pale walls of the facility in Göppingen, in the quiet spaces between fear and healing, Erika began to rejoin the world—not all at once but piece by piece. Some might call it a miracle, but Christa knew it was something slower and stronger, more lasting: the work of love, carried out in hours and days, in touch and presence.

Landesstelle Württemberg-Baden
für die
politisch Verfolgten des Naziregimes
Stuttgart

Fragebogen 1

(Bitte deutlich ausfüllen)

Ort *Kornwestheim* Kreis *Ludwigsburg*

Name *Dindinger* Vorname *Erika* geborene *Dindinger*

geb *24.7. 1924* Geburtsort *Bromberg* Staatsangehörigkeit *deutsch*

Beruf *Ingenieur* Branche *Chemie*

Selbständige Erwerbsbetätigung — welcher Art —

Led./verh./gesch./verw., Zahl der Kinder unter 14 J. —, über 14 J. —, Religion *evangel./i*

Wohnort *Kornwestheim* Straße *Weimar - Str.* Nr. *121*

Stadtteil — Bezirk —

Verhaftet am 1. XI. 43, kurz darauf verhaftet in *unbekannt* durch wen *Gestapo*

Emigration von *seit Einmarsch d. Alliierten* bis *auf weiteres* in *Kornwestheim* nach Kr.

Grund der Verhaftung oder Verfolgung (nähere Beschreibung) *Antinazistische Einstell.* *Verkehr mit Ausländern, Mutter stand als getarnte Jüdin in Verdacht. Ganze Familie stand von Anbeginn unter Beobachtung durch Gestapo.*

Fragebogen means "questionnaire" and was designed by the British and American Allies to rid Germany of anything "brown" (anything Nazi) in the postwar era. But the reality was that it was impossible to fire so many Germans with the expertise needed to rebuild the country. Consequently, many old Nazis returned to their jobs.

The allies used these questionnaires routinely. The one imaged here was to determine any of Erika's Nazi affiliations.

Hellmuth and Christa, forlorn and spiritually wounded following the death of Joachim and the mental breakdown of Erika, in Stuttgart, 1946.

CHAPTER THIRTY-EIGHT

ONWARD TO FREEDOM
(1948)

GERMANY STAGGERED THROUGH THE YEARS after the war, scarred by hunger, shattered cities, and a shaken sense of moral direction. Life was difficult there, haunted by suffering that had left no place untouched. Entire cities had been leveled by bombs. Industries were destroyed. Homelessness was rampant. For Tatjana and Adi, the question was not only what they needed to survive but what future remained for their children.

Christa, just twenty-three years old, was bright, talented, and restless. In the Germany of 1948, her potential had no room to grow. When the Hebrew Immigrant Aid Society—HIAS—offered passage to America for displaced persons, Tatjana and Adi pondered the decision with heavy hearts.

Finally, a decision was made: Adi would remain behind in Stuttgart with Hellmuth, who was preparing for medical school, and Erika, who was still institutionalized for ongoing care. For Christa, though, the only path forward was across the ocean.

So, on March 11, 1948, Tatjana and Christa stood on the deck of the SS *Marine Jumper*, once a US Navy troop carrier, now filled with exiles bound for New York. The air was filled with mingled scents of saltwater and diesel, undercut by faint sobs and shouted goodbyes. The docks of Bremerhaven buzzed with the frantic energy of families grasping hands until the last possible moment. For many, this was a final parting.

Tatjana clung to Christa's fingers as though her grip might bridge the separation that awaited them. On the dock below, Adi stood with quiet dignity. His broad frame seemed unchanged, but Tatjana recognized the anguish in his eyes and the heaviness in his posture. Beside him were Hellmuth and Stefan, waving and smiling for her sake, though their faces betrayed the ache of parting.

Tatjana committed the image to memory: Adi on the dock, straight-backed yet weary, the boys at his side. The ship's horn cut through the morning air, low and mournful, as the *Marine Jumper* pulled slowly from the pier. Adi raised his arm in response, his hand trembling slightly as he waved. From the deck, Tatjana could see the sheen of tears on his cheeks. He looked both proud and unbearably small as the distance widened.

Tatjana raised her free hand in return, her movement slow, almost mechanical, as if willing the gesture to hold back the separation. Beside her, Christa pressed a handkerchief to her face, shoulders heaving in quiet sobs, her own tears catching the wind and salt spray.

Just before they boarded, Adi had pulled them close, his voice breaking as he tried to steady himself. "Look after each other," he had said simply. "And remember, you'll carry us with you."

Now those words echoed in Tatjana's ears, the raw plea of a husband and father left standing on the shore: *You'll carry us with you.* And they would, just as they were carrying the slender spoons engraved with Christa's and Erika's initials.

The engines shuddered through the deck, and Tatjana held tighter to Christa's hand. Behind them, the outlines of Bremerhaven blurred into the endless horizon. The expanse of the Atlantic lay ahead, gray and restless. Her daughter's grip was warm and fierce, as if she, too, understood that their strength must come from one another now.

As the shoreline dissolved into mist, Tatjana forced herself to look toward it once more, straining to fix every detail in her mind. Among those images clustered the memories of war, of family loved and family lost. She knew they would not fade. They would travel with her, carried silently across the ocean.

The first days aboard the ship brought new routines and new faces. Their cabin was cramped, the bunks stacked so close together that Tatjana could feel every movement. Mornings began with the clang of trays and the cries of seasick children. Conversations rose and fell in a dozen languages.

Christa watched and listened with growing curiosity. Fear gave way, little by little, to the novelty of the voyage. The vast Atlantic stretched outside the portholes, endless and bleak, its motion a constant reminder that there was no turning back.

In the common room, Christa drifted toward a circle of young passengers like herself: Mira, a Polish girl, had a quick laugh and a box of paints she guarded as closely as her passport. Lev, a Ukrainian boy whose violin case never left his side, its battered wood polished smooth by his hands, spoke little, but when he played, the melodies seemed to carry stories too heavy for words. Sara and David, twins from Hungary, finished each other's sentences; their closeness defied a world that had tried to separate them.

The ship's mess hall offered them a kind of refuge. In one corner stood an upright piano, its damaged keys uneven but still capable of song. Christa lingered there one afternoon, her fingers hovering uncertainly above the keyboard. At last she pressed down, and a phrase of Chopin rose into the air. Then Beethoven, then Liszt, with Lev joining her on the violin. Passengers fell quiet, some closing their eyes, others humming softly. For a few minutes, the ship was more than a vessel of exile. It was a hall of shared memory and fragile hope.

When the music faded and Christa drifted into laughter with her new friends, Tatjana often slipped away to the deck's edge. There, with the sea stretching endlessly before her, she wrote letters to Stuttgart—pages filled with the ache of absence, the uncertain outlines of hope, and gratitude to the HIAS, whose help had made this passage possible. The ocean wind snatched at the pages as she wrote, the salt flecking her ink.

Evenings brought another rhythm. Tatjana often joined a circle of women from different countries, their shared losses weaving them together without need for common words. She translated for a Russian widow, who recounted how she survived the siege at Leningrad; helped a Polish mother confide her worries about her children; and shared fragments of her own story for a Ukrainian family. With her languages—Russian, German, Polish, Hebrew, Ukrainian, and English—Tatjana became a welcome bridge among her fellow travelers.

As the days passed, the ship grew into a small world of its own. Communities formed quickly as friendships were sparked over trays of soup in the mess hall or during quiet hours on the deck while watching the horizon blur into mist. Sometimes, Tatjana marveled at the strangeness of it all. Poles, Germans, Hungarians, Jews, Catholics, Protestants—once divided by enmity—were now leaning together against the same rails, carried by the same restless sea.

On the fifth day, the calm broke. A storm rose without warning, heaving the ship like a toy. Waves smashed the deck; wind screamed down the corridors. In their cabin, Tatjana wrapped her arms around Christa, whispering steady words she scarcely believed herself, waiting for the storm to break, as trunks crashed and metal groaned. The air stank of damp wood and fear.

Each pitch of the hull dragged Tatjana back to another night, years earlier—the roar of rifles in the forest, the glow of burning trees, the press of Adi's hand pulling her forward, out of Russia. Both storms had threatened to swallow everything she loved.

By dawn, the violence ebbed. Pale light slipped through the porthole, and Tatjana exhaled. The light gave her permission to hope again.

After the storm, any remaining barriers among the passengers seemed to loosen. What was the point of stiff reserve among people who together had faced the storm? In the mess hall, Mira sketched quick portraits, Sara and David taught the others dances from home, and the music returned with new urgency. Laughter mingled with anxiety as people began to imagine what awaited them on the other side.

The voyage stretched on, filled with small rhythms of community and long hours at the rail. Passengers pressed against the wind, straining for signs of land. Excitement built, tempered by fear. What if America was harsher than they expected? What if it was not ready for them? Still, hope proved stubborn.

Then one morning—March 23, 1948—the cry went up: "Land ho!" Cheers erupted. Tatjana and Christa hurried to the bow.

Out of the mist, the skyline of New York emerged—steel and glass rising against the pale sky. And there, torch lifted high about the harbor, stood the Statue of Liberty.

Tears clouded Tatjana's vision. She had seen this figure in photographs, yet standing here now, salt spray on her face, the reality was almost overwhelming. She clasped Christa's hand until her knuckles whitened.

"We're here," Christa whispered, her voice catching.

"This is the start of our new life," Tatjana whispered in return.

Behind them, the Atlantic stretched like a long, unbroken thread, binding them to the people and lives they had left behind. Before them lay the vast unknown—a new culture to navigate, new customs to learn—and underneath it all, a promise of peace, freedom, and the chance to build something beautiful from what they had lost.

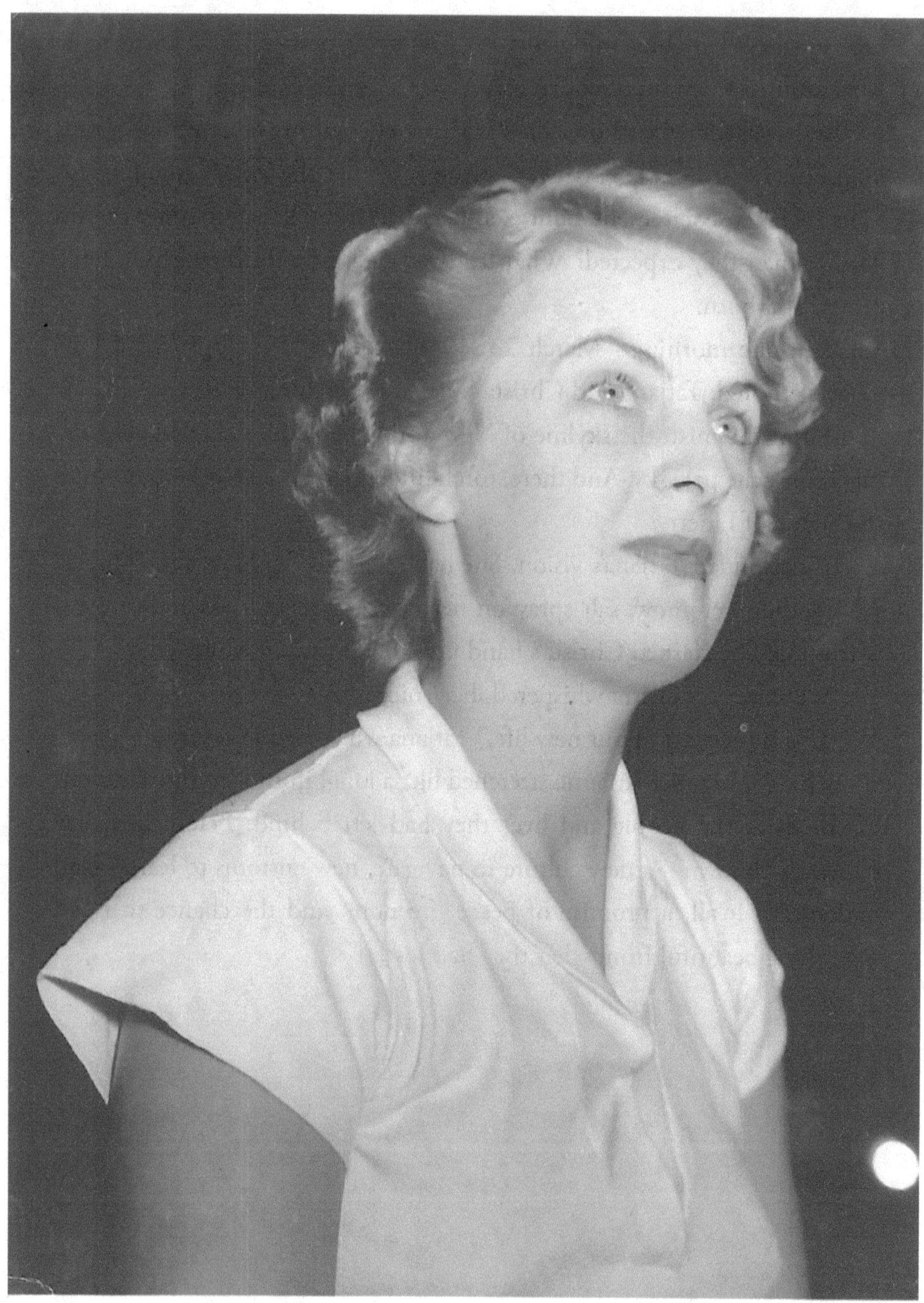

Christa in America, 1949.

REFLECTIONS (2022)

IT HAS BEEN MANY MONTHS since I first opened the cache of letters and documents tucked away in my grandfather's two small suitcases. In searching for the mother I lost, I have uncovered a story far more complex and heartbreaking than I ever imagined. Within those fragile pages lies a journey through one of history's darkest periods—not only a chronicle of war and survival but an intimate record of how love, duty, and fear shaped the choices my family made.

As I carefully gather the letters, treating each one as the priceless treasure it is, I feel a renewed sense of purpose. The choices my family made reverberated far beyond their own survival, shaping the legacy I've inherited. Their story—my story—was never just a chronicle of loss but also a reminder of how ordinary people carve paths forward even through darkness.

But where will these private letters and documents take me now? What would my family want me to do with their precious story?

Since that moment with my cousin Helga in Stuttgart, I have devoted months to translating these private family letters and documents. The oldest letters exchanged between my grandparents Adi and Tatjana date back to pre–World War I Russia, where their forbidden love took root in secret. Holding these letters, I feel the enormity of their courage—not abstractly but in the ink and creases of the paper itself. Before they were parents or grandparents, they were simply Adi and Tatjana: two people willing to risk everything for love.

My dear grandfather **Adolf Gustav Dindinger** stood at a remarkable intersection of European history and moved in the highest circles of power as a young man. His presence was part of my childhood world, and both his silences and his stories—when he told them—were equally revealing. His intimate knowledge of the Romanovs later drew him into the Anna Anderson trials of the 1960s, where he testified about the Imperial Family and the Grand Duchess Anastasia. Years later, quite through serendipity, I met Anna Anderson (then Anna Manahan) while I was a surgical resident at the University of Virginia in Charlottesville.

After World War II, Adolf turned again to building. When the family resettled in Stuttgart in 1946, he became one of the chief engineers of the Wagenburg Tunnel, completed in 1958. To carve stone into passageways was, perhaps, his own act of reckoning with devastation. He died in Stuttgart in 1981.

Among the letters in those two suitcases lay photographs of my beloved grandmother **Tatjana Wiczewski Dindinger**—smiling, though now I recognize how much she concealed behind that expression. To me, she was always *Mamus*, an endearing Slavic word for Mama. She was my blessing, though I was not privy to her wartime experiences at the time. Tatjana's journey is a story of survival and endurance—of returning, against all odds, to the hearth and heart of family. She endured loss upon loss—through the Russian Revolution, the Bromberg Death March, the death of her son Joachim, and her imprisonment at Bergen-Belsen. She survived so that others might escape, including her sister Fania, whom she helped to reach Palestine.

Faith carried my grandmother through where strength alone might have failed. Her survival required secrecy, passing quietly through a world that would have condemned her for being Jewish. It must have taken extraordinary strength to carry that hidden truth, wearing the cloak of Geheimnis even within her own family. As a child, I loved her deeply; now, I love her differently, having glimpsed, through these letters and photographs, the resilience and quiet bravery that defined her. She died in Rhode Island in 1975, still holding to her belief that all things are possible. Her strength didn't announce itself. It simply endured.

As I move deeper into the collection, I am plunged into the war through the eyes of **Joachim**, the uncle I never met, whose writings from the Eastern Front are the greatest gift—and raw in a way I never expected. His early letters brim with patriotic fervor, echoing the naïve belief that he was serving a just cause. I feel as though I am standing beside him on those frozen battlefields of the Eastern Front, where winter came early that year of 1941.

But as the war drags on, his tone shifts, and his handwriting grows uneven and slanted; each page reveals a young man wrestling with doubt, his orders colliding with his conscience and the values he had been raised to hold dear. In the end, he served the Resistance even as he served in the Wehrmacht. His life ended in a crossfire near Pekari, Ukraine, on October 1, 1943—but his spirit had been broken long before the bullet. Joachim was the family's anchor and their light; his story ended too soon, swallowed by war. His undoing was itself a kind of sacrifice, one that haunts me as much as his death.

Hellmuth, his younger brother, reveals through his letters the contradictions of a Luftwaffe pilot. He describes the thrill of flight, shadowed by the grief of loss, and his compassion endured even as he flew for the Axis. Reading one particularly poignant passage where Hellmuth recounts the day he lost his friend Urs after a troop transport plane was shot down, I feel the blunt truth of war more directly than any history book could convey:

> *One moment he was there . . . the next, nothing—just a plume of black smoke spiraling toward the ground. We are told we fight for the Fatherland. But in that instant, I understood that the only thing we fight for is each other.*

Though he survived the war and later became a physician, malaria contracted in North Africa claimed Hellmuth in 1966 at the age of forty-five. I remember my grandfather's heavy words announcing his death, noting with profound grief that this was the second son he had lost to the war. Hellmuth lies in rest in Bern, Switzerland, with his wife, Doris Christ Dindinger, and his best friend, Siegfried Boss.

Another set of letters illuminates a different kind of bravery: coded exchanges between Joachim and my aunt **Erika**. Each message peels back the secrecy of their part in the Resistance, revealing the shadow war waged from within. Erika—brilliant, determined, fearless—threw herself into the cause with unrelenting resolve. Joachim, though bound to the Wehrmacht as a reconnaissance soldier, became her secret ally, passing along crucial intelligence that could have cost him his life with every word.

Erika's resistance efforts included the sabotage of her own professional work, which surely cost her dearly given her profound love of science. I contrast her moral clarity with Operation Paperclip: a secret US initiative that whisked Werner von Braun and more than 1,600 German scientists to America, washing away their complicity in exchange for their expertise. Their rockets, once aimed at London, later rose over Cape Canaveral, blurring justice with a stain on the ledger of Allied victory.

My thoughts then turn to the letters of Erika and her beloved Stefan—a story of love and resistance intertwined, of both devotion and defiance. Their letters reveal their work in the Home Army and later with the S.O.E. between 1939 and 1945; nearly half the war intelligence to reach the British came from Polish sources like them. Each page reflects their willingness to risk everything for the freedom of others.

The Resistance comes alive most vividly through Stefan's words: urgent, shadowed by close escapes and narrow triumphs. Yet what strikes me most is not the danger itself but his steady hope—his belief in a future free of fear and his devotion to Erika, which gave his risks deeper meaning. "Each act of resistance, no matter how small," Stefan wrote, "is a declaration that we do not accept tyranny. It's a way of saying we still believe in a better world and that we are willing to fight for it."

I first met Erika in Stuttgart in 1970, when she mistook me for my mother. She guided my hand to the drill holes in her skull—remnants of Gestapo torture. I could not comprehend such cruelty then, but I understood enough to know that her war never ended; it merely shifted to an internal battlefield. Had the realities of PTSD been known in 1946, she might have lived a very different life—one where she and Stefan could have married and born children. As it was, no one knows what happened to Stefan in the years that followed. Erika lived quietly as a stenographer, bearing visible and invisible scars, until her death in Stuttgart in 2002. She is buried at her father's feet.

The letters that touch me most, however, are those written by my beautiful mother, **Christa**. From Hohenlychen, her notes reveal the innocence of a teenager whose daily life was entwined with the darker reality of the hospital's hidden operations. Her voice is bright, her concerns those of a young pianist intent on mastering her art:

> *Today I played Beethoven's* Moonlight Sonata *for the patients and some of the staff. They said I have the hands of a true artist! I practice every day when I am not having therapy on my knee. Someday I will perform in a grand concert hall in Vienna, and you will be in the front row.*

Reading these words now, I am struck by the contrast: a young girl pouring her energy into Chopin and Beethoven even as the world around her was bent on destruction. I can almost see her face alight with the joy of music, her fingers gliding over the keys—unaware of the horrors hidden within the walls of Hohenlychen and its ties to Ravensbrück. She could not have known that her physician, Dr. Karl Gebhardt, was a cold-blooded killer.

My mother carried a different kind of courage from that of her siblings. Her extraordinary talent at the piano brought her to an audition with Toscanini himself, who chose her as his soloist. Yet she stepped away from that path to raise a family. As a child, I only saw what was lost. Later, I came to see it differently: Hers was the courage to choose love over acclaim, to build another kind of legacy—one of devotion and endurance. My mother died in 2008, yet her love is still with me today. It is what led me to discover the two small suitcases that began this journey.

Learning the full truth of the lives of the Dindinger family has changed me in ways I did not expect. Each revelation has drawn me deeper into their world, and with every fragment of history I've uncovered, my sense of belonging has deepened. I am struck by the duality of their existence: each living a seemingly ordinary life while concealing extraordinary burdens. They preserved a semblance of normalcy amid the chaos of war—sharing meals, writing letters, even laughing. That ability to hold on to small joys, to compartmentalize while carrying the weight of secrets and fear, continues to astonish me.

I often wonder whether I could have done the same—whether, in their place, I would have found the courage to endure.

With all I have uncovered, I find myself drawing unavoidable parallels between their world and mine. The circumstances of their struggle are bound to the 1940s, yet the questions they confronted—about freedom, dignity, and moral responsibility—remain timeless. Their story has become a mirror, reminding me that the fight against injustice is never neatly confined to the past. It shifts shape, reappears, and asks us—each in our own way—to respond.

As the sun sets over my library, with the letters and photographs spread before me now, I feel the weight of responsibility. These are not only stories of another era; they are lessons still alive, asking us to remember what ordinary people can endure, resist, and achieve. These are not just my family's stories; they are stories that can remind and inspire us all. Yet they have become a part of who I am, shaping me as a daughter, a niece, a granddaughter, and now as custodian of their memory.

This story does not end with them. It continues in me—and in those who read and remember. What I found in those suitcases is not just a family chronicle but a legacy. With every step forward, I carry them with me, not only to honor that legacy but to live it.

Even in the darkest years, this family found ways to endure, to resist, to insist on their humanity. They were on the right side of wrong in a conflicted world. That legacy is not theirs alone. It asks something of us still.

ACKNOWLEDGMENTS

MY JOURNEY OF DISCOVERY WOULD never have begun without my cousin Dr. Helga Müller-Freigang's gift of my grandfather's two small suitcases. Her deep love for my grandfather and her generosity in sharing these treasures have helped to make this book possible.

Of course, we all stand on the shoulders of the historians and novelists who came before us. The works of Harald Jähner, Alex Borsino, Volker Ullrich, and Richard DiNardo helped illuminate the path I walked in researching and writing this book. I am forever grateful.

I first met Dr. Richard DiNardo through his thoughtful foreword of *Men of Barbarossa*. We developed a beautiful friendship as he educated me about Joachim's role with the Armored Bears. With Rich, so many doors were opened through the world of books. He thoughtfully guided me in my quest for historical and military accuracy and insight. His encyclopedic mind is only matched by the size of his heart.

Dr. Julie Glowacki, my Harvard research professor and eternal friend and mentor, has been steadfast in her erudite review of my writing. My early training in the art of the scientific method and her encouragement helped bring this novel to fruition.

Barbara Easley, my beloved German figure skating coach, explained the endurance of this beautiful sport even during the height of the Allied bombing. I miss you, Barbara.

Patricia Cornwell, internationally acclaimed bestselling author and friend, encouraged me to proceed with my writing endeavors. I remain grateful.

Robert Goldsborough, Nero Award–winning author and former editor of the *Chicago Tribune Sunday Magazine*, has become an invaluable resource and an unwavering supporter of my book. His encouragement and friendship are precious to me.

Sergio Porto deserves special thanks for his loyalty and belief in all that I do. He is both the designer of my beautiful book cover and my inspirational support.

Ruth Leanna Hillelson, MD, FACS

ABOUT THE AUTHOR

A NATIVE OF RHODE ISLAND, whose early years included the study of piano and competitive figure skating, Dr. Ruth Leanna Hillelson went on to devote her life to the art and science of plastic and reconstructive surgery. She was among the first female undergraduates at Johns Hopkins University, where she directed a National Science Foundation research grant at the age of eighteen. She completed her medical education at Harvard University, authoring a seminal research paper on tissue flap necrosis and salvage.

Dr. Hillelson's surgical training included residencies and postgraduate fellowships in general and plastic surgery at the University of Virginia,

Johns Hopkins, and the University of Kansas, along with advanced training in craniofacial and maxillofacial reconstruction at the University of Virginia. She achieved international acclaim for her techniques in breast reconstruction after mastectomy and her innovations in radiofrequency skin tightening and has lectured in this field across three continents. Drawing on her background in chemistry and skin physiology, she also developed a line of bioactive skin products, Iridesse Skin Care. She currently serves as Chief of Plastic Surgery and Aesthetics at the Hillelson-Whipple Clinic in Richmond, Virginia.

Both memoir and history, this book continues Dr. Hillelson's lifelong pursuit of knowledge into a more personal dimension, reconstructing her family's journey through terrible tragedies, narrow escapes, resistance efforts, and the lasting scars of survival. Reflecting years of tireless effort and dedication, it chronicles the extraordinary courage of her grandparents, her uncles, her aunt, and her mother, who risked their lives to resist the Third Reich and aid the Allies during World War II. The book stands as both a tribute to her family's bravery and a testament to Dr. Hillelson's ability to intertwine personal narrative with academic depth as only a scientist can do.

Dr. Hillelson lives in Richmond, Virginia, with her husband, Dr. Terry L. Whipple; their two charming and affectionate dogs; and their two beloved horses.